An American in Leningrad

Also by Logan Robinson/
The Russian Republican (RSFSR) Code
on Marriage and the Family
(translation)

Logan Robinson

AN AMERICAN

IN LENINGRAD

W. W. Norton & Company

NEW YORK / LONDON

Copyright © 1982 by Logan Robinson
Published simultaneously in Canada by
George J. McLeod Limited, Toronto.
Printed in the United States of America
All Rights Reserved
First Edition
Library of Congress Cataloging in Publication Data
Robinson, Logan
An American in Leningrad.
1. Leningrad (R.S.F.S.R.)—Social life and customs.
2. Leningrad (R.S.F.S.R.)—Intellectual life.
3. Leningradskiĭ gosudarstvennyĭ universitet
imeni A. A. Zhdanova. IUridicheskiĭ fakulʹtet.
4. Robinson, Logan. I. Title.

DK557.R6 1982   947'.4530853   81–22377
AACR2

W. W. Norton & Company, Inc. 500 Fifth Avenue, New York, N.Y. 10110
W. W. Norton & Company Ltd. 37 Great Russell Street, London WC1B 3NU

1 2 3 4 5 6 7 8 9 0

ISBN 0-393-01520-3

For my parents,
Alis Rule Robinson
and Landon Graves Robinson,
with love.

Contents

Acknowledgments

The idea for this book was conceived the moment I received a preparatory fellowship to study Soviet law the spring of my first year at Harvard Law School. That was eight years ago, in 1974. Since then innumerable teachers, friends, and colleagues have contributed to my knowledge of the Soviet Union and to this book. Although detailing all of their assistance would take a separate volume, some individuals and organizations must be mentioned.

I owe a great debt to the International Research and Exchanges Board, the organization that sponsored my two years of preparatory study at Harvard and my exchange to the Soviet Union. Under the leadership of Allen H. Kassof, IREX wages a lonely battle against the "ostrich" school of foreign policy, which asserts that because the Soviet Union is difficult to deal with, the prudent course is to know as little about it as possible.

This book was begun at the Documentation Office for East European Law at the Law Faculty of the University of Leyden in the Netherlands, where I worked after leaving Russia. Professor F. J. M. Feldbrugge, one of the great European authorities on Soviet law and dissent, gave me much encouragement. William B. Simons, editor of Leyden's *The Soviet Codes of Law*, on which I worked, was unflagging in weeding out, in the many drafts, much that was misleading or ill-taken. More than that, he was a true friend during the dreary Dutch winter when the first chapters were created. Ewa Suchanska and Andries van Helden were fountainheads of knowledge concerning things Slavic.

Of the many souls who shouldered the arduous task of teaching me Russian, Joseph N. Rostinsky and Slava Paperno stand out. Nancy Fehsenfeld, a fellow Leningrad exchange student, shared some of these experiences if not necessarily these opinions. Leonid Rivkin gave me many insights on the Russian psyche both before I left and after my return. John N. Hazard of Columbia University, the dean of American scholars of Soviet law, always had time for consultation during my years of preparation. Serge L. Levitsky, in reviewing the manuscript, gave me the benefit of his decades of experience with the Soviet Union as businessman and savant. Other leading authorities in the field such as Peter B. Maggs and George Ginsburgs, will, I hope, forgive any scholarly peccadillos they may discern.

General James M. Gavin, Lincoln Kirstein, and the late Richard Baxter of Harvard Law School and the International Court of Justice encouraged me to persevere. Harvey Simmonds of the Eakins Press and Anne Marie Talamo were of great assistance in the early days of manuscript preparation.

A special debt is owed to Eric Swenson, my editor, for transforming two rough chapters and an outline into a beautiful book and for taking a chance on this author.

My greatest thanks of all are to Edrie Baker Sowell for her support and affection while this book was being researched and written—from bitter winter mornings in Leningrad to late nights at the word processor in Manhattan.

Those friends and colleagues still in the Soviet Union will remain unnamed but not unappreciated.

Introduction

This is a book about Leningrad, the city, and some of the people I knew there. It so happened that I was there in law school, to be exact, at "the Civil Law Faculty of Leningrad State University Named for A. A. Zhdanov." Some of the people I knew were in the law school, and some others were involved, through no choice of their own, with Soviet law. But this book is not about Soviet law, at least not in a scholarly sense.

The law school has had some distinguished alumni. Peter Ilich Tchaikovsky and Igor Stravinsky studied law at Leningrad—at that time known as St. Petersburg—and later one Ulyanov passed his bar examination there after he was expelled from the University of Kazan for, they say, some kind of radical activity. Ulyanov's older brother had been a prominent radical, so prominent that he was hanged in the courtyard of the Schlüsselburg fortress as the bomb maker in an attempted assassination of Czar Alexander III. Later Ulyanov began publishing certain political writings which were to have great impact in Russia, but by then he had begun to use his pen name—Lenin.

This book, however, is not about the great luminaries of Soviet Leningrad or Czarist St. Petersburg, but about the everyday people I knew in the city. To me they were a special kind of alumni. The great adventure and the great stress of being an American postgraduate student in the Soviet Union has emblazoned Leningrad on my mind in deeper hues than the other cities in which I have lived. Companions in hardship and laughter, the people I met in Leningrad will always have a special significance for me.

This book is about the rich life of Leningrad: the student life in the dormitories, the social life with intellectuals, dissidents, and everyday people. My studies were in Soviet law, but this involved more than classes in jurisprudence. There were the formal aspects—classes at Leningrad State, talks with my advisor, visits to lawyers' offices; but also there was the darker side of Soviet justice—confrontations with the KGB at art exhibits, my own arrest for taking pictures in a grocery store, border searches, and reprisals against human-rights activists. I was not studying Soviet law as an end in itself but as an avenue, a system of analysis to discern general principles of Soviet society and the character of the Russian people.

When I was preparing for university in Leningrad, I found several interesting books about Soviet life, but they were all written by Moscow-based foreign correspondents. American graduate students have been going to the Soviet Union in small numbers for many years, yet the student experience is largely ignored. This is in part the result of discreet Soviet blackmail. To write accurately about life in the Soviet Union one must, of course, write of both the good and the bad. But publishing stories critical of Soviet society exposes the writer to the wrath of the Soviet government. For a Russian this would mean a charge of disseminating anti-Soviet slander. For an American, it means the risk of never again being given a visa to the Soviet Union. As an aspiring commercial lawyer, I was willing to run this risk. But for a student of Russian history to lose all access to archival materials in the Soviet Union, or for a doctoral candidate in Russian linguistics to be cut off from the country where the language is spoken, is no laughing matter.

Competition in academia is intense. American Sovietologists who become *personae non gratae* in Russia are placed in the embarrassing position of having to rely on their students, who can freely tour the USSR, for first-hand comments on the Soviet scene. Launching one's academic career by severing all one's primary sources is not an auspicious beginning. Thus, the Soviet Union subtly polices American Soviet scholars.

But leaving the foreign correspondents to do all the writing is unfortunate. Foreign correspondents live with their families in comfortable, American-style apartments in special Moscow "ghettoes" for Westerners. These special residential complexes, like that on Moscow's Kutuzov Prospect, are patrolled around the clock by the KGB. As a student, I lived in a small room with a Russian roommate, in a Russian dormitory. I had an advisor and attended classes as a regular Soviet law student would. Students simply do not rate the surveillance and espionage efforts lavished on the diplomats, businessmen, and foreign correspondents. As a result, I enjoyed relative anonymity and the freedom that accompanies it.

I discovered another disappointing uniformity in American books about Soviet life. Those books supposedly about life in Russia were really just about life in Moscow. This might not seem important, but the difference between Moscow and Leningrad is greater than that between New York and Chicago or between London and Liverpool. The Soviet Union is a highly centralized state, and its center is in Moscow. Decisions, even down to what a small Leningrad factory will produce, are made in Moscow. The foreign community in the Soviet capital is multitudinous. There are more than one hundred Western foreign correspondents. There are scores of embassies with hundreds of employees; most international airlines and several dozen big Western firms and banks have offices in downtown Moscow. A constant stream of foreign diplomats, businessmen, and official delegations flows through the city. In the Soviet Union all international trade is a state monopoly, and all but two of more than sixty Soviet foreign trading organizations are in the Soviet capital.

The Soviet leadership lives in Moscow and wants it to be a prosperous city. In addition, because the Kremlin knows that most foreigners' impressions of the Soviet Union are really just impressions of Moscow, the Soviet capital always receives top priority: in construction and housing, in consumer goods available in the stores, in quantity and quality of foodstuffs. The rows of high-rise buildings along Moscow's Kalinin Prospect are unique in the Soviet Union. Only a strict system of residency certificates prevents the majority of the Russian people from moving into Moscow. As the Russians say, "Moscow is always on display."

Leningrad—is vastly different. Despite its population of four million, it is, owing to Soviet centralization, a provincial town. In terms of housing or food and consumer goods in the stores, Leningrad is years behind Moscow. Even telephone calls made abroad from Leningrad, or to Leningrad from abroad, must first be approved by Moscow. A friend once attempted to call our dormitory in Leningrad from Western Europe. He ordered the call and was told, as is normal, that the connection would be made the next day. On the following day he was told by the Leningrad operator, "Moscow says your friend is not here." In Leningrad, the Western world is represented by a few consulates and two one-man airline offices (Finnair and SAS). There had been one foreign correspondent. Emil Sveilis, of United Press International, arrived in the fall of 1976 as the city's first Western correspondent. He spent two years in Leningrad under such harassment that the wire service decided not to refill the position.

Not surprisingly, it is precisely because Leningrad's foreign community is small and its political stature is low that it is a better city than is Moscow to get to know the Russian people. Yet Leningrad, capital of the Russian Empire from the time of Peter the Great to the fall of Nicholas and Alexandra, the home of Pushkin, Dostoevsky, and Gogol, is often ignored by Western observers of the Soviet Union. It is true that many tourist groups visit Leningrad's museums, but beyond this the city is virtually forgotten. What is written by Americans about life in Russia today is written about Moscow, and while it is true that Moscow is a showcase, in the Soviet Union, what is in the display window is not necessarily what's in the store.

I went to the Soviet Union under the auspices of the International Research and Exchanges Board (IREX). Based in New York City, IREX administers exchanges with the Soviet Union under the umbrella of the USA-USSR Intergovernmental Agreement on Cultural and Educational Exchanges. Funding for IREX comes partly from private sources, such as the Ford Foundation, and partly from governmental sources, such as the U.S. International Communication Agency. I went to Leningrad for ten months on the Graduate Student/Young Faculty Exchange with the Ministry of Higher and Specialized Secondary Education of the USSR. Traditionally, fifty Americans are proposed each year. A few candidates are always rejected by the Soviet Ministry of Higher Education, usually without any stated reason. For each American accepted, one Soviet student is placed in a university in the United States. Most of the Americans exchanged are fifth- or sixth-year graduate students in Russian history or literature, but the other fields in my year were as diverse as library science, mathematics, and even physical education. The Soviets who come to America are normally somewhat older and study the physical sciences or engineering. Their families stay behind. About half the Americans are placed in Moscow, slightly less than half in Leningrad, and the remainder in such smaller cities as Kiev and Tashkent. In 1976–77 twenty

American exchange students, with an additional ten spouses and children, were placed in Leningrad.

This had been the pattern for many years. Now, however, owing to the troubled relations between the two countries, the number of exchangees has been cut almost in half. In 1980–81 only eleven Americans were living in my former dormitory. Following Soviet moves against Sakharov and the invasion of Afghanistan, the USA-USSR Intergovernmental Agreement was not renewed. The exchange continues on an interim basis without a formal agreement, but its future is in jeopardy.

American law graduates on the exchange are particularly rare. It is difficult for an American lawyer to prepare properly. Russian language study and courses in Soviet studies can rarely be included in a traditional law-school curriculum of torts, contracts, and property. Some American exchange students have studied Soviet law, but with few exceptions they have been political scientists and not lawyers. There are obstacles to law study on the Soviet side as well. Law, because it is contemporary and closely connected with politics, is a sensitive category in Soviet eyes, and rejection rates for proposed law students are particularly high. Following my exchange year, a candidate in law was rejected by the Soviet Ministry of Higher Education without explanation, a sad finale to several years of preparation. Since the "chill" in U.S.–Soviet relations following the invasion of Afghanistan, no American lawyer has gone to Leningrad on the exchange.

In 1974 I received a preparatory grant from IREX to study Russian language and Soviet law. At the time I was a first-year student at Harvard Law School. I studied Russian at Harvard and for two summers at the Russian Summer School at Middlebury College, Vermont. In the fall of 1975 I was nominated for the exchange by IREX and accepted by the Soviet Ministry of Higher Education the following spring. While in Leningrad I received a grant of 225 rubles a month and a shared room in a dormitory. I arrived at the Leningrad airport from Helsinki on August 9, 1976, and left the Soviet Union on a Russian cruise ship from Odessa on June 4, 1977. As a tourist, I returned to Leningrad on October 25, 1980. Much had changed in the intervening three and a half years, and the final two chapters of this book are about those changes.

Although I have used the terms "Russia" and "the Soviet Union" almost interchangeably, they are not, strictly speaking, the same thing. The Union of Soviet Socialist Republics is made up of fifteen republics of which the Russian Soviet Federative Socialist Republic is only one. Theoretically, each republic is sovereign and even has the constitutional right to secede from the USSR. In reality, the Russian Republic is by far the dominant one, with approximately three-fourths of the area and one-half of the population of the Soviet Union. Leningrad is in the Russian Republic. Moscow is the capital of both the Russian Republic and the USSR.

There is a similar important difference between the Russian people and the Soviet people. Only about half of the people in the Soviet Union are ethnic Great Russians, and only this half speaks Russian as a first language. To say that someone is a Soviet is not to say he is a Russian. A Soviet citizen may be anyone from a fair-haired Balt to an Oriental Uzbek.

As is necessary in any book about personal experiences in the Soviet Union, alterations in some names and details have been made to protect Russian friends.

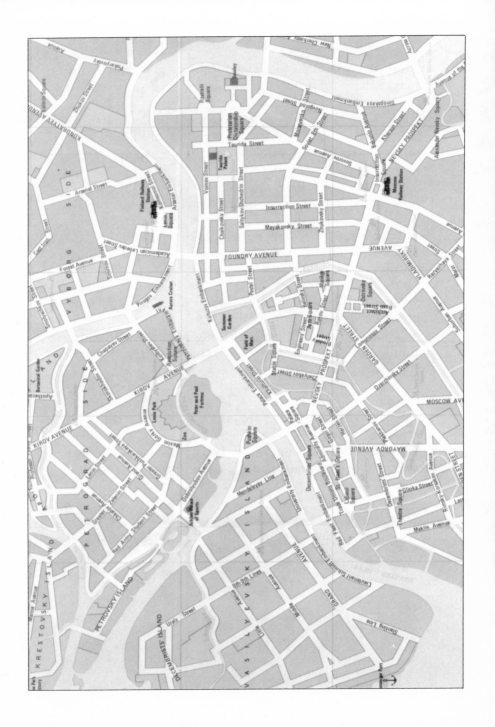

An American in Leningrad

One /

Leningrad State

University

I had been in Leningrad almost two months before I met my advisor and began my studies at the law faculty. In August, my first month, we exchange students had language instruction and orientation; September is harvest month in northern Russia, and the university is supposed to help with the crops. Although even professors are expected to pick up a few potatoes, most of them manage instead to slip away to the Baltic coast to catch the last sunshine before the onset of winter's darkness. Several exchange students tried to find their faculty advisors in September, but with no luck. Technically the university was open, and the advisors were required to be in. If you went to the faculty, you were always told that your professor was sick or had just left. "Come back next Monday," they said. Since the professors were officially in Leningrad, their secretaries were careful not to tell a foreigner that their bosses were still frolicking in Estonia or helping their relatives in Karelia sell the produce from the family garden. I suspect that everyone was in on the joke except the exchange students.

I myself was somewhat delayed by not knowing where the law faculty was. It was not with the main university buildings on University Embankment. Finding out was not an easy matter. Of the approximately one hundred Russian and one hundred foreign students in my dormitory (all of the foreign students were from countries in NATO or from other developed capitalist countries—a student is housed according to his country's military alliance), I was the only one studying law. There is certainly no such thing as a university information center at Leningrad State, and inquiries at the bookstore and in the dormitory produced no useful information.

This was not entirely surprising. Students at Leningrad, as is also typical in Western European universities, study in only one field. If a student's field was Russian literature, he would go to that faculty only and never set foot in another department. What was surprising was not that the Russian students in the other faculties did not know where the law faculty was, but that they had no idea how to find out. I could have made an appointment with the dean of the university, waited a few weeks, and then asked him, but this seemed ridiculous and to be used only as a last resort.

Contributing to my lackluster performance in this search was a certain intimidation I felt in the whole endeavor. I had become accustomed to the city, the dormitory, and my roommate. Leningrad is spectacularly beautiful in the late summer, and there were museums, parks, and palaces to be visited. It was my first time in Russia, and I wasn't going to fall into the trap of thinking that since I had a whole year, I could save everything for later. I was making friends and enjoying all the *mir i druzhba* (peace and friendship) fellowship in those early days in the dormitory. We had a small library at the American consulate, and I had borrowed *The 900 Days*, Harrison Salisbury's epic about the tragic blockade of Leningrad during the Second World War. An American girl on the exchange whose doctoral thesis was on Pushkin introduced me to his fantastic stories of eighteenth-century Russia. I was leading the unhurried intellectual life I had never had time for at Harvard or Cornell. My Russian was improving daily, but I still worried, wondering whether my Russian or I myself was up to the shock of Soviet law school.

By October, the university was slowly awakening. Most of the Americans had met their advisors, and I knew my time had come. I had met a number of Russians outside the dormitory by this time and asked if they might help me find the law school. A few discreet telephone calls were made and I soon had my answer: building number seven, line twenty-two. It was right in our part of town, on the same residential island, perhaps a twenty-minute walk from the dormitory.

The next morning, October 9, I set out. When I reached the building I was not surprised that no one had known where it was. Line number twenty-two was a muddy back street not far from the harbor. Technically it was only one side of the street—the left side as one faced the Neva River. The other side of the street was line twenty-three. It was at the very end of a group of streets laid out by Peter the Great on the large Vasilevsky's Island. By Peter's orders, these lines were all to have had canals dug between them; hence the different numbers. Some canals actually were dug, but after Peter's death they were refilled for hygienic reasons.

Trolley car number twenty-six, on its way to St. Isaac's Cathedral and the Winter Palace, splashed along the broken pavement. Line twenty-three consisted mostly of boarded-up abandoned construction sites; line twenty-two was a row of faceless gray buildings with no markings except their street numbers. On the law school itself were two signs, neither of which identified the building as the law school: one was a white tin circular building marker with the number seven; the other, stenciled on the building's wall in blue, read, "This side of the street especially dangerous during artillery barrages." The Germans had been that close, and the city council had left this sign as a reminder.

I found a door and went in. Inside sat the omnipresent

babushka, one of the stout Russian women of grandmother age who seem to sit inside every door in the Soviet Union. She was chewing on a piece of bread and didn't acknowledge my presence. I started to wander. On the walls were a couple of signs for DOSAAF, the student paramilitary organization, and for Komsomol (Communist Union of Youth) meetings: still nothing that would identify the place as the law school. On the second floor was more activity. Students were milling about, and I found a sign that said "Dean's Office." Walking in, I explained to the secretary that I was the new exchange student from the United States and had come to see the dean. She asked me to take a seat and disappeared into the dean's office. When she returned she said that we needed to find another official, who was called the "dean for work with foreigners." She was not sure who that was for this school year, however, and I should return in a few days when they had everything sorted out. Thus ended uneventfully my first visit to the law faculty of Leningrad State University.

On my second visit I was taken to see Comrade Victor Fedorovich Sidorchenko, the dean for work with foreigners. He was pleased to see me but had no idea who I was or what I was supposed to do. I found this perplexing. About eight months earlier, when I was still in law school in Massachusetts, the American exchange committee in New York had written me an urgent request for thirty copies of a document called an *anketa*. I had already been accepted for the exchange on the basis of a long proposal and interviews in Russian and English.

This *anketa* was a kind of questionnaire outlining my research proposal and stating the archives and interviews I would need. It also contained an academic autobiography. Fifteen copies were to be in English and fifteen in Russian. I was given a week to have it back in New York. No one at the law school had seen one of these. For that matter, no one had even told them I was coming. To this day I wonder who received those fifteen "urgent" Russian copies of my *anketa*. I'm sure the Ministry of Higher Education in Moscow has a few, undoubtedly the Leningrad City Council of Working People's Deputies has several, and the KGB at all its central, city, regional, and district offices certainly got their share; but no one thought to send one to the law school.

Comrade Sidorchenko was basically a kind man. His legal specialty was maritime salvage law, and he had just come to the law school from a maritime research institute. I could not help feeling that his new job was a demotion. He was about fifty. We talked a long time, mostly about life in the United States. He was interested in American legal education and asked me how Americans could afford education. Like many Russian scholars, he had read in Soviet journals about the high cost of education in America, but had never been told about state schools, work-study programs, scholarships, or federally insured student loans. He knew about costs in the West but nothing about wages or incomes. He evaluated Western goods and services in terms of how long he, Victor Sidorchenko, would have to work at his Soviet salary in order to acquire them. A fifty-year-old dean at a top American law school might receive between $50,000 and $70,000 a year. I do not know exactly how much Sidorchenko made, but I am sure it was not less than 175 rubles a month and not more than 250. At the official exchange rate, converted to a yearly basis, this would be between $2,800 and $4,000 a year. At the black-market rate, a ruble cost between twenty-five and thirty-five cents; thus if Sidorchenko actually converted his salary into dollars he would receive at the most $1,000 for a year's work. Given his Soviet reference point, America looked like an expensive place indeed.

Sidorchenko ground no ideological axes in our discussions. His interest in the West was open and sincere. We got along very well, and after an hour or so he told me that he wanted to be my advisor. This posed a rather delicate diplomatic problem. I did not even know what my "advisor" was supposed to do, and Sidorchenko, as a new arrival, seemed about as integrated into the law school as I was. I thought it might be better to find someone on the regular teaching staff. Nor was maritime salvage law my strong hand.

I knew the name of one professor on the law school faculty—Olympiad Solomonovich Ioffe. Ioffe had published over thirty books, some of which I had seen in Western international-law libraries. He was the head of the civil-law faculty in Leningrad, reputed to be the best in the Soviet Union. I told Sidorchenko that I really thought I should talk to Professor Ioffe before I made any decision and he—reluctantly, I felt—took me to Ioffe.

Professor Ioffe always treated me very well. Even when critical he had a certain charm. He was heavy and not tall—a little Russian bear—and seemed the only person in the place capable of making a decision. At that first meeting he brushed Sidorchenko aside, saying I would be in his department and he would find me an advisor. He asked me how old I was and what degrees I held. He was very impressed when I told him I was twenty-six and had a doctorate in jurisprudence. I explained that this was quite normal under the American system, that law school was exclusively a graduate program and the doctorate was the basic degree. In the Soviet Union, more in accord with the Continental system, one goes to law school immediately after high school. The first degree after five years of study is simply called a diploma. Then students are assigned a place to work for two or three years, often in developing areas of the USSR. In order to be admitted to graduate school, a student must take another test and be accepted by the Soviet Ministry of Higher Education. The first graduate degree, called the candidate's degree, usually takes three years and includes course work and a thesis. A Soviet degree of doctor of science, in this case juridical science, usually takes many years to earn. There is no additional course work, but the dissertation must be a major contribution to the field. I told Professor Ioffe that he shouldn't consider me at the same academic level as a Soviet doctor. He said, "Well, we shall see, we shall see," and told me to come to the departmental meeting on the fifteenth of October to meet my advisor and be introduced to the faculty.

Professor Ioffe had all the characteristics I came to recognize in the successful Soviet bureaucrat. He was friendly, actually jovial, loving a little light repartee. Successful Soviet bureaucrats no longer have the doctrinaire, deathly serious, self-righteous approach I gather they had during the Stalinist period. Now they have, in informal situations at least, an almost light-hearted style that makes them thoroughly disarming. They are quite open in criticizing selected aspects of Soviet life. A conversation might proceed in the following manner: "What! It took you four weeks to assemble all the signatures to apply for a weekend trip to Novgorod and then your request was denied? Shocking, this bureaucracy of ours; it's better in your country, I know. Ah, yes, this is the land of bureaucracy, all right; it was much worse before the Revolution, and then the war was so hard on us."

I came to call this phenomenon the "if I can only get to the czar" theory of Russian bureaucratic relations. The minor officials with whom one dealt on a daily basis were, in general, overweight, slobbering nincompoops who were afraid to provide any assistance or make any decisions whatsoever. They would keep one standing in line interminably, not show up for appointments, and lie at every opportunity, whether the situation demanded it or not. They had no sense of responsibility to the public, treating them with disdain and derision. A Russian friend of mine finished law school and was happy to receive a clerical post at Leningrad City Hall. It was not really a "law" job but entailed helping citizens fill out various forms, some involving requests or complaints. On his first morning at work, one of his co-workers poured some of the previous night's cold tea from the samovar into his cup. "Why should I want some of yesterday's tea?" he asked. "Because, silly, when one of those bastards gets in here and starts complaining about how you're not working hard enough on his problem you just point to your cold glass and say, 'Listen, you, I'm working so hard I don't even have time to drink my cup of tea!' "

They also explained to him the "hare in the winter" theory of dealing with the public. If you kill a big Russian rabbit in the winter, you are supposed to let it hang out in the cold for a time before you attempt to cook it. This preserves and slightly ages the meat so that it becomes both succulent and easy to work with. Similarly with the public, he was told. If you let someone in to see you right away, he is likely to feel very important and demand and threaten and pound the table. But if you let him sit out in the cold waiting room with everyone else for a while, he comes into your office hungry, tired, and cowed. You can do anything you want with him. Two or three hours was considered appropriate refrigeration.

If, however, you could ever get through the barrier of minor officials, the higher-level bureaucrats were often cordial, refined, even solicitous—if not always helpful. You were brought to feel that "well, things may be a mess here but at least these upper-level guys are all right." In time I realized that this was not in fact the case. What was occurring was simply a twentieth-century rerun of the famous eighteenth-century trick the czars loved to play on the peasants. For centuries the Russian peasants suffered under an incompetent, avaricious, and unenlightened official class; but the peasant did not view the czar as incompetent or avaricious, and thought him "unenlightened" only in regard to the condition of that particular peasant and the corruption of the czar's officials. "These small guys are a bunch of bastards," the Russian peasant would say, "but if only I could get to the czar . . ." The czar was usually every bit as bungling and greedy as his underlings, but in the eyes of the peasants he was always czar-father. In fact, as Mussorgsky's opera *Boris Godunov* and various peasant revolts show, the Russian peasants could suffer any calamity but one— having a false czar on the throne. Time and time again, this brought them to revolution; their cause was to reinstate their father, the true czar.

In its modern variant the schema is not much different. Most of the time one deals with low-level officials. Sometimes they stall a request by claiming they haven't the authority to do something and the petitioner must see someone else. More often they give out wrong information and run you around town. Much time is wasted, but if you don't give up you may finally get through to someone in authority: the "czar" receives you and does what he can. You are bitter about the preliminary problems with those subaltern idiots, but not bitter about the system itself. In reality the "czar" can pretty much control whether and when you'll get to see him. In fact, he was probably the one who directed that the earlier obstacles be placed in your path. Yet the image of "czar-father" lives on.

The organization responsible for foreign students at Leningrad State (besides their individual faculties) was Inotdel, Russian shorthand for foreigners division. Everything that a foreign student hoped to do had to be approved by Inotdel, including things presumed by Westerners to be automatic—such as leaving the city, changing dormitory rooms, or visiting a historical archive. There is considerable bureaucratic enmity between the faculties and Inotdel, and as is common in the Soviet Union there are no standardized procedures or published instructions. Exchange students are batted around among their own faculties within the university, in my case the law school; the institution whose facilities they hope to utilize, such as an archive or library; their own embassies and consulates (trying to help where they could); and, finally, Inotdel.

After a year of frustration with Inotdel, I wrote this description for the handbook prepared for the following year's American exchange students:

The basic function of *Inotdel Leningrad* is to make foreign students as inefficient as possible. The method used is partial reinforcement, developed down the street from *Inotdel* by Pavlov in the late nineteenth century. It is true that Pavlov only experimented on dogs, but much has changed in the Soviet Union since the Revolution. If, for example, *Inotdel* never processed a request, the consulate would complain, then the American exchange committee would protest, and eventually the whole program would be in jeopardy. Alternatively, if *Inotdel* facilitated requests, promptly denying the impossible ones, foreign students could simply get on with their work. Apparently, neither alternative is acceptable. The only way, then, is to occasionally grant a request and to occasionally not make any mistakes. Not only does this ensure that Joseph K. will run around gathering signatures and looking for someone to help him, but also that he will wile away the hours trying to figure out what *Inotdel* really wants. Speculation as to why Vadim Anatolyich (the bottom-most official) facilitates one visa to Moscow and stalls on another for a month is parallel to speculating why one player drew an ace and another the queen of spades. Indeed there may be a reason, but the basic reason is to keep you guessing and to keep you playing.

For example, in order to go to Moscow one must first submit a "petition" to get a visa from *Inotdel*. After I obtained the signature of my advisor and the dean of the law school, to go to Moscow as duly recorded and planned six months previously, *Inotdel* decided that I also needed the signature of the Dean for Work with Foreigners [Sidorchenko] and that no one else could sign for him. He, of course, was in Moscow at the time. (I could not go to Moscow to get his signature because I did not have a visa: Catchka-

22.) This experience would lead one to believe that *Inotdel* really respected all those signatures: not at all true! Another time, on the blank spaces of a signed "petition" for a study request, an *Inotdel* official changed several items and added a visa to Riga which was completely unrelated to my petition. What my advisor and the dean had initially agreed to had been completely disfigured, while new and unrelated requests were simply tacked on above their signatures.

Often the foreign exchange students would argue over which university's Inotdel was the worst in the Soviet Union. It was as if it were some kind of special honor if your university had the stupidest and most insensitive administration of all. It is more than mere loyalty to my alma mater that makes me feel Leningrad deserves first place. Admittedly, however, Moscow's Inotdel could give them quite a contest. A Dutch friend of mine was given a scholarship to Moscow to study a *living* Leningrad poet. After a year's research and writing he was refused a short visit to Leningrad to meet the poet, because Moscow Inotdel did not think it would be useful for his work.

After one had made first contact with the faculty, the next issue on the academic agenda was the Scientific Plan. Every person in the Soviet Union is supposed to have a plan. No organization is too small, no individual too insignificant, to be without a plan. Scholars are no exception; in fact, as Soviet scholarship is considered "scientific," scholars are expected to have a scientific plan. In theory this makes good sense. The scientific plan is the document that outlines one's research and scholarly objectives for the coming academic year. It also details what interviews the scholar would like to have, what study trips to other cities will be necessary, and to what archives or other Soviet institutions the scholar needs access. At the end of the year, there is another Soviet ritual called "plan fulfillment." Every organization from machine shops to lawyers' offices must go through this year-end accounting and report to higher authorities, detailing to what extent they have "fulfilled the plan." I too would be expected to prepare an *otchet*, or accounting, at the end of the school year. This can lead to endless inefficiencies, as rewards in all types of endeavor are based not so much on actual output as on plan fulfillment. Article 152-1 of the Russian Criminal Code makes "padding" your plan an antistate action punishable by up to three years in prison, but few Soviets I knew lost much sleep over this. They knew that they would never have to falsify their *otchet* if from the first their plan's target was easily reached. The lower the goals set, the higher the chances of fulfilling or slightly overfulfilling your plan. For a factory or an individual really to work at full capacity is to court disaster. The next year's targets will be based on this past production and set even higher. The factory or individual will eventually fail to fulfill the plan and suffer for it. The wise Soviet citizen knows a thousand tricks to keep his quota low and his plan easily fulfilled.

For the exchange students, failure to fulfill one's scientific plan was no great threat, as we would all be heading home shortly after our year-end accounting. Drafting the scientific plan did, however, pose certain very real dangers. We had absolutely no information on the form for our scientific plan or the rules that governed it. It was in Inotdel's interest to keep things vague and contradictory so as not to inhibit any of their subsequent policies. All information about the plan was passed by word of mouth. When our little band of twenty Americans arrived in Leningrad, a few American students remained from the preceding year's exchange, all in the process of leaving. They counseled us sternly on the importance of getting everything even vaguely applicable into our plan, because what is an innocent-looking document in the fall could become an obstructionist monster in the spring, when Inotdel nonchalantly informs you that they will not grant any visas or study requests not mentioned in the scientific plan. Having a request in your plan certainly did not guarantee it would be granted, but at least Inotdel would have to come up with some excuse. You would still be in the running. We were urged, therefore, not only to include everything we wanted to do, but everything we might want to do; to list research visits to institutes we'd never heard of and excursions to cities we couldn't find on the map. After all, nine out of ten requests might be denied, but even making a request was impossible if it had not been included in the scientific plan.

All of this was marvelous advice until you tried to get something into your scientific plan. The problem was that you didn't write your plan in consultation with Inotdel, but with your faculty, which had very different ideas on what a plan was to encompass. You were whipsawed. The faculty would say, "This is a scientific plan. You need only put your research objectives here, which you can alter as the year progresses." At this point you could visualize yourself appearing a few months later in front of an Inotdel official saying, "But my advisor told me . . ." and his saying, "Well, you probably misunderstood—request denied."

This is merely an example of how a complex bureaucracy can thwart any initiative, but there is room to maneuver if the petitioner is both very knowledgeable and very clever; and believe me, many Russians I met were both very knowledgeable and very clever. But for a poor foreigner just off the boat, the Soviet bureaucracy is a jungle.

I arrived at the faculty on Wednesday afternoon, October 15, and met the advisor to whom Ioffe had assigned me, Valentina Fedorovna Yakovleva. We were to have many interesting conversations as the year wore on, but on that day we barely had time to say hello before the faculty meeting began. There were perhaps twelve middle-aged men sitting around a conference table. My advisor was the only

woman. On chairs against the walls were five or six junior
members, all about my age. Professor Ioffe was at the head
of the table and started the meeting. He introduced me as
their "distinguished colleague from America," and then
asked for my scientific plan. My advisor said that we had
just met and had not yet written my scientific plan. Ioffe
exclaimed, "Well, we can't do anything without a scientific
plan," and ordered us to go into the back room and write it
up immediately. So, the document that was supposed to
rule my every action for the next academic year was thrown
together in five minutes while the faculty waited. I was ter-
rified. I knew it was critical that I ask for the right things,
but I had no idea what to ask for. I proposed three months
in Moscow; she said two were enough. I asked for a trip to
Tbilisi; she countered with Sochi. Meanwhile papers flew,
documents were stamped, and suggestions were shouted
from the other room. It reminded me of a tobacco auction.
When we presented the paper Ioffe said, "I don't think trips
are supposed to be in a scientific plan." Someone else said
that in his experience they did belong, but interview requests
did not. A man across the table said no, it was precisely the
other way around. General debate and impassioned argument broke out all around the table, my fate wafting about
the room on one thin sheet of paper. During a lull in the
hubbub, I mentioned my fear that Inotdel might not allow
me to do anything that was not in the plan from the beginning. Some agreed that this could be a problem; others said
the integrity of the form must be preserved. After more
debate, Ioffe called the meeting to order and suggested a
compromise. I was to have two plans; a strictly "scientific"
one to please the formalists, and a "cultural plan" to include
everything else, from trips to Central Asia to tickets to the
Kirov ballet. Everyone applauded this masterstroke; my
advisor and I wrote it up quickly—still squabbling over time
in Moscow; and it was read, voted on, and approved.

Two things intrigued me about all this. First, that the

law faculty in particular was extremely helpful in all of these early procedures. Students in other faculties had advisors who were literally afraid to sign any study request, fearing that a mistake might do them political harm. They treated their advisees as untouchables, reasoning that these foreign devils could not possibly help their careers but could conceivably ruin them. Their advisees were viewed as embarrassing stigma. When I asked my Russian friends why I was doing so much better, they said that the law faculty was much stronger politically than the other faculties. History and literature pretty much had to do what Inotdel told them, but the law faculty had power and prestige of its own. Had not Vladimir Ilich Lenin himself taken the bar there?

The second point is that my all-important scientific plan was drawn up without reference to any other documents. There had been other documents. Almost a year earlier I had prepared a five-page proposal of what work I wished to accomplish during an academic year in the Soviet Union. I was then invited to New York by the American side of the exchange, the International Research and Exchanges Board, to defend and explain this proposal, first in English and then in Russian. It was on the basis of this proposal and interview that I was accepted for the exchange. Then there were the vanished thirty *ankety*. Each spring the Soviet and American sides sit down and negotiate. On the basis of these proposals and other information, the Soviet side accepts or rejects the American candidates. Every year some are rejected outright, some are given city placements they do not wish, and others are told to rewrite their proposals. Yet when we actually drew up my plan, this document was never mentioned. The detailed proposal so carefully constructed—intended to run the perilous diplomatic gauntlet between an American academic selection committee and the Soviet Ministry of Higher Education—was suddenly a dead letter.

When I first went to the faculty I asked where I might be able to buy a Civil Law Code. The professors told me that there were none available at that time and one simply had to be there when some appeared. I asked where this "there" might be and they said, "Oh, you know, when the trucks unload at the bookstores." I explained that I really needed a copy and asked if there were any way they could use their influence to get me one. About six weeks later, I was presented with a copy of the Civil Code of the Russian Soviet Federated Socialist Republic. I was very thankful for this book, which was indispensable for anyone studying civil law. For someone without the good offices of the law school, finding any kind of legal code was almost impossible. Despite my weekly trips to bookstores to see what was available, not only in Leningrad, but in Moscow and other cities as well, I never saw a law code for sale. There were books about the law codes, but never the law codes themselves.

An identical situation holds true in the field of literature. It is possible to find many books of literary criticism, but never the authors' own works. In the Leningrad "House of Books," on Nevsky Prospect, the biggest bookstore in the city, it was impossible to find an edition of any classical Russian author. Once I asked one of the administrators why this was so. She told me that there were many people in the Soviet Union and there was a paper shortage. Behind us stood a virtual mountain of books by Marx, Engels, Lenin, and Brezhnev, not only in Russian but in every language of the civilized world. There were political books, children's books, technical books, maudlin stories of socialist realism by Soviet authors, and literary criticism. I found it ironic and sad that in Russia, the land of the endless *taiga*, the dense Siberian forests, Tolstoy is not published because of insufficient paper.

The sad truth is that the great writers of nineteenth-century Russia are published in the Soviet Union, but not to be sold to Russians, rather to be sold for hard currency in stores like the Four Continents in New York, or in Russia to foreign tourists in the Beriozka dollar stores. During Christmas vacation, I spent hours in Russian bookstores in Paris buying books that were published in the Soviet Union but unavailable there. In the city of Pushkin, Gogol, and Dostoevsky, a person without connections or foreign currency (illegal for Russians to possess) simply cannot obtain books by these authors. It is not that they are not "honored" in the Soviet Union. In fact, there are statues and museums dedicated to them. It is difficult to find a Russian city without a Gogol Street and a Pushkin Square, and no Soviet cultural official would begin a lecture on Russia's contributions to the world without reciting a litany of their names. Yet when it comes to making their works available to the common man, there is a paper shortage, and political books are considered more appropriate.

The way one shops for books (and for that matter anything at all) in the Soviet Union is through fortune, persistence, and serendipity. The concept of going to a bookstore to buy a particular book at a particular time does not exist in the mind of the Soviet consumer. You drop by the bookstore and see what they have. If you really like books, you go to three or four bookstores a week and cultivate friends who work there. To increase my chances, I would make agreements to look for books in fields my friends were studying and they would do the same for me. Sometimes a Russian friend would present me with a book and a hilarious story about how he got it.

"But Volodya, where did you get this book? I've been looking for it all year!"

"Well, you know down there at Gogol Metro Station? There's an old babushka with a little cardboard table who sells postcards. Sometimes she has a few boxes of books, and just as I was passing she opened a box and pulled out five copies of Pushkin's *Captain's Daughter*. Well, before I could get across the corridor some guy scooped up all the copies. But then another fellow grabbed him by the collar and yelled, 'You can't have all of them,' and a scuffle broke out. The first guy dropped one of the books and in the confusion I got a hold of it, threw down the money, and ran." Even telephone directories must be obtained in this way, and the situation for legal textbooks was no better. One had to be at the bookstore when an edition came out. I was able to get a textbook on international law and one on labor law, but despite searches, I never once found one on civil law.

Given the great difficulty in finding codes and textbooks, lectures are by far the most important element in a Soviet legal education. Every Thursday, Professor Ioffe gave a class in Soviet civil law for second-year students. Since Soviet legal education is an undergraduate program, these students were about nineteen years old if they had not done their military service, and twenty-one or twenty-two if they had. (All Soviet males are required to serve two years in the army or three in the navy, but exemptions do exist.) Perhaps one-third of the class of one hundred were women. I went to class unannounced, both because I did not want to attract any notoriety among the students and because I did not want to let Ioffe know I was there. I do not believe he would have conducted the class differently if he had known I was there, but still I wanted to have as nearly as possible a "laboratory" situation. I arrived early and sat in the back of the room.

During the class the students took notes, or at least some of them took notes. The deportment of the majority of the class was less than mature. Many read papers or punched at their neighbors and talked. Ioffe was a popular teacher and joked with the students during those Thursday-afternoon classes, although frequently his jokes seemed to be designed to avoid straight answers to sensitive questions. One day he was lecturing on what Soviet citizens may own. While there is no private ownership of producers' or "capi-

(*top*) Leningrad from the northern bank of the Neva River. In the foreground is the sailing ship *Kronverk*, now used as an exclusive bar. The Greek-revival building across the river is the former stock exchange.
(*bottom*) The Law Faculty of Leningrad State University.

(*opposite, top*) Sign on the wall of the Law Faculty. The large sign reads "Citizens! During artillery barrages this side of the street especially dangerous." The white marble sign reads, "In memory of the heroism and courage of the Leningraders during the 900-day blockade of the city, this inscription has been preserved."

(*opposite, bottom*) Valentina Fedorovna Yakovleva, professor of civil law, my advisor (with the author).

(*above*) Nevsky Prospect and Dom Knigy (The House of Books), Leningrad's biggest bookstore. In reality it offers little beyond technical and political literature. The crown of the building reminds the viewer of the building's original purpose, as the Russian headquarters of the Singer Sewing Machine Company.

(*top*) One of the little shops with drawn curtains. Here one could buy foreign goods and high-quality Soviet products, unavailable to the average Russian, for special D-series certificate rubles. Prices were only a fraction of those in regular stores. I was able to buy my certificate rubles for dollars at the U.S. consulate. It is generally believed that high-level Communists receive part of their salary in this currency. It therefore matters less in the Soviet Union how much money you make than what kind. Some rubles are more equal than others.

(*bottom*) Identifying sign placed on the law-school entrance after I complained to Zhenya about how difficult it had been to find the school. The sign reads, "Leningrad Order of Lenin and Order of the Red Banner of Labor, State University named for A. A. Zhdanov JURIDICAL FACULTY."

tal" goods in the Soviet Union, one may own consumer goods. In Soviet terminology, ownership of producers' goods is called private ownership and private property, while ownership of consumer goods is called personal ownership and personal property. "Personal" property may even include a car (though relatively few Soviet citizens own a car).

This distinction is basically known to every Russian over the age of ten, and I was surprised that Ioffe felt that it required a lecture. There were, however, gray areas which held some intellectual interest. One student asked whether as it was all right to own a car, it was also all right to own a truck. This was interesting because ownership of a truck is an invitation to engage in private hauling. The Georgians who live in the rich agricultural lands along the Turkish border (their name comes from St. George, their patron saint) are notorious for engaging in this practice. In fact there are stories about Georgians building entire roads in the middle of the night in order to truck their fruits and vegetables past Soviet roadblock checkpoints. Ioffe answered: "Well, as they say in Georgia, you can, but you'll get into trouble if you do!" The students roared.

The next question was tricky: could Soviet citizens own foreign currency? Article 137 of the Russian Civil Code specifies that foreign currency and financial instruments expressed in foreign currency may be acquired only with special permission. But Ioffe did not answer with this citation, perhaps because he wanted to avoid the obvious follow-up question: why were Soviet citizens required to have this special permission? (Poles, by contrast, are perfectly free to own foreign currency, have bank accounts in U.S. dollars, and shop in the hard-currency stores.) Instead Ioffe gave a series of hypothetical examples to show how a Soviet citizen might acquire foreign currency legally and what would happen in each case. One of these examples was from his own experience. If any of his books were sold abroad, the hard-currency earnings would be received by the All-Union Copyright Agency (VAAP). They in turn would issue him D-series coupon-rubles to shop in special stores where foreign goods were available and prices were low. These coupon- or certificate-ruble stores were an interesting socialist phenomenon. They sold high-quality food and liquor at one-tenth the price a Russian would pay in the regular stores, if he could even find what he wanted. I had access to them because I was on a governmental exchange and could buy for hard currency the necessary coupon-rubles from the U.S. consulate. These stores were different from the Beriozka stores, where tourists paid directly in hard currency. Beriozkas were principally for souvenirs, not fresh produce. The coupon-ruble stores had no signs but were known for their pale yellow curtains that prevented the unprivileged Russians from seeing in. Because diplomats had access, the stores were also referred to as "diplomatic gastronomes." On the black market, D-series coupon-rubles were worth from six to eight regular rubles. It was generally assumed that high officials received a portion of their pay in this currency.

The student then said he knew there were legal ways to acquire foreign currency, but he wanted to know if its mere possession could ever be construed as illegal. At this point, Ioffe made a characteristic joke. He said, "Oh, I see our black marketeer is really interested in this question." The class laughed and the questioner flushed red. Although it was said in a friendly way, this was no laughing matter. Article 88 of the Russian Criminal Code establishes deprivation of freedom of from three to eight years, with compulsory confiscation of the financial valuables plus possible confiscation of other property, and possible exile (i.e., to Siberia) of from two to five years, as the punishment for currency speculation. In serious cases, involving large sums or recidivism, the penalty may be death. Ioffe gave yet another example of a legal way to acquire foreign currency—by working in Soviet missions abroad. In this case, the official upon his return is expected to turn over his hard currency to the state and receive D-series coupon-rubles. Ioffe finished the inquiry by saying, "Enough questions from black marketeers," and returned to his lecture.

Despite tactics such as this, Ioffe was basically a good lecturer with a kindly, avuncular style. His classes were always entertaining. Once he said, "You know, if you get permission from the state you can even own a plane." "What kind," one of the students yelled from the back, "a Foxbat?" Even Ioffe laughed. (This was the type of fighter in which a young Soviet pilot had escaped that fall to Japan, a tremendous embarrassment to the Soviet Union.) Ioffe was probably the most popular teacher at the law school.

Classes were nothing like at Harvard. There was no Socratic question-and-answer method, nor was there any analysis of actual cases and decisions to illustrate legal reasoning and techniques. Lectures reminded me of the way I was taught history in high school: there was no attempt to develop a historical method or make historians out of us— we were told the facts, and during examinations we were expected to give the facts back, not with analysis, not with differing interpretations. Some teachers would use the West as a comparative framework upon which the Soviet Union had improved. They would say such things as "Under bourgeois systems they do this, but here in the Soviet Union. . . ." At Leningrad the students took notes and, at the end of the term, an oral examination. If they did not know an answer the professors would often give them little hints. In Soviet education there are few failures. The state needs the graduates, and it reflects poorly on the professor if any of his students fail. While there were some bright students, my impression was that the overall level of legal education was very low. I must repeat, however, that Soviet legal education is at the undergraduate level, and therefore a direct comparison with American legal education is not fair to the Soviet system. The greatest weakness in Soviet legal education seemed to me to be its failure to develop a critical or analytical approach. The students were taught to recite the rather vague Soviet codes and nothing further.

For the rest of that semester I met with my advisor every second week. First we would take care of administrative problems. Her signature was the initial step in my submitting any official requests I might have. The most important of these were requests simply to leave the city. We were not supposed to go more than thirty kilometers (eighteen miles) from the center of Leningrad without a visa. It took me, with an American passport, six weeks of negotiations with Soviet authorities to receive permission to leave the country for three weeks at Christmas. (For a Soviet citizen to obtain a visa to leave the Soviet Union would have required years of effort, probably ending in failure.) After this we would discuss what I was reading and any questions I had on Soviet law. Inevitably our conversations drifted to current events and politics.

My reading assignments were a continual source of frustration. In the West I had access to any Soviet law book I desired. The collection at the International Law Library at Harvard was very good. Some Western institutions, notably the Documentation Office for East European Law at the University of Leyden in the Netherlands, have libraries that are vastly superior to those in the Soviet Union itself. This is because of the considerable difficulty of using a Soviet library and the Soviet practice of removing books whose contents or authors fall into ideological disrepute. In fact, one is not permitted to take old books out of the country, without special permission for each book. During my student year this prohibition applied to any book published before 1946, but in the fall of 1980 the ban was brought forward thirty years to encompass any book published in the Soviet Union prior to 1976. My feeling was that I had not come to the Soviet Union to read books more readily available in the West, but to do that which could be done only on the soil—to see Soviet law in practice.

My advisor's position was understandably quite the opposite. Valentina Fedorovna Yakovleva wanted me to behave as a normal Soviet graduate student would, to read texts that would deepen and refine my sense of Marxist-Leninist jurisprudence. Moreover, my advisor had no particular contact with, or love for, actual legal practice. She was a professor and viewed courts, consultation offices, and commercial arbitration as somehow retarded caricatures of a grand theoretical model. I felt she honestly never really understood why I wanted to see all those sordid things when there were books to be read.

The Soviet academic legal community is more cut off from lawyers in legal practice than is the American academic legal community. This is owing in part to the different and superior status the Soviet academic lawyer has in the Soviet bar generally. An American practicing lawyer has exactly the same degree as a law professor, a doctor of jurisprudence. By contrast, a Soviet practicing lawyer has an undergraduate diploma while a professor has possibly ten more years of academic study and two higher degrees. While the highest-paid American lawyers are certainly those with lucrative private practices, it is the Soviet academic lawyer who garners the highest salaries and fringe benefits (although many practicing lawyers supplement their earnings by payments "on the side"). This makes it less tempting for a Soviet academic to mix his scholarly duties with private practice, as is common for American attorneys. As all Soviet lawyers are assigned to one particular institution, it would be difficult structurally as well. Although my advisor promised she would help me to see Soviet law in practice, she never did. Everything I later accomplished in this endeavor I did unofficially and never discussed with Professor Yakovleva either before or after the fact.

Our relationship was on the whole a positive one. She

asked me about my family and how we lived. When I told her my mother was fifty-two, she was very pleased; she was exactly the same age. The most remarkable thing about her, and for me perhaps the most valuable, is that during my whole time in the Soviet Union she was the only Party-line Communist I knew. The people in the dormitory were in the Komsomol; they could not be in a dormitory with foreigners otherwise. In fact they could not even be in Leningrad State University otherwise. But their political opinions seemed to vary depending on how loudly the radio was playing and what other Russians were present. Among the people I met around Leningrad—for the most part artists and professional people—I couldn't find a single Communist. That is not to say all of these people were critical of their government; some were and some weren't. But the Marxist-Leninists I thought I would meet by the droves simply were not there.

After discussing my reading, my advisor and I would talk about life in our countries and, inevitably, politics. One of these discussions involved the problem of motivating people under a socialist regime. I was not talking about that small percentage of scholars, artists, and careerists who do their work out of artistic or professional motivation. I was concerned about the average person with a clerical, trade, or labor job, who in the West is motivated primarily by material incentives. In the Soviet Union, the "carrot" of material gain is gone, or at least "withered away" (unlike the state itself), but so is the "stick" of destitution. If someone has no job and refuses to take one, he will eventually wind up in a work camp on charges of parasitism. But if you have a job and simply show up occasionally, you will never be fired. You will be cajoled to work harder, and harangued occasionally, but nothing more. With some exceptions, the Russians I observed did not work hard, and Russian bosses did not make them work. People have the duty to work but also the right to a job. Laboring jobs all pay poorly, they all pay about the same, and everybody gets paid. To watch Russians at work is a study in organized inactivity. Most people seem to drift, doing as little as possible.

I raised this problem with my advisor. I said that except through the Communist Party bureaucracy or the university hierarchy, there seemed to be no way to improve one's position, and as a result people paid very little attention to their work. Her answer was an emotional one from her own experience. She asked how I could make such a statement when she, now a professor on the law faculty, was the great-grandchild of serfs "tied to the land." Her great-grandmother had been an unschooled peasant babushka from the village. How could I then say there was no chance to improve one's position? She was so pleased with her rebuttal that she determined to use it despite the fact that I had excluded the university from my criticism. In the interests of our continuing good relations, I did not counter her argument with the embarrassing truth that Soviet peasants—as they were not at that time issued internal passports necessary for travel, and had to receive the permission of their collective farm in order to leave their job—are still very much "tied to the land." The restrictions on the issuance of internal passports are only now beginning to change, and by 1982 all peasants should have passports. However, restrictions on changing jobs still keep the population from moving about. Residence in the large cities requires a special permit. I asked her if such advancement was also possible for the workers. She then used an argument I was to hear many times in the Soviet Union and which continues to fascinate me: "Man does not live by bread alone." She did not use that exact word, "bread," but said that man does not live by "material things" alone.

Marxism-Leninism purports to be scientific, materialistic, and antireligious. Yet it seems that Soviet Communists cannot defend their system without arguments that are emotional, antimaterial, and religious. In factories, giant signs proclaim, "Lenin lived, Lenin lives, Lenin will always live," or "Lenin is more alive than the living." Even Aeroflot, the Soviet airline (affectionately known to us as Scareaflot or Aeroflop) had advertisements that said, "Lenin flies with us." The night of November 7, the anniversary of the Bolshevik seizure of power in 1917, several of us were having dinner in the dormitory with some of the Russians. After more than a few glasses of wine a pimply-faced Russian, feeling very patriotic, began lecturing us on Soviet achievements since the Revolution. At one point, someone asked him why, if the Soviet system was so successful, the standard of living was so low. He had a meatball on the end of his fork and began waving it in the air. "Now, take this meatball, for example. I know the meat is bad—you don't have to tell me it's bad, I've lived here all my life—but under communism we believe in the future."

I discussed this with my advisor. Marx argued that there was nothing morally wrong with capitalism, that it was in fact a necessary stage in economic development. It would inevitably fall owing to its own "internal" contradictions. These contradictions resulted in uneven development, concentration of capital, and the increasing size and misery of the industrial proletariat. Socialism would relieve these contradictions and usher in an era of plenty. Soviet reality falls quite short of this expectation. I asked my advisor how she could justify a system on economic grounds which year after year proved incapable of producing goods for the masses. Her response was that economics had nothing to do with production of goods but with relationships between people. If you had no capital and worked for someone else who did, then you were exploited—by definition. But if only the state had capital and everyone worked for the state, then you were not exploited—also by definition. I asked her what she meant by "exploitation," when an American worker had ten times the disposable income of a Soviet worker doing the same job. She responded: "Man does not live by bread alone."

I did not disagree with her final statement. Coming from someone who held religious or spiritual values it would have been normal and understandable, but coming from a "historical materialist" it seemed hypocritical. When the Soviet Union could not measure up on the facts, I was told that I must "believe": believe in the future, believe in Lenin, believe in the people, believe in anything, but just believe. I found this a curious position for a "scientific atheist."

On other occasions Valentina Fedorovna Yakovleva would respond to any question about the Soviet system with immediate attacks upon the West. Once I asked if she thought there was any possibility of the Soviet border becoming more open. She shot back that there was no intention of opening the border to let drugs come in from the West. She mentioned three Americans in transit from Southeast Asia to Europe recently arrested in Moscow with drugs. (The story had received much attention in the Soviet press.) She told me that drugs were the great problem with which my generation would have to struggle and that the penalty for anyone selling drugs must be death, as this was equivalent to murder. I reminded her that there were different types of drugs, some more harmful than others. She said no, there was no difference, and the legal penalty must be death regardless of the circumstances. I saw very little connection between this and a more open Soviet border.

I encountered this style of argument frequently among Soviet official people. The response would have no logical connection to what one had said. Here, for example, the arrested Americans were in transit to Europe, not supplying the Russian market. The opium in their possession had very likely come from communist Laos or socialist Burma. Only a month before, most of the North Korean diplomats in the Scandinavian countries had been expelled for drug smuggling. In any case the Soviet Caucasus has plenty of opium and marijuana of its own, both grown and used. Nor was I advocating that people crossing the border not be searched—I myself was once searched for two hours by three customs men—but only that they, and their books perhaps, be allowed to go through.

She told me that she was not the only one who had such political views. I could ask any professor on the law faculty, she said, and they would all have identical opinions. I pointed out that from a Western perspective this was precisely the problem, that for us, diversity of political views and discussion were encouraged, not suppressed. She allowed that although 30 percent of the law professors were non-party (she herself had been a member since the Second World War), it would be impossible for someone with different political views to become a professor.

Though I do not doubt the sincerity of her convictions, I found her unable to carry on a discussion without extreme emotional agitation and spectacular non sequiturs. In our conversations she displayed no ability for abstraction or dispassionate analysis, relying instead on rhetoric, party slogans, and derisive laughter. Despite her sense of accomplishment in having risen above the lot of her great-grandmother, she acted more the part of a babushka from the villages than what she in fact was: a professor on the finest civil-law faculty in Russia.

Victor Sidorchenko and I also had periodic talks during the first semester. As dean for work with foreigners in the law school, he represented stage two in the procedure for processing requests and visas. He had four hours of "reception" a week which, to my continual consternation, he would rarely honor. When he finally came there would always be an angry line of Cubans, Vietnamese, and Eastern Europeans outside the door. Several times when his signature was essential the faculty would organize manhunts to find him. Later I would be told he had slipped down to Moscow without telling anyone. For a time I was able to convince the dean of the law school to sign for Sidorchenko, but Inotdel eventually complained, saying that Sidorchenko's signature was necessary as well. The motivation behind this fascination with signatures was that Inotdel understood very well that if they sent someone to get the signatures of any four Soviet officials chosen at random, one would certainly be sick and another would be in Moscow. It would take a month to collect them all.

When I actually would get in to see Sidorchenko, he was always very friendly. He accorded me higher status than the other students he was responsible for, probably because I was an American. The basic rule of thumb is that the worse your government's relations are with the Soviet Union, the better you are treated by the authorities. Citizens of "fraternal socialist countries" get very shabby treatment indeed. On a personal level, Americans are particularly well liked. I traveled all over the Soviet Union that year and met all sorts of people, yet I never once encountered any anti-American sentiment. To the contrary, as soon as I told people I was an American their eyes would open wide and practically glow at the thought of having an American friend. This was particularly impressive considering the daily diatribe against the United States in the Soviet press.

Once when I entered Sidorchenko's office he was talking with a Mongolian student about dormitory conditions, and motioned for me to sit down. Mongolia, large, poor, and sandwiched between Russia and China, is politically a Russian protectorate. In private conversations, Russians even refer to Mongolia, Bulgaria, and East Germany as their sixteenth, seventeenth, and eighteenth republics. Many Mongolians study in the Soviet Union, but their relations with the Russians on a personal basis are not good. The Mongolians consider the Russians to be drunken brutes, while the Russians—inclined to dwell on their successful defense against Western invaders, Charles XII, Napoleon, and Hitler—cannot quite forget that they were less fortunate when the attack came from the East. During the Mongol invasion of Europe, Batu, a grandson of Genghis Khan, crossed the Urals in 1236. After massacring the populace of the principality of Riazan, Batu attacked and destroyed the seat of the Russian grand prince at Vladimir in the winter of 1237–38. In a few months the Mongols had conquered the strongest area of Russia—the only successful winter invasion of Russia in history. Turning south, the Mongols then leveled Kiev and established a yoke over Russia which was to last for more than two centuries.

This particular Mongolian was telling Sidorchenko that if the Mongolian students were required to live six to a room, they preferred that all the Mongolians be together and not mixed up with the Russians. They weren't complaining about the crowding in the dorms, but did not want to live with filthy drunkards. Rather than having three Mongolians and three Russians in each room, they wanted six of their own people. Leningrad State's policy was that all foreigners should have Russian roommates except married couples, and Sidorchenko's problem was to refuse the Mongolian's request as diplomatically as possible. Sidorchenko, himself a Ukrainian, countered that it was good to have Russians in your room because even drunken Russians at least spoke Russian, and it was important for foreign students to improve their Russian. They then argued about how many Russians were necessary in each room. Sidorchenko eventually said he might be able to reduce the number to two per room, and the Mongolian left.

Sidorchenko was a reasonable man and not a bad diplomat. In dealing with foreign students, he was dealing with people who in every case came from countries that were richer, freer, or at the very least warmer than Russia. One of the arguments he frequently employed was some variant of the "Think how much worse off you could be" argument, which is used with great success against native Russians. Its corollary, the "Nobody's complaining but you, comrade" argument, was also quite popular. The new dormitory in Peterhof is an example of the "Don't complain, it could be worse" defense.

The university was, we were told, building a new and modern dormitory at Peterhof, where Peter the Great had built his Russian Versailles. This would have been good news considering the tenement we were living in, but Peterhof was a full two-hour trip each way from the university. Any trip to the faculty, the library, the consulate, or any cultural event would have entailed a long commute, frequently in freezing weather. This, added to the other inefficiencies—standing in food lines and chasing after signatures—would have made our lives useless for anything beyond physical survival. The new dormitory, which was supposed to improve our living conditions, instead had turned into a threat, silencing any criticism about our current situation.

My Russian next-door neighbor told me about his summer experience in a student work camp in the forests between Leningrad and Moscow. His Komsomol group and student groups from Poland and Cuba were doing construction work under very primitive conditions. They didn't mind the hard work so much but grew increasingly unhappy about the poor facilities and poor food. There were five toilets for several hundred people, and no separate facilities for women. The food was atrocious even by Soviet standards, and the cooking arrangements so unsafe that several students had been severely burned. Boiling pots of soup were placed on rickety chairs on wobbly wooden floors, for want of kitchen tables. Finally the students complained, and one of the leaders of the Komsomol was dispatched from Moscow. Despite the fact that Komsomol literally means "Communist Union of Youth," its leadership is in its fifties (admittedly, this is still a full generation younger than the septuagenarian politburo). A meeting of the Komsomol was called from which the Poles and the Cubans were excluded. Lev, from Moscow, balding and overweight, took the stand. "So you are complaining, comrades," he began, "after all the party has done for you. Don't you know what things were like for your parents' generation? You don't like your food, but they had no food. Did they complain? No, they were too busy fighting for your country's survival, so that you could live in peace and prosperity. Do you realize that this is the only camp in the whole Republic that has complained about conditions? At the other camps, as soon as I get within three miles of the place I see signs praising Lenin and the Soviet leaders. But not here, no, not here. Here there is just a chorus of dissatisfied children." The actual dressing down lasted an hour, and afterwards the members of the Komsomol felt horribly embarrassed and disgraced. The complaints ceased; the food stayed bad and the kitchen unsafe. Later, when my neighbor was back in Leningrad, his friends told him that they had also complained about conditions in their camps, and had been told that they were the only ones complaining.

Sidorchenko employed similar arguments in our conversations. I complained that Soviet procedures made academic life difficult for no apparent reason. We were not allowed, for example, to bring our own books into the library. Everything had to be checked: coats and umbrellas in one place, books and briefcases in another—both checkrooms with long lines and harassed, underpaid checkers. Then we had to get in another line to present our library cards, which were like small hardbound passports. We were then given a long, narrow sheet of paper. The code of any book we requested would be stamped on this paper. To get something to eat or drink one turned in the library card and strip of paper and went downstairs to the buffet. This entailed at least a twenty-minute wait in line if in fact the buffet was not closed owing to "sanitary day," "free day," "accounting day," "break," "technical reasons," "repairs," or one of the other myriad occurrences which managed to keep most things in the Soviet Union closed most of the time. The books in the library were all on closed reserve and usually needed to be ordered a day ahead. One had to be certain to be there the next day to pick them up or be prepared to start the process anew. Every hour we had to abandon the reading room in order to let the library staff open all the windows. The icy winds from the Gulf of Finland would pour in, ostensibly airing the room. We used to call this procedure "Blow your house down."

Worst of all from my point of view as a foreigner was that we were not even allowed to bring in our dictionaries. There were dictionaries available in the library but they were written by Russians, for Russians. Based on the British English of Charles Dickens's time, they were old and of poor quality.

Sidorchenko calmly listened to my tirade and in a fatherly way finally responded, "Well, just be glad you've at least got a library card." I asked him what he meant. "It's really a great privilege. I know there are inefficiencies in the libraries but at least you can use them. A Soviet citizen can't even get into the *public* library without a university degree, and as for BAN, the library you use [Library of the Academy of Science], that library is only for members of the Academy of Science, or at the very least, graduate students working on advanced degrees." I was floored. "What do people do who don't have university degrees?" I asked. "Oh, they have readers' halls with technical and political literature. They aren't very large collections, of course, but if someone's work requires something special, he is given it."

Earlier I had mentioned that studying in the dormitory was difficult. There was a separate study room but it had no lights, no chairs, and only four desks for two hundred people. In my room the electric socket was broken, there were no parts to fix it, and it caused my light to blink on and off like a Broadway billboard. At that time of year there were only five hours of dirty gray light from dawn to dusk. I did not mention to him that my roommate was usually drunk and swaggering about the room or crying in the corner. Sidorchenko dealt with these problems summarily. "Sure, there are problems in the dorm, but just be glad you're not a Mongolian."

Sometimes the walls have ears in Russia, and in small things a foreigner can unexpectedly achieve tremendous results. I complained a few times in the dormitory about how hard it had been to find the law school. I even said to my roommate that I thought it disgraceful that the law school did not even have a sign to identify it. On my very next visit to the faculty there was a man on a tall ladder outside the main entryway. He was putting up a series of gold-painted letters: Leningrad Order of Lenin and Order of the Red Banner of Labor, State University named for A. A. Zhdanov JURIDICAL FACULTY. I felt I had made my contribution.

Two /

Dormitory Life

When I arrived in Leningrad from Cincinnati via Boston, London, and Helsinki, I was met at the airport by an official from the American consulate. The Soviet customs officer asked only if I had any literature in my suitcases, and when I said no, he waved me through without any inspection. As luck would have it, I had arrived just in time for the new exchange students' official reception at the American consulate. Most of our group had come the week before; I had been delayed by the Ohio bar examination. Before going to the consulate, we went by the dormitory to drop off my things. This was my first look at dormitory number two at 25 Shevchenko Street on Vasilevsky's Island—my home for the next ten months.

My room was number fifty-eight on the fourth floor of the undistinguished, five-story, light gray brick building. My roommate-to-be was not there, but his possessions were scattered around the room. They branded him "Westernizer," and this for me was a disappointment. Since Peter the Great's time there has been a tension in Russia between the "Westernizers" and the "Slavophiles." By the nineteenth century these two groups had established themselves as philosophical movements. Proponents of both groups thought Russia had a great historical mission, but the Westernizers believed it could be accomplished only in the context of European civilization and Western institutions. The Slavophiles found the West spoiled and decadent and felt that the nation must look to the East and to Russia's own past for guidance.

From one glance it was clear that my roommate was a "Westernizer" in the extreme. American rock-and-roll albums were spread around the room; bottles of Alka-Seltzer lined the shelves. Foreign books and toiletries were everywhere. This was all the more surprising because in Russia these items can be obtained only on the black market. Had I come so far to return to a "Little America"? From the small library it was clear that my roommate not only read English but that the language was his major subject in the university. I put down my suitcase, guitar, and typewriter, and went with my escort to the consulate.

Half an hour later I was standing at the Marine bar of the American consulate, hoisting a Heineken, surrounded by old comrades from the Russian Summer School at Middlebury College, Vermont. After the reception some of us went down Liteiny Prospect to the Volkov Restaurant. My first meal in Russia consisted of a big bowl of meat soup (*solyanka*), black caviar from the Caspian Sea, chicken croquette, sliced tomatoes with sour cream, black bread—and vodka. For me, at least, summer in Leningrad was not to be a time of deprivation. We continued our revel back at the dorm until three in the morning. I then dragged up the stairs to meet my new roommate. We were to share an eight-by-thirteen-foot room for the next ten months.

His name was Yevgenii Alexandrovich Komkov, or simply, Zhenya. (The initial *Zhe* in *Zhenya* is pronounced like the final *-ge* in the word gara*ge*.) He was a graduate student in English—English historical linguistics to be exact—and his English was very good indeed. In my first few months of getting to know Russia, he was certainly the Russian I got to know best, and my impressions were very much colored by him. It turned out that Zhenya played the guitar,

as did I. The records, Alka-Seltzer, and other foreign products were presents from a string of American and British
roommates he had had during his four years in the dormitory. During those early days he was a one-man cultural-
orientation committee. He showed me where things were
and how they worked, providing me with all sorts of information from nuances of Russian syntax to where to get a
cold beer.

As the year progressed our relationship deteriorated. This
was not the fault of either of us, but was to some extent
inevitable, the result of the enormous psychological stress of
spending a year in a very small room with someone from a
radically different culture. Our little room, our agreements
and disagreements, became a microcosm of the relations
between our countries. Détente slid into cold war. Looking
back on the year, I can describe not one but two Zhenyas.
My relationship with Zhenya displayed the ambiguity in
many relationships between foreigners resident in the Soviet
Union and the Russian people.

Zhenya was from the small town of Saransk, south of
Gorky. Gorky itself is some three hundred miles due east
of Moscow. (Called Nizhni-Novgorod before the Revolution, Gorky is closed to foreigners and is presently the place
of "internal exile" for Nobel laureate Andrei Sakharov.)
Outside of the great tourist cities of European Russia, the
level of development is essentially that of the eighteenth
century. Saransk is a muddy little town where the horse-
drawn plow and log cabin still figure prominently. Saransk
and the towns like it were referred to by the cosmopolitan
Leningraders as the *glush*—the sticks, the provinces, the
backward areas.

Probably the first time we drank vodka together—and
there were many such times—Zhenya told me about his
father. Zhenya's father was nicknamed "the Bear." He had
been a prisoner of war but had escaped from the Germans
and made his way to Switzerland, where he was interned.

Zhenya told me that after the battle of Stalingrad, the Swiss respect for the Russians increased remarkably. Zhenya's father was released. He decided not to sit out the war comfortably in neutral Switzerland, but to cross the border into occupied France. He spent almost a year hiding with anticommunist Russian émigrés, and eventually, crossing the Mediterranean, made his way across North Africa to neutral Turkey. Over the Black Sea, he returned home to the Soviet Union. He did not receive the hero's welcome he had expected but instead was immediately arrested.

Zhenya's father was fortunate. Most returning Russian prisoners of war were sentenced as traitors and bundled off to Siberia. But with the war on Hitler's eastern front still raging, Zhenya's father was offered a choice—Gulag or a *shtrafnoi* (punishment) battalion. The *shtrafnoi* battalions were used to do the most dangerous fighting. Indeed, they were to fight until they no longer existed as a battalion. Individuals who survived were pardoned. Two weeks later Zhenya's father was in the eastern suburbs of Budapest. Hungary had been a German ally during the war and Budapest was still in Axis hands. The battalion was told that they were to spearhead the effort to cut Budapest in two. The city would have to be taken street by street and house by house. Zhenya's father was a big man, big enough to hold a floor-mounted heavy machine gun in his bare hands. In the *Götterdämmerung* battle, the Russian battalion fanned out across the rooftops of buildings held by the German and Hungarian defenders. To capture the lower floors, six men would lower "the Bear" down the side of the building with his heavy machine gun blazing. When the fighting was over, there were twenty-seven men left in the *shtrafnoi* battalion—there had been twelve hundred. Zhenya's father was given a full pardon and returned to Saransk. Later he joined the Party, took a degree in engineering, and became a figure of some importance in the small town.

Zhenya was a bright pupil. He was not only talented in

his studies but was a good artist and musician as well. In the Pioneers and then in the Komsomol, he was always appointed art director. He graduated from his community college with a gold medal for having all fives (the equivalent of all A's) and received a Lenin fellowship to the University of Leningrad. The stipend carried the highest award possible, ninety rubles a month. Tuition was free, but there was a small dormitory-room rent of thirty rubles each semester.

Life in the NATO-pact dorm was a new world for the scholarship student from the *glush*. He was not like the other Russians. He was a linguist; he was curious and friendly. He was invited to the foreigners' parties to sing and play guitar. He soon found himself with a succession of foreign girl friends. It did not take long for him to incur the envy of the other Russians. The dormitory president (not elected but appointed by a higher Party committee) publicly criticized Zhenya's conduct. Zhenya was told to be friendly with the foreigners but not to become friends with them. This put him in a difficult position. This denunciation reinforced his feelings that he could trust the foreigners more than he could his own countrymen. Just as many of the Russians resented him for his French girl friends and American albums, he had come to hate them for their stupidity and toadyism to the Party officials. Increasingly he became both critical of the Soviet Union and paranoid about his position in it. He read all of the books and newspapers the foreigners brought home from their consulates. He started to drink—heavily.

Zhenya relished his time in Leningrad. He never studied but continued to triumph over the idiots who got into Leningrad on the strength of their fathers' Party records. He knew, though, that his triumph would be short-lived. Without connections, and with his loyalty perhaps subject to question, when the time would come for employment, it looked as if it was back to Saransk. A lecturer there received 120 rubles ($160 in 1976) a month, no French girl friends, and no Alka-Seltzer. There was no chance of his being chosen for an exchange program such as mine to the West: the Soviets rarely send anyone other than established mid-career scientists and engineers on exchange.

Zhenya had considered the possibility of marrying one of the foreign girls in the dormitory and explained to me what a Soviet male goes through when he applies to marry a Westerner and to emigrate. Usually the authorities say he can't be permitted to go because he has served in the army (as he must) and hence knows military secrets. Even those who did little more than peel potatoes for two years are refused because of their knowledge of "military secrets." Zhenya told me a joke about the refusenik (i.e., one who applies to emigrate and is refused) who is told by a KGB officer that he can't go abroad because he knows a crucial military secret. He responds, "But comrade colonel, we have no military secrets." "Precisely," reports the officer; "that's our military secret." Zhenya's case was different. Because of his high marks and poor eyesight, he had not been in the military. But he told me this would not make it much easier for him. The imagination of the authorities was boundless, and they would just find another excuse.

Some of the reluctance to let males emigrate had nothing to do with communist ideology but sprang from the deep-rooted Russian cultural belief that the wife should follow the husband: if a Western woman married a Russian man, the couple should stay in Russia. Of course no one wants to do this, especially the Soviet husband, who half the time sees his foreign wife principally as a ticket out of the USSR. While it is possible to get a man out, the Soviet authorities make it very difficult. Zhenya knew that if he applied to emigrate he might never be allowed to go, and meanwhile the repercussions for his family would be disastrous. His father would be thrown out of the Party and probably lose his job. Even if Zhenya received permission the process might take two years, during which time he would be unable to find work. Furthermore, Zhenya was sophisticated enough to have no romantic illusions about the position of an émigré in Western society and the struggle to start life again in a foreign land. No, he concluded; for a woman this might be a solution, but for a man it would not do. A marriage to a Leningrad girl might at least secure a place for himself in the city and prevent his being forced back to the *glush*.

While he thought he drank, and when he drank he became both emotional and violent. Once he started choking me because I had left the door ajar as I had entered the room— he was convinced the other Russians were spying on him. After such outbursts he would apologize profusely and tell me, with tears and embraces, that his genius had been wasted on his filthy, backward country. Every month Zhenya would stand in line on the first day possible to receive his stipend. For the next three days he would be on a drunken binge. He would take a girl out to a restaurant the first night and insist on paying for everything. Drunken and laughing, he would stagger back to the dormitory, half of his month's stipend gone. The next day he would wake up with an enormous hangover and head for an outside beer stall to queue up with thirty or forty other hungover Russians. Each stall had a woman dispensing beer with a hose from a huge tank behind the shed. This tank was in turn filled from what appeared to be a miniature gasoline truck, dispensing beer from its hose in place of petrol. Each woman had only a few mugs, so the customers would have to wait for someone ahead to finish drinking. After a few mugs Zhenya would head to the public baths, then back to the beer stall, and finally back to the dormitory to sleep it off. That night there would invariably be a party somewhere. By the third day his entire month's stipend would be gone. He would take back his old wine and vodka bottles for money to buy soup. Then he would start borrowing. People realized that they would never again see money lent to Zhenya; I never saw mine, nor expected to.

By the middle of the year, a new problem made Zhenya increasingly difficult to live with. Zhenya had always had trouble with his eyes. His thick horn-rimmed glasses had broken in several places. He had tried to replace them but had been told that there were no eyeglasses in the city and he would have to wait to be included in the production plan for the next year. His old glasses, hanging together with the help of tape and paperclips, gave him constant headaches. He could read for only an hour or two each day. Vodka, he said, eased the headache and made his eyes stop aching. An invitation from anyone at any time to have a drink brought Zhenya on the run.

Zhenya's attitude toward the Soviet Union vacillated with the issue and his mood. Often when our late-night conversations turned to politics, he would turn up his radio and tell me stories of outrageous corruption and duplicity. This "turning up the radio" ritual was a continual facet of Soviet life. As soon as someone wanted to introduce a sensitive subject, he reached for the radio. It was as much an automatic response as turning on the lamp when one wanted to read. Zhenya suspected there were microphones in the room but said—correctly, I believe—that they were there to pick up the conversations of the Russians. The foreigners' opinions were expected to be critical. If Zhenya and I wanted to do something together, he would leave earlier and wait for me at the bus stop. We would return by different routes. He would tell me stories about his occasional and fleeting contact with the Russian upper class, about big bashes on Western liquor and imported delicacies paid for from the state's foreign-currency reserves. He told me about the time he had caught a suspected informer listening at the door and had beaten him severely. He said that he had been abroad one time, to Bulgaria, but having had to endure so many commissions and investigations in order to go even there, practically a Soviet colony, he planned never to go abroad again.

Our roommate situation gave me a revealing glimpse into Soviet psychology. All of the rooms on the north side of the dormitory were for two people. Married couples on the exchange lived in these rooms. The rooms on our side, the south side, were slightly larger and were for three people, normally one Russian and two foreigners of different nationalities. Our third roommate had never shown up. Zhenya said he was a Soviet Ukrainian who was nominally registered but had in fact left the city some time ago. Zhenya had succeeded in bribing the dorm commandant not to put anyone else in the room. Zhenya and I discreetly paid the thirty rubles per semester dorm rent for our inconspicuous third rooommate. I must admit it was a bargain. A third person in that room would have given each of us about five square yards of *Lebensraum*. At least with only two we each had our own desk and the occasional private moment. This arrangement was top secret, and I was instructed to say that of course we had a third roommate and that if there were any questions they were to be taken up with Zhenya.

One night in November I threw a spaghetti party with another American exchange student, Nancy Fehsenfeld. The occasion was my having passed the Ohio bar examination. Spaghetti is a great treat in the Soviet Union because it is rarely available in the stores for the common people. We bought all sorts of Western products from the diplomatic store and invited friends, both Western and Russian. One of the Russians we invited was Vera, Nancy's roommate. Vera was thirty-five and a first-year graduate student. She was studying German, but the only thing anyone had ever heard her say in German was "I'm not so dumb as I look." That night she certainly proved her point. After

(*opposite, top*) The author in the dormitory shortly after arrival in Leningrad.
(*opposite, bottom*) The large building on the left is our dormitory, Shevchenko
Street 25, Building 2.
(*above*) Zhenya, my roommate.

Room #58, the dormitory room I shared with Zhenya for the year.

enjoying the food and drink and general conviviality, she began to question me about our third roommate. I was as evasive as possible, but she would not let the subject drop. She conducted the whole cross-examination in a joking manner, with an "I can keep a secret" style. The next morning we received a visit from the woman in charge of passport and room registration about our third roommate. Vera had denounced us. After the woman had left I was fuming, but Zhenya was quite calm and said to me quietly, "You know, I don't think it was very wise of Vera to tell all those jokes about Jews and other Soviet minorities last night, I mean considering that you foreigners were here. After all, what kind of an impression would it give you? She was very careless last night." Zhenya would not discuss it further, but we never got a third roommate and Vera never came back to our room or even set foot on our floor again.

There was something in Zhenya's character that made me uneasy. Was he, as he said he was, an oppressed, misunderstood person whose only crime was that he got along with people, including foreigners? Or was there a darker side? Had he in fact been placed in the dormitory as a very effective informer, a *stukach?* He never studied, his English was excellent, and he had always had American and British roommates. If in fact he had been censured for contact with foreigners, why was he permitted to continue living in the NATO-pact dorm? I asked him this last question and he explained that it was because of his father. As long as his father lived he would not be totally denounced, but when his father died he would surely be swept away. There were rumors, however, that Zhenya had been in the dormitory twice as long as the four years he claimed. One night he said that the Soviet Union had never annexed any Bulgarian territory, as they had that of their other European neighbors (Finland, Rumania, Germany, Poland, Lithuania, Latvia, Estonia). I pointed out that he was confused in his geography: Bulgaria was not their neighbor; they had no common border. I thought it odd that he did not know this—his one trip abroad, he had told me, had been to Bulgaria. I asked him how he had gotten to Bulgaria, but he refused to talk about it. I had caught him in a lie, but why had he lied? Perhaps there was a second Zhenya, an agent in training not bound for Saransk but having grander plans. Perhaps all the stories of oppression were designed only to endear himself to the American community. One never knows. This may be wild paranoia on my part (an occupational hazard of Soviet studies). One never knows.

Upstairs on the fifth floor was a young man named Sasha. He was also from the *glush*, from Siberia in fact, but unlike Zhenya he was proud of it. Sasha was a very positive character, the strong, silent type. He was always the first to volunteer for dormitory projects or to assist the foreign exchange students. Unlike Zhenya, Sasha did not wear his feelings on his shirt-sleeve, but kept very much to himself. Sasha's viewpoint was one I found characteristic of the students from Siberia. It was what might be called the "true communist" point of view. Sasha considered himself a fervent communist in a time when the Party no longer practiced what it preached. To him, the leaders of the CPSU, the Communist Party of the Soviet Union, had deserted the spirit of communism and no longer applied its principles in their daily lives. These "old believers" felt that the party bureaucrats of Russia's European cities were destroying everything the Bolshevik Revolution had fought for. The *apparatchiki* were turning the party into a new aristocracy, rife with nepotism and privilege. Sasha told me that only in Siberia did the people still have the true spirit of sacrifice and sharing—a communism as pure as the Siberian snow. While everyone else at the university was desperately trying to stay in Leningrad and avoid being assigned to the "virgin lands" for the mandatory three-year service that graduates must perform, Sasha longed to flee Leningrad for the endless *taiga*. His Siberian puritanism extended to sexual relations as well. While the other Russian students were promiscuous in the extreme, Sasha sought true love. Sasha's Siberian philosophy was mildly reminiscent of that of the mountain-states Westerners whom I had met at Harvard Law School. They too felt the big Eastern cities to be decadent and bureaucratic and longed to return to the pure, simple life of the Rockies.

During the year, Sasha became increasingly disappointed with Brezhnev's leadership. That fall Brezhnev had his seventieth birthday, and some thought he was preparing to retire. Brezhnev was constantly in the news, receiving a decoration for one accomplishment or another. Sasha quietly complained to me, "Look at this, he has been on the front page of *Pravda* every day for two weeks. He even made the East Germans give him a medal for the victory over Germany. You'd think he personally won the war. I don't understand it." Sasha said, "Stalin was denounced for the 'cult of personality,' but now there are two movies playing about Brezhnev's life, and the bookstores are brimming with books by him and about him. His picture is everywhere. I frankly don't think he has any intention of stepping down but will have to be forced down or die in office like all the others."

Events that spring seemed to prove Sasha right. Nikolai Podgorny, longtime president of the Soviet Union, disappeared without so much as a "thank you" for fifty years of service to the Party. We knew something was happening when *Pravda* did not come out on time one day. When it finally appeared there was a one-line explanation: "Podgorny . . . relieved of all duties." Brezhnev, already general secretary of the Communist Party and marshal of the Soviet Union, took the unprecedented step of assuming Podgorny's presidency himself. Not even Stalin had held the positions of both chief of state and leader of the Party. Sasha was greatly depressed by Podgorny's fall from power and disappearance. Podgorny, Sasha told me, was the last of the "men of the people" who had tried to resist the elitism of the Brezhnev clique. Podgorny had been the last of the Khrushchev protégés. "Brezhnev and his group denounce Khrushchev as a bumpkin and a corn farmer," said Sasha, "but he was very popular among us bumpkins and corn farmers. He really cared about us, while all Brezhnev cares about are his Moscow and Ukrainian cronies."

Upon hearing of Podgorny's fall, Sasha went immediately to the local propaganda store to buy a cardboard folder, called a *papka*, full of wall-size pictures of all of the members of the Politburo. Sasha hoped to get one before the picture of Podgorny could be removed. He was too late; sales of Politburo *papki* had been suspended while the propaganda stores awaited further instructions from Moscow. Sasha was bitterly disappointed. He told me he was very lucky to have his old pictures of Khrushchev. They were now collector's items, almost impossible to obtain. He advised me to buy some pictures of Brezhnev before he too became a nonperson.

It was not by coincidence that Zhenya and Sasha were from outside Leningrad. All of the Russians in our dormitory were. Students from Leningrad were expected to live at home. In order to live in our dormitory, with exchange students from developed capitalist countries, the Russian students had to be approved by a Party commission. I do not know how severe this commission was, but certainly it screened out anyone of questioned political sympathies. Despite the fact that ethnic Russians constitute only half of the population of the Soviet Union, no students from other nationality groups were living with us. We were not intended to hear late-night lectures exposing Russification in non-Russian republics. There were no Soviet Jews in our dormitory. By process of elimination we were left with non-Leningrad, politically approved, ethnic Great Russians. The age range was roughly twenty-five to forty. Many were studying foreign languages or purely ideological subjects, such as the history of the Communist Party of the Soviet Union. Many of the men had been officers in the Red Army. Our Russians seemed as a group to be in the university and in the NATO dormitory primarily owing to their political loyalty rather than for any particular academic ability or achievement. Among the group were some smart people, certainly including my roommate. On the whole, they were older and more settled than most people in the university. Many had left wives and children back in the *glush* to come study in the big city.

The people in the dormitory, as provincials from the Soviet countryside, represented a long tradition of those who had gladly slogged their way out of the Russian villages to get their education in Leningrad or old St. Petersburg. It may be a dying tradition. In October 1976 G. V. Romanov, the Party leader of Leningrad and at that time the youngest member of the Politburo (born February 7, 1923; his family name, the same as that of Russia's last dynasty, is the butt of many local jokes), called a meeting of Leningrad establishment intellectuals. In his speech, a major denunciation of the liberal trends in the artistic and academic community, Romanov said that there were people in Leningrad who called themselves artists and poets but had no diplomas to prove it. They were doing nothing for the city and should be crushed. What particularly worried the intellectual community in Leningrad was that Romanov "suggested" that Leningrad University should be for Leningraders alone—outsiders should not be allowed to matriculate. Romanov's "suggestions" are virtually law in the city. If such a policy were to be maintained for ten or fifteen years, then without the stimulus of the brightest outsiders Leningrad State would lose its position as an elite university and drift into provincial torpor. Moscow's partial victory of replacing Leningrad as the cultural center of Russia would be made complete.

Our dormitory, like most buildings in the Soviet Union, had a strict method of controlling who was allowed inside. About fifteen feet from the front door was a clerk's office in a glass enclosure having full view of the only outside door and the two internal staircases. Someone was on duty from six in the morning until one o'clock the following morning. At one, the outside door was locked, bolted, and chained shut. There were no other exits or fire escapes, and the lower floors had barred windows. Security was so tight that the Westerners were concerned about how we would get out of the building in the event of fire. The dormitory commandant assured us that fires were not a problem in the Soviet Union. If they had been, he maintained, we would have read about them in the newspapers and Soviet officials would have taken precautionary measures. Despite this assurance, from the fifth floor of the dormitory we could frequently see black smoke billowing up around the city. To allay our fears the authorities put up a sign urging parents not to let their children play with matches.

Anyone entering the building who was not recognized as a resident had to pass by the glass enclosure and leave his passport before going upstairs. Soviet citizens carry internal passports for identification. Residents had to stop and pick up their keys. The keys were four inches long, ending in a simple ungrooved metal piece which went in the keyhole to turn the bolt. The room number hung on an attached metal disc. It took little time to realize that the keys had nothing to do with privacy or protection of property. There was one key for each room, even though the rooms were for two or three students. With few exceptions, all the keys opened all the rooms. Sometimes it happened that every other key in the building opened the door to a room except the one with the room number on it. The keys were in reality little flags to enable the dorm commandant and the other residents to have a general idea which rooms in the building had an occupant present. I was surprised to learn that when one left one's room to go to another room, the practice was to lock the door and leave the key in the lock. When I asked Zhenya why this was done, he told me it was to let the other roommates know, when they returned, that one of their roommates was already in the building. Why this was important for them to know I am still not sure. Many doors, hinges, and bolts were in such disrepair that one either could not lock them or could not open them when they were locked. My door was broken all year (as were my window and my electric wall socket). My repeated pleas were to no avail. When workmen came they would claim not to have the parts necessary to make the repair.

I recall how midway through the year my right knee began to ache for no apparent reason. If the weather was damp it was particularly painful. I was convinced that at the ripe old age of twenty-six I was being laid low by rheumatism. After some months I deduced the cause of my pain. The only way I could get my door to close was to pull it shut with my left hand while turning the key with the right. Still it would need a little jolt to get the locking bolt to drop in the catch. I would give the door a little jolt—with my right knee. It never hurt when I did it, but the cumulative effect of two or three little jolts every day put my kneecap in agony. When at last the connection dawned on me I switched to using the toe of my boot (subconsciously desiring to kick the door in altogether).

None of my Russian friends from the neighborhood ever came to the dormitory, which they feared. Few of them allowed me to call them from the dormitory phone. All of them asked me never to refer to them by name when in my room. To them the dormitory was a nest of *stukachi*, vicious informers. One could call this paranoia, but if so it is a paranoia so widely shared that Russians say it comes to them "with [their] mother's milk."

The degree to which our activities within the dormitory were monitored had a particularly strong impact upon thoughts of courting Russian women. There is an old maxim that the best way to learn a foreign language is from a foreign girl friend (there are more ribald equivalents). While there is much to be said for this approach, the situation of a Westerner in the Soviet Union is rather different from the "American in Paris" hypothetical. As if by coincidence, the Russian girls in our dormitory were a hopelessly unattractive lot. Our Soviet girls were older than those in the university generally. In their mid thirties, they averaged twenty pounds overweight, and seemed to spend most of their time boiling cabbage in the communal kitchen. They were all very kind and helpful, and generally made a much better impression than did their male counterparts. Still, there was not a beauty among them, and few who could even be called "plain." This "coincidence" in dormitory assignments seemed to reflect a conscious decision on the part of the Soviet authorities to discourage romantic involvement.

It was quite possible to meet attractive Russian girls around the city, but there remained a very real problem as to where one could spend time with them. Any Russian girl entering the dormitory would have to leave her internal Soviet passport with the clerk, who would then certainly note down all her biographical information in the daily log. Once she was upstairs there would be the problem of one's Soviet roommate, who would do everything possible to ascertain who this girl was, how you had met her, and the nature of your relationship. Getting him to leave would be ticklish.

Within a few days the girl would certainly be cautioned by someone, either at her work or at the university, about seeing a foreigner. Phone calls would have been made. Worse, she might be told to go ahead with the relationship but to let the authorities know from time to time whom her new foreign boyfriend was seeing and what he had to say. Sadly, as soon as one attempted to bring a girl into the dormitory, she would be unwillingly forced into one of two predicaments. Either she would be put in a compromised position at work or school because of seeing you, or she would be impressed into service as an agent.

If one could not bring a Russian girl friend back to the dorm, what alternatives were there? No one had cars, and the parks were covered with snow for much of the year. Could one take her to his American friends? I was close to several people who worked in the American consulate and had acquaintances in the Swedish consulate as well. Emil Sveilis, the UPI correspondent, was a good friend, as was the local SAS representative. But all of these people lived in compounds or blocks of flats that were guarded at all times by the KGB. A militiaman sat in an all-weather guardhouse and logged in every vehicle and person who approached the residence. Everyone who lived in the compounds took it for granted that their apartments were bugged. To bring a Russian girl into this situation would be no different from taking her to the dorm. Her every move would be observed and reported.

What then about one's Russian friends? Unfortunately, to bring a Russian girl to the home of a Russian friend who did not know her would be to commit the greatest possible *faux pas*. I met many Russians during my stay, and I would soon be introduced to their Russian friends, but it was always made clear to me that I should never bring another Russian to their homes. This peculiar pattern of relationships I called the "wedge theory" of East–West acquaintances. I would meet one Russian, perhaps the friend of another Westerner. This Russian would be the apex of the wedge. He would introduce me to his friends and they would introduce me to theirs, all this radiating out from the initial contact. These other Russians were usually relatives or well-trusted friends of years' standing—never casual acquaintances. Within one wedge of friends you were never to mention that you knew someone in another. Sometimes I would even hear the name of an acquaintance from another wedge mentioned in conversation, yet I would never say, "Oh, I know him." Despite what many Westerners think, the average Russian in the street without a party or defense position is not afraid of contact with foreigners. In fact they consider contact with foreigners a great social plus. It is other Russians that they fear and distrust. As Zhenya summed it up, "I can talk freely to foreigners, but never to my own countrymen or in their presence, for in the back of my mind is always the question 'Will they denounce me?' " If I had brought an unknown Russian girl to the home of a Russian friend, we would all have spent a tense evening in stony silence.

The final courting possibility would be her place. This might be all right, but it was inconceivable that she would have her own apartment, even if she were a working doctor or lawyer. It would be unlikely that she would even have her own room. As an unmarried woman in her twenties she would customarily be living not only with her parents and younger brothers and sisters, but also her grandparents and an older sibling with spouse and baby. Possibly even her divorced former husband would still be living there, waiting to get another housing assignment. You would certainly be welcome for tea anytime you could find a place to sit down. Moreover, the whole extended family would probably think you were fantastic, the most interesting social event in years. Granddad would break out the *samogon* (home-distilled vodka) and tell you how he had used a Thompson machine gun and rode in a Willy's Jeep during the war. Every evening you could huddle around the radio and listen to the Voice of America's Russian-language broadcast. All of this would be great fun but hardly conducive to an intimate relationship.

None of these inconveniences was insurmountable, but the harsh Soviet economy threw up more subtle barriers. Unfortunately, in the narrow sense of physical appeal, few Russian girls are attractive by Western standards. The diet is poor. Most people subsist on bread, potatoes, cabbage, and vodka. Fresh fruits and vegetables are not available at all in Leningrad for the larger part of the year. Meat was often available in the big cities (if you got to the store early and fought the lines), but it was of the fattiest utility grades. On a diet like this it is hard to keep one's figure. Compounding this is that many women have no particular desire even to try. Culturally, the Russians, who throughout their history have often not known where their next meal was coming from, associate being big with being beautiful. This is true not only of bells and cannons, but applies to women as well. In fact, the Russian word for thin is the same as the word for bad, *khudoy*. Moreover, Soviet women work very hard. Their day is long and their pay is low. The good jobs, managerial and administrative posts, are reserved for men. Jobs in construction and heavy labor, usually done by men in the West, are often women's work. At the end of a long workday the Soviet woman stands in a seemingly endless queue to get food for the family dinner, usually while the men in the family are resting and tippling vodka at home. By the time a Russian woman is thirty she looks as if she's forty-five.

Difficulties do not stop with diet and hard work. There is an enormous problem with getting good clothes in the Soviet Union. A Soviet young person will pay his whole month's wages (100 to 150 rubles) for a new pair of black-market Levi's. I initially thought this an incredible amount to pay for a status item, but the other options are equally appalling. Russian trousers cost 40 rubles and wear out in a season. They sag, have no shape, are poorly sewn, and are dirty gray or brown in color. Considering their relative life expectancies, a pair of Levi's costs little more and looks much better. Even if one is not style conscious or is even anti-style, it is difficult from a Westerner's perspective to ignore the shabbiness and poor fit of Soviet clothing. Cosmetics are an even greater problem. If Soviet women simply wore no makeup it would be all right, but Soviet youth is very emulative. Soviet girls want to look like French girls but can't get French products. Instead they use Soviet products: lipstick like wall paint and perfume that Westerners wouldn't use for disinfectant.

If one were to get involved with a Soviet woman and want to take her to the West, it could be done only after a long, expensive, and emotionally demanding diplomatic skirmish with the Soviet government. But a woman would be easier to get out of the country than a man would. During my stay, the average time it took for a Western spouse to get a Soviet wife out was six months, for a husband it took four times as long.

All of these factors tend to discourage Westerners from romantic interest in Russian women, but none of them would thwart true love. There were some lasting involvements and an occasional marriage between the Russians and the Westerners in our dormitory. In the end what kept me from any romantic involvement with Russian women was the very great psychological pressure of living in the Soviet Union. Sitting in a small, cold dormitory room with a rarely sober Russian (who wants you to tell him everything you did that day, every day), the darkness, the lack of food, the vitamin deficiency, the frustration, the cold—all make one reluctant to add the cultural experience of a complicated relationship with a Russian woman. In the American Leningrad group there were six single males on the year-long exchange. Of the six, two could not stand it and left; a third slipped on the ice and fractured his skull; a fourth ended up in a Russian drunk tank with diagnosed liver damage, the result of a continual vodka bash. The two of us who fared the best had steady American girl friends from the start who, it seems, kept us fairly sane.

Three /

Venice of the

North

Most cities grow slowly, their exact origins lost in unrecorded history. Not Leningrad. It was founded, as St. Petersburg, on May 16, 1703. It is younger by seventy years than Boston or New York, an unusual status for a major European city.

St. Petersburg was founded on the delta of the Neva River. The Neva is short. It flows only forty-five miles from Lake Ladoga, the largest lake in Europe, to the Gulf of Finland. The Gulf of Finland opens onto the Baltic Sea. The delta of the Neva comprise 110 islands. The area is a marsh, a northern swamp only a few feet above sea level. In fact, the word "neva" means "swamp" in Finnish. It was a curious place to found a capital. No other city of its size—the current population is four and a half million—is so far north. It is farther north than Juneau, Alaska.

St. Petersburg was founded by one man with a mission, and until 1924 the city bore his name. That man was the Romanov czar Peter the First, known as "the Great." With him began a new period in Russian history, known as the St. Petersburg Era or the Imperial Age. This period ended abruptly in 1917.

At the time of Peter's birth Moscow was not only the capital but the very heart of Russia. Landlocked except for one arctic port frozen six months of the year, the land giant was surrounded by its seafaring enemies: in the north the powerful Swedes controlled the Baltic; to the west Russia's hereditary enemy the Poles sealed off Western Europe; and to the south lay the Ottoman Empire, master of the Black Sea and much of the Ukraine. But hundreds of miles inland behind its huge Kremlin wall, Moscow was secure. This was the home of the Great Russian people and the home of their first family, the Romanovs. Everything was in Moscow—the cathedrals, the icons, the patriarch of the Russian Orthodox Church—every religious and hereditary symbol of his majesty the czar. Yet by the end of Peter the Great's life, Moscow had been politically abandoned. There was a new capital in the remote north, built under the very guns of the marauding Swedish navy. In wanting to leave the protection and tradition of Moscow, Peter stood alone. St. Petersburg was the product of his iron will. There is no other major city in the modern world that has been so totally the conception of a single man. To understand why Peter deserted Moscow and created his new capital, it is necessary to understand the world of his Moscow childhood, the world he would leave behind.

Peter's father, Alexis, was only the second of the Romanov czars. Alexis married twice, first to Maria Miloslavskaya, who bore him thirteen children. Maria died in childbirth in 1669, and to the regret of her Miloslavsky relatives, who owed their preeminence at court to the czar's marriage, Alexis began looking for a new wife. The Miloslavsky position was particularly insecure because it was not clear that any of Maria's thirteen children would succeed their father and become czar. Most of them had died in infancy. The surviving sons, Fedor and Ivan, were lame and sickly. Alexis's daughter Sophia was intelligent and strong but, because she was a woman, was not even under consideration. A woman had never ruled Muscovy, and the daughters of the czar, born too high to marry, traditionally spent their lives in prayer and embroidery in secluded apartments of the Kremlin palace.

Alexis chose as his second wife Natalya Naryshkina, who sixteen months later gave birth to a healthy baby boy, christened Peter. This situation—the older Miloslavsky sons ill and the younger Naryshkin son healthy—pitted these two extended boyar (high noble) families in a life-and-death struggle for the Russian throne. On Epiphany in 1676, Czar Alexis caught a chill, and as often happened in those times, the "chill" proved fatal: Fedor became Czar Fedor III, and the Miloslavskys were temporarily in control.

The six years of Fedor's reign passed quietly for Peter and his mother. The child Peter learned to read and write, and studied geography from a giant globe in his room. When the sickly Fedor died in 1682 he had no son, and for the first time in the young Romanov dynasty, there was no clear successor to the throne. The normal choice would have been Fedor's sixteen-year-old brother Ivan, the son of Maria Miloslavskaya. Ivan, however, like his brother Fedor, was weak. He had a speech impediment, and was lame and partly blind. By contrast, ten-year-old Peter was active and healthy. When the patriarch of the Russian Orthodox Church asked the boyars who should rule, the Naryshkin supporters urged that rule from a sickbed should not be continued. The patriarch threw the question to the Moscow crowd gathered in the Kremlin's Cathedral Square. The answer came back, "Peter." Peter's coronation was a severe blow to his half-sister Sophia Miloslavskaya. She had been Czar Fedor's confidante and advisor. To lose now meant she must return to a cloistered existence, but to win and place her incompetent brother Ivan on the throne meant she could rule all Russia as Ivan's regent. Sophia organized a revolt of the palace guard against Peter's family, the Naryshkins. The slaughter took place in the Kremlin before the eyes of the ten-year-old czar. His mother's guardian was thrown onto spear points; his uncle was hacked to pieces. Peter and his mother were not physically attacked, but it is said that the boy czar was made to walk through the blood of his slain family. The power of the Naryshkins was broken. The political result was that Ivan became senior czar with Peter as junior czar in a co-czar arrangement unique in modern European history. Sophia ruled as their regent.

This incident had profound consequences for Peter and for Russia. The Kremlin atmosphere of blood feuds and intrigue, and the slaughter of his family before his very eyes left Peter seething with hatred for Moscow and all that it represented. However, even without the personal tragedy he had suffered, there was reason enough for the inquisitive, energetic young czar to detest seventeenth-century Moscow. It was a city of theocracy, ritual, and suspicion, a thoroughly backward barbarian capital, its population so illiterate that one could have assembled all of educated Moscovy in a large living room. Peter at that point did not know where his capital would be, but he knew one thing—it would not be in Moscow.

During the seven years of Sophia's regency, Peter was left to grow up in the countryside, wandering and exploring. An old Dutchman taught him how to use a sextant, and thrilled him with stories of Europe. Together they happened upon an old boat, and Peter learned to sail. In the company of foreign craftsmen Peter built boats and talked of distant lands and foreign ideas. Russia had for centuries looked to Byzantium as its cultural wellspring. Peter now saw it was in the direction of Western Europe that the Russian nation must be led. To accomplish this he nurtured the thought of building a new city, a "window on the West." Peter would become the supreme Westernizer of Russian history.

As Peter grew into manhood, confrontation with Sophia became inevitable. In 1689 the Naryshkin camp sensed an impending coup, and Peter withdrew to the protection of the Trinity–St. Sergius Monastery. From this holy sanctuary Peter rallied support to his cause. Defectors to Peter's side daily took the forty-five-mile road from the Kremlin to the monastery. Sophia's support evaporated, and Peter became czar in fact as well as name. Ivan remained a figurehead co-czar until his death in 1696, and Sophia, the first woman to rule Russia, was ensconced in a convent to live out her days.

Despite this great victory, Peter's interests did not immediately turn to ruling, but for the next few years he pursued the great passion of his life, sailing and the sea. Peter knew that to open his country to the West he would need a modern navy and merchant marine, and he set out to visit the one saltwater port that Russia possessed, Archangel, on the White Sea, only 130 miles south of the Arctic Circle. In 1693, when Peter set sail on the White Sea, it was the first time in history that a Russian czar was on saltwater. Peter knew that Archangel alone, frozen in ice for half the year, would not suffice to make Russia a seagoing nation. For that, a port on the Baltic was necessary. But the Baltic was controlled by the then "Mistress of the North," imperial Sweden.

As his thoughts turned to nation building, Peter embarked in 1697 for Western Europe on his "Great Embassy." Although he traveled incognito and pretended not to be the head of the delegation, young Peter stood six feet, seven inches tall, a giant by the standards of the day: his disguise fooled no one. Peter's principal reason for this unprecedented journey by a reigning czar was to learn the seafaring trades and bring back master craftsmen for his technically impoverished nation. Fascinated with the idea of making Russia a modern nation and a seapower, he wanted to visit the great maritime nations, Holland and England. But Peter also had a diplomatic mission. He hoped to shore up a faltering alliance against the Turks, and it was during the Great Embassy that speculation began about a new alliance.

Augustus II, King of Poland, raised the possibility of a joint attack on Sweden. A victory would permit Russian access to the Baltic.

Sweden, its borders much larger than they are today, had become the dominant military power in northern Europe. Controlling Finland and the eastern Baltic, it blocked Russia's access to that important sea. Sweden also had large territories in what is today Germany and Poland. Only one of the great rivers emptying into the Baltic, the Vistula at Danzig, was not under Swedish control. In 1700 Denmark and Poland-Saxony allied and declared war on Sweden. The moment was ripe. Charles XI had died and the Swedish throne was in the hands of his teenage son. In typically impetuous fashion, the day after he announced a peace treaty with Turkey, Peter officially joined the alliance against Sweden and entered what is today known as the Great Northern War. It was from the ashes of the Great Northern War that St. Petersburg was born.

At first the war went poorly for Peter. Charles XII of Sweden, though merely eighteen years old, was a brilliant field commander. Charles first knocked the Danes out of the war, and then in a blinding snowstorm on the Baltic coast defeated the Russians at Narva. Some say that the Swedes could have marched straight to Moscow, but they did not press their attack and instead turned to fight the Poles. Peter was given a chance to regroup and applied total energy to the task. Every aspect of the nation's life was bent to the war effort; church bells were melted to make cannons. Within a year of the defeat at Narva, Peter had a new army in the Baltic. With the Swedes fighting in Poland, Russian forces captured the Swedish fortress of Noteburg, where Lake Ladoga empties into the Neva. Peter renamed the new Russian fortress Schlüsselburg—the key to his campaign to make the Neva a Russian river. With the Lake Ladoga source of the Neva secure, Peter needed a fortress near the Gulf of Finland to protect the river's mouth. On

May 16, 1703, Peter founded the Peter and Paul Fortress on the former Hare Island in the Neva delta. The legend goes that Peter cut two strips of sod and, laying them in the form of a cross, announced, "Here shall be a town." A hole was dug and a box of relics of Russia's patron saint, Andrew, was buried in the ground. As yet unnamed, St. Petersburg was born in this humble way.

The Swedes were eventually able to subdue the Poles and turn their attention back to Russia. But this time Peter was ready. In 1709 in an open field at Poltava in the Ukraine, Peter at the head of his army met his Swedish adversary. All of Europe assumed that the undefeated Charles would annihilate Peter and that Russia would be swiftly carved up by its enemies. But Charles had been wounded and was too weak to command. In one of the great watershed battles of European history, the Swedish army was destroyed. Peter returned to subdue the Baltic area and captured Riga, Tallinn (Reval), and Vyborg, thereby securing the approaches to St. Petersburg. Russia replaced Sweden as the dominant power in northern Europe. In 1712 the capital of Russia was moved from Moscow. Peter's dream had been realized; he had his "window on the West," a major naval port, and a modern nation state. When a final treaty of peace was signed with Sweden in 1721, Peter the First became Peter the Great—the "czar" became the "emperor."

None of the nobility, including Peter's family, wanted to move from the comforts of Moscow to this unconstructed "capital." Not only was the new "city" situated on a pestilential bog, it was on enemy territory, harassed by Swedish armies and ships every summer. Peter forced the Russians to come to the new city. Any noble family that owned more than thirty families of serfs was required to build a house in St. Petersburg on a site determined by the noble's rank. Noblemen with over 500 serfs were required to build two-story houses. The style of the house was also prescribed.

There were to be none of the Byzantine domes and shingles of Moscow. The estuary islands such as Vasilevsky's Island were planned in a grid. Peter wanted none of the labyrinthine alleys of Moscow but, instead, numbered parallel streets. South of the Neva was the mainland part of St. Petersburg. It was here that Peter built the first Winter Palace.

Later, during his visit to the French capital in Versailles, Peter was so impressed with the three boulevards leading to the Place du Palais that he decided on a similar arrangement for his capital. In keeping with his position as founder of the Russian navy, Peter did not center his three boulevards on the Winter Palace but on the central building of the admiralty. The summer palace of Peterhof, barely begun at the time of Peter's death, had as its stated purpose the surpassing of Versailles in grandeur. Peter was so determined to have the principal buildings of his city made of immutable stone rather than the wood of Moscow that by imperial decree in 1714 no stone buildings were permitted to be constructed anywhere else in Russia. Some nobles, already impoverished by Peter's wars, managed to escape this enormous cost by building their houses of wood covered with stucco to look like stone. Peter insisted that the streets were to be paved, and therefore everyone entering the city had to bring paving stones or pay a heavy fine. A man arriving by cart had to pay a "toll" of three paving stones, each weighing at least five pounds.

The early days of St. Petersburg were grim. Fire and floods ravaged the city, and in 1715 a woman on Vasilevsky's Island was eaten by wolves in broad daylight. Unskilled workers were drafted from all over Russia to serve in the building corps for six months. They lived in ghastly conditions, crowded together in muddy huts. Disease was rampant among them. Of those who survived the epidemics many died in construction accidents or drowned in the rickety boats used to ferry materials across the Neva. It is a measure of Peter's determination, and of his cruelty, that there were far more Russians killed in the construction of St. Petersburg than in the victory over the Swedish army at Poltava. Estimates range from 25,000 to 100,000 laborers who died constructing the "city built on bones." While others cursed under their breath, Peter's love for the hostile city increased. To his friend Prince Menshikov he wrote, "I cannot help writing you from this paradise; truly we live here in heaven."

Although Peter fought wars and founded a capital city, he above all else wanted to be remembered as a reformer. His reforms affected the root and branch of Russian life. After him, even the Russian calendar was never again the same. In 1672, when Peter was born, the Russians—despite being devout Christians who even referred to Moscow as the third Rome—calculated their years not from the birth of Christ, but from their estimate of the beginning of the world. Finding it hard to believe that the world had been created at a time of year when Moscow was locked in frozen darkness, the Russians had their new year begin not on January 1, but at harvest time, on the first of September. It was Peter who forced the Russians to adopt the Julian calendar then in use in Western Europe. One December he decreed to his countrymen that as of that January first it would be the year 1700 and not the year 7208 as they had assumed. Ironically Russia adopted Western practice not long before the West itself decided to change. In 1752, thirty-seven years after Peter's death, England left the Julian calendar and adopted the Gregorian. Not wishing to follow again the chronologically fickle West, Peter's successors remained with the Julian calendar. The Julian calendar was less accurate and, compared to the Gregorian, lost about a day every century. As a result the Russian calendar lagged increasingly behind that of its Western neighbors. By the twentieth century it trailed by almost two weeks. It is for this reason that the Soviet holiday commemorating the "Great October Revolution" (i.e., the storming of the Winter Palace) is celebrated not in October but on November 7. Following the Revolution, in January 1918, the new Bolshevik government adopted the Gregorian calendar, which is now standard throughout the world.

The eighteenth century saw fantastic architectural expression in St. Petersburg, ranging from baroque at the beginning of the century to neoclassical at the end. Although it is Peter the Great's city, only the Peter and Paul Fortress truly reflects the architecture of his time. Peter was a man of simple and somewhat military tastes. The Leningrad the visitor sees today is more the creation of Catherine the Great and her grandchild Nicholas the First. The Winter Palace itself was built and rebuilt five times. The czars, in keeping with Peter's custom of luring foreign specialists to Russia, imported the best architects of Western Europe to their capital. Money was of no consequence. Many of the leading architects were Italian, a fact of some embarrassment to the present the-Russians-did-everything mentality of the Soviets. Domenico Trezzini of Lucano had been the favorite of Peter the Great, coming under contract as Peter's "master of building, construction, and fortification." Trezzini's greatest achievement is the baroque Cathedral of Saints Peter and Paul with its 400-foot spire. Count Bartolomeo Rastrelli came to Russia at the age of ten with his father, a sculptor invited by Peter the Great. Rastrelli was responsible for the Winter Palace, the Smolny Cathedral, and Catherine's summer palace in Pushkin. Carlo Rossi, born in Florence, built the General Staff building on Palace Square and the Mikhailovsky Palace, which now houses the Russian Museum. Giacomo Quarenghi built the Smolny Institute. Originally a school for well-bred young ladies, Smolny became Lenin's headquarters during the Bolshevik Revolution. Its name derives from "smola," meaning "tar" or "pitch" in Russian, because it had been the site of Peter's tar stores for shipbuilding in the early days of St. Petersburg. Even Charles Cameron, a Scotsman who designed the interiors of Catherine the Great's Palace at Pushkin and the nearby summer palace at Pavlovsk, was Italian trained. Although attention naturally focuses on the more monumental structures, Leningrad is practically littered with Renaissance palaces designed by renowned Italian architects.

It is this Italian architecture on an island city of canals and hundreds of bridges that has inspired the name "Venice of the North." The allusion, though flattering, is also misleading. The canals of Leningrad were designed for drainage and not commerce. One of the principal canals, the Griboyedov, is actually a river of the Neva delta. No colorful gondolas ply Leningrad's waters. While Venice is sultry and passionate, Leningrad is cold and serene. Leningrad is a city of monuments—long embankments, broad avenues, parks, and palaces. If one wishes to compare another city with the physical aspects of Leningrad, that city must be Paris. In Catherine the Great's day St. Petersburg was frequently referred to as the "Paris of the East." The architectural ensembles, enormous cathedrals visible from the quay, spacious gardens, broad boulevards sweeping to squares where former emperors straddle their prancing bronze steeds—this description could fit either city. Comparison stops with the architecture and city design, however. The visitor to Leningrad will not find the charming cafés, the high fashion, or the gourmet cuisine of France. Leningrad's beauty is a cold beauty, a forbidding grandeur, a distance. But there is a splendor there still—the gentility of a bygone glory.

The greatest jewel in the cultural crown of the St. Petersburg era was its literature. But unlike architecture, which flourished because of the czars, literature prospered in spite of them. Many saw the icy hand of Nicholas I behind Pushkin's early death in a duel. Nicholas also ordered the exe-

(*opposite*) The Peter and Paul Fortress with the spire of the Cathedral of Saints Peter and Paul (Trezzeni, 1713–1721) inside. Built for protection against the Swedes during the Great Northern War, it is Leningrad's oldest structure. After the loss of its military importance the fortress became the Russian Bastille. The first prisoner was the Czarivitch Alexis, Peter the Great's son (Peter had him tortured to death here in 1718). Many important figures in Russian history were to follow: the writers Radishchev, Chernyshevsky, Dostoevsky, and Gorky; political reformers and revolutionaries such as the Decembrists, Lenin's brother Alexander prior to execution, and, after the Bolshevik seizure of power, the ministers of the liberal provisional government.

(*above*) St. Peter's Gate, an extrance to the Fortress of Peter and Paul. The emblem is the Romanov double-headed eagle.

(*opposite, top*) Petrodvorets (Peter's Palace). Having visited Versailles in 1717, Peter the Great set about surpassing it in splendor. The palace was finished by Rastrelli in 1750, after Peter's death. It was completely destroyed by the Nazis and has been painstakingly rebuilt since the war.

(*opposite, bottom*) The palace grounds of Petrodvorets in winter.

(*above*) The facade of the Winter Palace. Built by Rastrelli between 1754 and 1762, it was the former residence of the czars and now houses the Hermitage Museum.

(*above*) St. Isaac's Cathedral, named for Saint Isaac of Dalmatia, a Byzantine monk who was Peter the Great's patron saint. Designed by the French architect Montferrand, it took thirty years to build (1818–1848). More than 220 pounds of gold were used just for the plating. The equestrian statue is of Czar Nicholas I, in whose reign (1825–1855) much of the cathedral was built.

(*opposite, top*) Griboedova Canal and, in the distance, the Church of the Savior on the Spilled Blood, built on the spot where Czar Alexander II was assassinated by a terrorist's bomb on March 13, 1881. Its design was modeled on the Church of Basil the Blessed on Red Square in Moscow and is distinctly non-Leningrad. Despite its medieval appearance, it was finished in this century, in 1907. The Soviets leave it closed and in permanent scaffolding.

(*opposite, bottom*) View across the Neva from Vasilevsky's Island of the former building of the Senate and Synod, and the cupola of St. Isaac's Cathedral.

cution of Dostoevsky for radical activity. Dostoevsky was imprisoned in the Peter and Paul Fortress waiting to be taken out and shot when a horseman rode up with an imperial pardon. The sentence was commuted to imprisonment and hard labor.

Although many Russian writers suffered at the hands of the czars, without one particular czar there might have been no Russian literature at all. Before Peter the Great, there was not only no Russian literature worthy of the name; there was scarcely a Russian language to support it. The early Russians, obsessed with thoughts of their own salvation, wrote almost exclusively about religious subjects. Their written language, known as Church Slavonic, was the language of the orthodox clergy. Of Bulgarian origin but adapted to Russian speech, Church Slavonic was cumbersome and bookish. The peasants did not speak Church Slavonic but a common idiom that, while sufficient for an agricultural existence, had neither the forms nor the vocabulary for a modern literature.

Peter knew that his country could never learn science, navigation, or architecture with the archaic linguistic forms of the clergy or the idiom of the peasants. Undaunted, Peter set out to reform the Russian language. He created a new alphabet of Slavonic, Greek, and Latin letters and instituted Arabic numerals to replace the Slavonic ones. Peter searched the peasant language for resources, and when they were insufficient, borrowed terms from Dutch or Swedish. Once the "window to the West" was open, new foreign terms poured in daily. St. Petersburg rapidly became a Tower of Babel. The Russian language was in such a chaotic state that Peter even toyed with the idea of eliminating the native tongue altogether and making all his subjects speak Dutch. The first newspaper appeared in Russia only at the beginning of the eighteenth century, its first number edited by—who else?—Peter the Great.

After Peter's death the language continued to progress. In 1755 Lomonosov, the son of an Archangel fisherman, wrote a modern Russian grammar. (Ironically, the oldest surviving Russian grammar was compiled by H. W. Ludolf, a German, and published at Oxford, England in 1696.) Then another foreign tongue began to rival Russian. In the century after the founding of St. Petersburg, Russia soaked up French culture like a sponge. Prior to Peter, the czar and the Russian nobility married only women of other orthodox Russian boyar families. From Peter's time on, the high nobles adopted the customary European practice of marrying foreign royalty. In the eighteenth century the preeminent influence on things European was France. Many educated people in the Russian aristocracy spoke to each other in French. They could not accept that cultivated people could speak to each other in the language of their peasants. This prejudice was in large measure due to the fact that the Russian language still had no modern literature. In the last year of the eighteenth century a man was born who would change all that. Alexander Pushkin, great-grandson of an Abyssinian slave, was born in St. Petersburg. The time was ripe for Russians to be reintroduced to their native language. The Napoleonic wars had turned the century-long Francophilia of the Russian upper classes into Francophobia. After the collapse of Napoleon's *grande armée*, Russia emerged as the leading military power on the Continent. Czar Alexander's armies chased the French all the way back to Paris.

As a lighter note in the Franco-Russian interchange, the Russian peasant soldiers, trying to get something to eat in Parisian eateries are reported to have given the French their word for short-order café, "bistro," from the Russian word for "quick." A French phrase also slipped into Russian, although certainly not with the intended meaning. The story goes that the beleaguered French soldiers, fleeing across

Russia and Poland, would knock on the doors of peasants, crying "cher ami" and begging for food. From this arose the Russian word *sharomyzhnik*, for one who lives off the labor of others.

As a result of the tremendous military victory, the Russians promptly exchanged their feeling of backwardness for a sense of pride in their native land. Suddenly Russians were interested in what their own culture had to offer. Pushkin showed the eager Russian nation that their language could be used with a clarity, cadence, and grace that were worthy of a world literature. Pushkin was the first to capture the power of modern Russian verse, the first in what came to be a sixty-year literary explosion. As the poet Theodore Tiutchev said in a poem devoted to Pushkin's tragic death: "You, like first love, the heart of Russia will not forget." Every book that refers to St. Petersburg seems to quote from Pushkin. He is the uncontested poet laureate of the Russian language.

Pushkin was mesmerized by his native city and its heritage. On the bank of the Neva in front of St. Isaac's Cathedral there is an equestrian statue of Peter the Great. Unveiled in 1782, it was commissioned by Catherine the Great and executed by the great French sculptor E. M. Falconet. The pedestal of the statue alone is a 1,600-ton cliff of solid granite. Peter's head is turned to gaze across the Neva to the Peter and Paul Fortress, where he first cut the sod to found the city. Inspired by this supremely lovely statue, Pushkin wrote his poem to the glory of St. Petersburg, the "Bronze Horseman":

"I love thee, daughter of Peter's genius; I love thy noble and severe face, and the mighty Neva flowing between its granite banks. I love the mysterious transparency and the pensive brilliance of the moonless nights, when I write and read in my room without a lamp, as sleeping silhouettes of the streets stand out against the sky and the spire of the Admiralty gleams."

Thus began the "Golden Age" of Russian literature, roughly 1820 to 1880, from Pushkin's first major poem to Dostoevsky's last novel. Throughout this period, the literature of Russia was unquestionably the literature of St. Petersburg. Pushkin, Gogol, Lermontov, Turgenev, Dostoevsky, and later Bely and Gorky—the list is staggering. Many of them wrote about the city at one time or another: Pushkin his "Bronze Horseman," Dostoevsky his "White Nights," Bely his *St. Petersburg.* Only Tolstoy of the world-class Russian writers avoided the embrace of the city, and even he used St. Petersburg as the *mise en scène* for his masterpiece *Anna Karenina.*

The name St. Petersburg was to last for over two hundred years. On August 1, 1914, imperial Germany declared war on imperial Russia. The First World War had begun. The city's Germanic name was changed on August 18, 1914, to its Russian equivalent, Petrograd. On January 26, 1924, five days after Lenin's death, the city's name was changed again. The city of Peter became the city of Lenin—Leningrad.

Born in time of war, the Great Northern War, St. Petersburg was spared the ravages of war for two and a quarter centuries. Peter's old antagonists the Swedes did briefly threaten the city in 1788, but no damage was done. The really destructive war of the nineteenth century passed Petersburg by: Napoleon wanted Moscow. In the course of that campaign, Moscow was first captured by the French and then burned, probably by Russians to deny the use of the city to the *grande armée.* In the First World War, the Russian army suffered more casualties than did any other combatant, but the front was far away from Petrograd. In 1917 Petrograd was the scene of two revolutions, but these revolutions were in the nature of coups d'état which did little to damage the city. By the standards of the time the city of Peter had been lucky. No foreign armies fought house to house; no street battles were waged over paving-stone barricades. The city of Lenin would not be so fortunate, and when the horror of war returned, Leningrad was to suffer longer than any other city in modern times.

Leningrad's misery started before the guns of the Second World War and was to continue after they were silent. Contrary to the spirit of Peter the Great, Lenin moved the capital of the Soviet Union back to Moscow. The change was to be temporary, necessitated by Leningrad's exposed position close to foreign borders. When Lenin died in 1924, the twentieth-century Soviet succession crisis, that of deciding which contender would become "Red czar," began to play itself out in familiar surroundings—the Moscow Kremlin. By 1934 Stalin had eliminated his principal opponent, Trotsky, and begun to consolidate his power. One man troubled him, however—Sergei Kirov, party boss of Leningrad. It was rumored that Kirov was more popular in the Central Committee of the Communist Party than its general secretary, Stalin himself. Stalin hated to lose popularity contests, and on December 1, 1934, Kirov was shot dead in his office at Leningrad's Smolny Institute. Using the pretext of Kirov's assassination, the secret police were given for the first time the right to execute accused persons without the delay of a trial. The Great Purges had begun. The first to go were the old Bolsheviks. Stalin accused Lenin's former lieutenants of being deviationists and Trotskyites. Gregory Zinovyev, a former Leningrad party boss, had already fallen from power. Still, scapegoats were necessary, and Zinovyev, at one time Lenin's right hand, was shot after a show trial in 1937. Thousands of Leningrad party members and intellectuals were rounded up, never to return.

In order to replace Kirov and to build a new party organization, Stalin ordered to Leningrad the second most powerful man in the Soviet Union, Andrei A. Zhdanov. Zhdanov, a Politburo member, was from the city of Nizhni-Novgorod, now known as Gorky. So close were the ties between Zhdanov and Stalin that Stalin's daughter Svetlana married Zhdanov's son, Yuri.

On August 23, 1939, an event occurred which many in the West had thought impossible: Hitler and Stalin signed a nonaggression pact. Communists and Nazis were suddenly allies. That agreement was accompanied by a secret protocol. The Soviet Union would be permitted to expand its influence in Eastern Europe. The Red Army promptly occupied Eastern Poland, annexed part of Rumania, and in November 1939 attacked Finland. Bent on plunder himself, Stalin ignored the growing danger. But Hitler continued to cherish his dream of a *Drang nach Osten* and, after consolidating his position on the western and Balkan fronts, turned his attention to the East.

Zhdanov had been the architect of the Hitler-Stalin pact. When Russian generals grew nervous about growing German troop concentrations on the Soviet border, it was Zhdanov who assured them that Germany "cannot and will not fight a war on two fronts." So confident was Zhdanov of Hitler's goodwill that when the attack came, as all intelligence reports showed it must, Zhdanov was vacationing in the sunny Crimea.

Stalin had been warned by his own intelligence service that an attack on the Soviet Union was imminent. Perhaps the greatest spy of the Second World War was a German newspaper correspondent in Tokyo named Richard Sorge. Secretly he was a Communist and an agent of the Soviet NKVD, a predecessor of the KGB. Sorge was a close confidant of the German ambassador to the court of the Japanese emperor. Owing to the military alliance between Japan and Germany, the ambassador was privy to secret military communications of the most sensitive kind. He unwittingly passed this information to his good friend Sorge. After a steady stream of intelligence documenting German attack preparations, on March 5, 1941, Sorge sent to Moscow an

(*above*) Pushkin's study. It was from this apartment, No. 12 on the Moika Canal, that Pushkin went out in January of 1837 to fight a duel over the honor of his child bride. He returned mortally wounded.

(*opposite*) A statue of Alexander Pushkin, poet laureate of Russian literature. In the background is the Russian Museum. Formerly the palace of Grand Duke Michael Pavlovich, younger brother of Czar Alexander I, it has been the central museum of Russian art and life since 1898. The icon collection is staggering. Though the Russian museum is sometimes overshadowed in the tourist's mind by the Hermitage, the Hermitage collection is basically one of Western European art and is similar to the great museum collections of those countries. The Russian museum is unique.

(*top*) Elijah Repin's painting of Stenka Razin, the great Don Cossack (Russian Museum). Stenka Razin led the first great peasant revolt against the Romanovs, in the year 1670. He is immortalized in Russian song and story.

(*bottom*) *The Volga Boatmen* (Russian Museum), probably the best-known work of Elijah Repin (1844–1930), considered the greatest Russian painter of his generation. The Volga boatmen were not themselves on boats, but pulled them in a primitive version of the work performed by mules on the Erie Canal. The young boy looking off into the distance is said to symbolize Russian aspirations for a better future.

(*top*) The Kirov Theater, named for the Leningrad leader whose assassination triggered the great purges of the thirties. Its ballet company is considered the finest in the Soviet Union. Nureyev and Baryshnikov danced with this company before defecting to the West.

(*bottom*) The cruiser *Aurora* at its permanent anchorage on the Petrograd embankment of the Neva. In October of 1917, the sailors of the *Aurora* joined Lenin and his Bolsheviks. A shot fired from the *Aurora*'s deck gun signaled the storming of the Winter Palace and the fall of the Western-supported Kerensky government.

interesting piece of microfilm. It was a photograph of the very telegram from the Nazi foreign minister, Joachim von Ribbentrop, setting forth the date for Operation Barbarossa, the attack on the Soviet Union. In what was perhaps the greatest blunder of the Second World War, Stalin paid no attention.

Far from Leningrad, at Samarkand, Soviet scientists had undertaken excavation work at the tomb of Tamerlane, the great warlord of Central Asia, conqueror of the Mongols. Unlike many ancient tombs, Tamerlane's had never been opened. There were two reasons for this. Unlike the pharaohs and Oriental emperors, Islamic leaders were not buried with gold or valuable objects. Robbers knew this and left the tombs alone. The other reason was the fear of an ancient curse. Tamerlane had been a savage and brilliant warrior, and it was said that the spirit of war followed him even to his grave. A massive panel of jade covered Tamerlane's sarcophagus, and, legend ran, the stone imprisoned the demon of Tamerlane's wars inside; whatsoever nation removed the jade barrier would unleash on itself the specter of war itself. In the third week of June 1941, Soviet archeologists lifted back the panel and opened the tomb.

On the night of June 21–22, 1941, at the summer solstice, when the northern sun turns midnight to day, the German army began to move across the Soviet frontier. Unprepared, the Red Army was thrown back across the whole of the country. The losses were staggering. So rapid was the blitzkrieg that within ten weeks the German Northern Army Group smashed all the way to the outskirts of Leningrad. The last remaining rail and highway link between the city and the Soviet front line was cut. As of August 30, 1941, the population of four million was in blockade. Leningrad was completely unprepared. In keeping with the strong Soviet predilection to centralize, the City Soviet (council) had stored what small food reserve the city had in the enormous Badayev warehouse complex—hundreds of wooden buildings built eight to ten yards apart. It could not have been a more tempting target. On September 8, 1941, the warehouses were firebombed by German planes. Three thousand tons of flour were lost. A sea of 2,500 tons of molten sugar flowed into the earth in such concentration that later the ground would be used to make tea. Surrounded by a hostile army, the city was left without food.

The blockade and siege were to last until January 27, 1944. By the time it ended the population was reduced from four million to 560,000. Some Leningraders were flown out; others escaped in winter over the frozen Lake Ladoga. Many fell victim to German bombs and artillery. But the greatest factor in reducing the city's population was starvation. Though the precise figure will never be known, during the almost 900-day siege, between a million and a million and a half Leningraders starved to death.

But Leningrad was not conquered. Owing to the courage of her citizens, the city survived. And even in the darkest of those 900 days, there were those who talked of a renaissance, such that the city, which had stood steadfast for Russia, would once again become the "window on the West." The Leningrad defenders looked forward to continued warm relations with the Western democracies, the Soviet Union's wartime allies. Leningrad, they hoped, would be returned to its position as the cultural if not the political capital, an international city. This was not to be. As Peter had loved the city for its Western cosmopolitanism, so Stalin for the same reasons despised it. Leningraders had emerged from their ordeal proud—too proud for the Kremlin. Leningrad was not to become the gateway to Europe; the "window on the West" was slammed shut.

Just as businesses in the West are sometimes named for their founders, purges in the Soviet Union follow the same practice. In 1944, when the siege was finally lifted and the Red Army carried the war back to Germany, Zhdanov left Leningrad and returned to Stalin's side at the Kremlin. Following the war, Zhdanov rewarded the city's heroism by presiding over a purge of Leningraders, especially of the intellectuals, which came to be known as the *Zhdanov-shchina*. Leningrad poets, writers, and scientists were rounded up. Those historians who refused to deny Western influence in Russia, those scientists who were not convinced that Russians had invented everything, and those biologists who did not teach that the son would inherit the skills learned by his father were eliminated. But, as frequently happens with purges, things got out of hand: Frankenstein's monster turned on Dr. Frankenstein. In August 1948 it was reported that Zhdanov himself had perished in the Kremlin, the victim of poisoning or deliberate medical malpractice. Immediately thereafter, what had happened to the Leningrad party organization of Kirov happened to those who had been associated with Zhdanov. Zhdanov's successor as Leningrad party chief, Mayor Popkov, disappeared. The party secretaries and factory heads, even the rector of Leningrad State University—as many as 2,000 courageous souls who had led Leningrad during the blockade—were liquidated. So total was Stalin's campaign to wipe out the memory of the city's heroism that even the Museum of the Defense of Leningrad was closed, its exhibits confiscated, and its director packed off to Siberia. Leningrad came to be known as the graveyard of Soviet politics.

How could a city that had shown such courage against the enemy be so savagely turned upon by those who were supposedly its leaders? How could anyone hate or fear a city so much that he would destroy its museum? There are those who speculate that the Kirov assassination, the *Zhdanovshchina*, and finally the purge of Zhdanov and his Leningrad associates followed in the long pattern of rivalry between Leningrad and Moscow—played out in this case by their party organizations. When Lenin moved the capital back to Moscow in 1918, all of the traits that Peter had hated—the provincialism, the suspicion, the greed—began to reassert themselves. For Leningrad there was to be no cultural rebirth from the ashes so long as Moscow held sway. In accordance with the central state plan, Leningrad was the last of the major Soviet cities to be rebuilt after the war.

There are many little ironies in the Soviet Union. Kirov, who was almost certainly liquidated on Stalin's instructions, has as his namesake many Leningrad institutions, from factories and bridges to the world-famous Kirov theater and ballet company. And Zhdanov, architect of the Hitler-Stalin Pact, who with war imminent left defenseless Leningrad to go on vacation, whose poor planning resulted in hundreds of thousands of deaths by starvation, who was Stalin's principal hatchet man first against the old Bolsheviks and then against the intellectuals, who more than any other man did everything possible to destroy Leningrad and its artistic, cultural, and intellectual heritage—this man, who did not deserve a cesspool in his honor, was given as his namesake Leningrad State University.

Four /

Life in

the Neighborhood

It seemed a pattern among the foreign students that
after a few months, when we had become accustomed to
the Russian students in our dormitory and more confident
in our knowledge of the language and culture, we would
begin to branch out into new activities and new friendships.
The starting point for all of this was our neighborhood, and
our neighborhood was on an island, the largest island in the
Neva, Vasilevsky's Island. Its name came from that of an
obscure lieutenant of artillery, Vasily Korchmin, who com-
manded a shore battery there at a time when Peter the Great
was still wary of an attack by the Swedish navy. Later Peter
gave the major part of the island as a present to his friend
the governor general of St. Petersburg, the Serene Prince
Alexander Menshikov. Menshikov's red palace, the largest
house in Peter's city, was used by the czar for formal enter-
tainments. It still stands on the embankment of the Neva
just downstream from the buildings of Leningrad State
University.

The mainland of Leningrad is on the southern bank of
the Neva. Vasilevsky's Island is to the north of the Neva's
main channel. Crossing the Neva in Peter the Great's day
was no mean feat. Its width and fast current made bridging
unfeasible, so transport was by ferry. If a storm came up
the inhabitants on the north and south banks of the river

could be cut off for days. To complicate matters, Peter, determined to instill seamanship in the Russian citizenry, decreed that the ferrymen must sail across the river without the use of oars. After a number of dignitaries, including the Polish ambassador, drowned while tacking across the icy river, Peter at last permitted the ferrymen to row.

Despite its isolation, Peter had high hopes for Vasilevsky's Island. Its eastern half was to be a New Amsterdam, a grid of intersecting boulevards called prospects, and canals. Peter's new French architect, Alexandre LeBlond, was ordered to get to work on the site immediately. Unfortunately, when Peter was away, the plan was quietly sabotaged by Prince Menshikov, who knew that if the island became the commercial center Peter envisioned, the czar might renege on his gift to the prince. The canals, to be used for commerce as in Holland, were somehow dug much narrower and shallower than LeBlond had instructed. They quickly turned into unnavigable mud sewers, carriers of nothing but disease. After the czar's death they were filled and became streets, called "lines," in keeping with the original designation. The wide avenues which ran vaguely east-west and perpendicular to the lines were known, literally enough, as the Great, Middle, and Little Prospects. Shevchenko Street was beyond the original lines and like them ran north-south. My dormitory was on Shevchenko between the Middle Prospect and the Small Prospect, on the western end of the island, not far from the harbor where passenger ships arriving in Leningrad would unload.

I heard about a local resident named Slava from an American friend who had lived in Leningrad before me. Slava was about thirty, a translator. He translated English books into Russian under contract from Soviet publishing houses. Slava had published a dozen translations, from classics like *Washington Square*, by Henry James, to books on marine animals and life in the Canadian Far North. Slava was married to Laura, who worked in a bookstore. She possessed a wealth of knowledge about Russian literature, but was overall of a practical turn of mind. While Slava sat at home with his books waiting for the next translation contract to come in, Laura brought home regular pay and did battle every night with the lines and with the shortages. But in her own way Laura was also a dreamer. The store where she worked was small, and she got to know the books in it as if they were a kind of extended family. There were idle moments in the shop when she could peruse the new titles. There were conversations with old friends who dropped in to see what was available. Within the confines of her world the gray reality of Soviet life could pass by unnoticed, as it did for Slava. Laura had her own little shop full of dreams to gain strength from.

Slava and Laura had a son named Maxim, who was eight at the time I made their acquaintance. Maxim was a cherub. Despite the fact that neither Slava nor his son had ever been beyond the borders of the Soviet Union, they spoke to each other exclusively in English. Slava had raised Maxim bilingually, partly so that Slava would have someone to speak English with and partly so that his son would have a valuable skill—particularly valuable if the family were ever to leave the Soviet Union. Speaking English with his son, translating Henry James, and consorting with the foreign community, Slava had created a little Western salon in his Leningrad apartment.

Slava lived at only a three-minute walk from the dormitory, a fact which admittedly played a role in our close friendship. Because the public transportation system is so crowded and poorly developed, because few people have telephones—and those who do are wary of foreigners calling them—keeping up a friendship with someone far from the center drains one's time and energy. Slava lived close enough that I never had to phone, I could just drop by, and if he was not home or was too busy to see me, the day was not lost.

Not every important historical building is restored. The city is a patchwork of brilliant and expense-be-damned restoration of a few buildings, while every-thing else deteriorates. This is the palace of the Serene Prince Menshikov, closest confidant of Peter the Great. In Peter's day it was the grandest mansion in St. Petersburg, used by the Czar for official state functions. Although it is the oldest major building on Vasilevsky's Island, it is now left to the elements.

(*top*) Russian friends. On the right, Slava Paperno, my Russian teacher. On the left, Tolya Putilin, a well-known abstract artist.

(*bottom*) Citizens in my neighborhood looking at offers to trade apartments. There is no free market, and the state is the only landlord. Those dissatisfied with their quarters could advertise to trade for another apartment. Money was not suppose to figure in the transaction, but it frequently did.

(*top*) The streets in Leningrad were under interminable repair. This view is typical of Vasilevsky's Island in winter.

(*bottom*) The ubiquitous Soviet beer stall. Customers would queue up in freezing weather for their half liter. Typically the woman in the stall would have only a few mugs, and customers would have to wait for those ahead to finish.

(*top*) A construction site near the dormitory. No work had been done there for eight years. Because no one feels the economic pressure to use urban land or heavy equipment such as these cranes in a profit-maximizing way, sites are simply abandoned if the manpower is transferred to a higher-priority project. The construction materials were just left to rust away in the harsh climate.

(*bottom*) On two or three occasions during the long winter, Leningrad received a large shipment of oranges. These were from Morocco. Although they were expensive, everyone would take down his net shopping bag and buy as many as he could afford. Leningraders knew that this was the only fresh fruit they would see until summer.

As my relations with Zhenya deteriorated, Slava's apartment became my home away from home. I dropped by three or four times a week, perhaps to have dinner, perhaps to bring Slava a Western newspaper, or perhaps for a game of chess with little Max. Although Slava had never been abroad and was a homebody by temperament, his work as a translator and his inquisitive mind made him the most worldly Russian I was to meet. I sometimes wonder whether I could have gotten through that long, hard Leningrad winter without Slava's quips about life in Russia and Laura's home-cooked meals.

Slava took great pleasure in watching me discover the little rituals of Soviet daily life. After any new experience I would report back to his place to discuss my latest adventure. He always had some witty sidelight to add perspective to the encounter. I remember one of my earliest experiences shopping in Leningrad. Back in the States I had been warned to bring a year's supply of toothpaste, but in all the dashing and tearing about at the time of the bar exam and taking leave of family, friends, and country for a year's sojourn behind the Iron Curtain, who thinks to pack ten tubes of toothpaste? Time caught up with me, however, and in the early fall my family-size tube of Crest gave its last.

There are fewer stores in Soviet cities than in Western cities of equivalent size, and as a result they are always thronged. The profit motive which would cause an entrepreneur observing customers lined up to get into one store to open another one across the street, does not play a role in the Soviet economy. As a result you can't get toothpaste on just any corner. You must know of a store that would carry it, and there is always the possibility that toothpaste, or any other item you might seek, would be entirely sold out citywide and remain so for months.

I had been informed by the other American residents in Leningrad that Russian toothpaste was usually available but tasted so bad that it was to be avoided at all costs. While I

was sure there was some truth in this, I have found that
when it comes to personal articles, most Americans are
firmly tied to their acquired tastes, condemning everything
else out of hand. Something like the taste of toothpaste is
drummed in by habit from an early age. In any case, all of
this was idle theorizing, because I had no choice. Unlike in
Moscow, there was no American shop in the consulate
basement. It was either go native or go without. Having
located a store near the Vasilevsky's Island metro stop, I
sallied forth to make my purchase.

One follows a unique procedure in buying something in
a Soviet store. There is a certain three-step, well known to
anyone who has shopped within the Soviet economy. I
approached the counter marked "toiletries." The salesclerk
was a young woman with a blond beehive hairdo. The
counter was surrounded by customers and I had to wait my
turn. When I got to the front, I asked for toothpaste and
she pointed to a small white tube in the glass display case
in front of her. She informed me that the price was eleven
kopecks. However, I could not simply buy the toothpaste
from this woman. She was qualified to handle goods but
not money. In order to take care of the financial side of the
transaction I would have to go somewhere else. Secure in
the information that what I wanted was available, and
knowing the exact price, I joined another line.

At the head of this line sat a cashier on a high stool in a
glass enclosure, armed with an abacus and a squat machine
that typed quantities and prices onto a thick roll of cashier's
tape. When I got to the front of this line I reported to her
that I wanted two tubes of toothpaste at eleven kopecks each.
Instead of tallying up the amount, she informed me that
toothpaste was thirty-two kopecks per tube. I was certain
that I had understood the salesclerk correctly, but I was far
from the counter where I had been told the price was eleven.
If I got out of line at the cashier's to try to verify the price
with the clerk, it would take me another twenty minutes to

get back where I was. Moreover, the cashier could still say I was wrong, and with long lines at both places, neither the clerk not the cashier was going to leave her post to dispute the price of toothpaste. The cashier slid a few beads across the abacus and I ponied up sixty-four kopecks for two tubes. She gave me a little tear from her cashier's tape which showed I had paid this amount. I would surrender this receipt to the clerk when I received my purchase.

I again joined the line at the toothpaste counter. After waiting for those ahead of me to be served, I handed the clerk my chit. She looked at it and said, "I told you toothpaste was eleven kopecks a tube, not thirty-two." "I know," I said, "but when I went to the cashier, she told me thirty-two was the price." The clerk grimaced and I wondered if I was going to have to start the whole process over again. Instead she exclaimed under her breath, "Damn that cashier," and pulled out a small cardboard carton from under the counter. Keeping it down on the floor so that other customers couldn't see, she fished out two tubes of imported Bulgarian toothpaste in brightly colored boxes. She handed them to me furtively, and whispered, "Don't tell the others." She had stashed this shipment away, hoping to sell it just to her friends. The cashier knew the Bulgarian toothpaste was available and, perhaps because I was a foreigner, wanted to see that I got some of it.

I was back out on the street with two tubes of Bulgarian toothpaste, and the whole process had taken only half an hour. I had done well. I grabbed the bus for Slava's in order to try my new purchase. With Slava standing by, I brushed my teeth with some of my hard-won prize. It was awful. It was hard to imagine a worse taste in a toothpaste. While Slava grinned, I tried some of his Soviet toothpaste for comparison. It was awful too, but no more awful than the Bulgarian. Both were variations on soap, with a few noxious chemicals thrown in for good measure. I asked Slava if he liked the taste of the Bulgarian. He said he had tried it before and thought it was awful. Why, then, I asked, if the Soviet toothpaste was awful at eleven kopecks, and the Bulgarian toothpaste was awful at thirty-two, was this clerk going to the trouble to hide away the imported stuff for her friends? Well, Slava pointed out, there is after all a certain status in brushing your teeth with hard-to-come-by Bulgarian toothpaste!

Not least among the activities I shared with Slava and his family was my continuing study of the Russian language. I had arrived in Leningrad with pretty good schoolboy Russian. Harvard and two summers at Middlebury's Russian Summer School had given me the equivalent of four years of college Russian. But as every American who has spent a junior year abroad knows, the American classroom is but a prelude to learning a language. Russian is an especially difficult language for an American. It is not the alphabet that makes this so. The Cyrilic characters look forbidding, but there are only thirty-three of them, many of which correspond to letters in the Latin alphabet. Nor does the relationship between spelling and pronunciation pose any great difficulty. Unlike the English alphabet, in which a given letter has numerous pronunciations—a *c*, for example sometimes sounding like an *s* and sometimes like a *k*—the Russian letters with rare exception are pronounced only one way.

What makes the Russian language so demanding is its grammar. There are three genders: male, female, and neuter. There are six cases: nominative, accusative, genitive, dative, instrumental, and prepositional. Words, primarily word endings, change depending on their usage in the sentence. If a noun, even the proper name of a person or a city, is the subject of a sentence, it will have its nominative, "dictionary" ending. As soon as the noun changes function and becomes, for example, the object of a preposition, its form will change. Even one's name changes forms as it changes function in a Russian sentence. When modified by numbers, even singular and plural are constructed in a bewildering manner. As would be expected, the endings of Russian nouns change in going from one of something to two of something (as in English, one year, two years). But two of something in Russian does not use the plural form. The plural actually begins at the number five. "Why five?" I had asked my teacher at Middlebury. Well, because the number two had always been felt to be a little different; it had a kind of dual quality. Okay, I thought, perhaps two is special, but then the plural should come at three, not at five. Yes, my teacher explained, but somehow, nobody really knew how, the two infected the three and the three infected the four, so now the plural comes at five. Infected, I thought; well, I was glad the epidemic had not spread further.

The fact that almost every word in a Russian sentence has a special ending permits the Russians to do something that can be done in English to only a very limited extent. In Russian, the words may be moved around within a sentence without changing their meaning. In English, the sentences "I had the dog trained," "The trained dog I had," and "I had trained the dog" all have different meanings. Moving the words around this way in a Russian sentence would not have the same effect. The Russian speaker would look to the ending of each word to tell him its relationship to the other words. Position in the sentence would not alter this. But, while the Russian sentences would all have the same meaning, the emphasis on each element would be altered, thus adding diplomatic and poetic nuances unknown to English.

To all of this, spoken Russian added another level of difficulty—the actual voice inflection and pitch of a sentence. It is quite possible for an American to speak grammatically perfect and even accent-free Russian and still be regularly misunderstood. When a native speaker of American English wants to ask a question, he slightly raises the pitch of his voice on the last syllable of the sentence. "Are you going *home?*" For a Russian, this pattern would reflect a command or a state of excitation. In a normal polite question, the Russian speaker raises his pitch in the middle of the sentence and then lets it drop down to neutral. "Are you *going* home?" This can lead to some confusing situations. For example, the buses in Leningrad were crowded beyond belief. If you did not begin pushing toward the door three stops before your own, you were carried a mile out of the way before finally wiggling free. In making your assault on the door anything was fair play: shoving, squirming, shouting, pleading, cajoling, or insulting. Anything, that is, except pushing your way past someone else who was also trying to get off the bus. Standard procedure was to ask in a courteous tone, "You're getting off the bus?" Unfortunately, in that hot, crowded, swirling black hole that is the back of a Russian bus, if the hapless American delivered this interrogative with an American stress pattern, the sentence would not be understood as a courteous request, but as an insistent command: "You're getting off the bus!"

This same problem afflicts Russians who are trying to communicate in English. The tendency of Russians to drop the pitch at the end of a declaratory sentence has the effect of making English-speaking Russians seem rude and bored. Many a Russian Beriozka (hard-currency store) clerk or Intourist guide whose "What do you want!" or "Where are you going!" is meant to be solicitous is thought instead to be rude. In stressing her English sentence as she would stress its Russian equivalent, she sounds to the American like a drill sergeant.

The American male who desires to learn correct Russian must overcome another dfficulty, this one of a psychological nature. Most American males speak in a monotone. Standard Midwestern American English is basically the John Wayne drawl. To speak with a sharp rise and fall in the pitch of your voice is indicative, in the mind of some, of a homosexual speech pattern. To learn proper Russian, an American male must give up his John Wayne drawl and make his voice rise and fall drastically in pitch throughout a sentence. It is a painful process. The problem of sentence stress and the different feelings it conveys is only recently, I am told, being explored by linguists. Perhaps when the concept is fully understood a diplomatic history could be written attributing many international fracas to misunderstood sentence stress.

At my urging, Slava agreed to become my Russian teacher. At first, in the fall, it was just the occasional lesson, but by midwinter, when there wasn't much else to do anyway, we were meeting every weekday morning. I would awaken just before nine, when it was still dark outside, and quickly wash up in the near-freezing communal basins at one end of the dormitory hall. I would dress as quietly as possible, so as not to wake the snoring Zhenya, and slip out of the dormitory just as the sun was rising. In the frozen stillness the only sound was the muffled crunch of my boots on the glistening snow. I would arrive at Slava's after a three-minute walk and go up to the third floor of his apartment building. Built in the so-called Stalinesque style, it had thick walls, false Greek columns, and undersized windows. Laura would already be off to work, and Slava, still in pajamas, would let me in. I would exchange my snowy boots for floppy indoor slippers called *tapochki*. While Slava washed up I would put on the kettle to make tea. After brewing the leaves, we would pour the tea over raspberry jam called *malina*, which Slava had made from berries picked that fall. *Malina* was about the only source of vitamin C afforded by the Leningrad winter diet. Usually we would have Finnish eggs for breakfast with black bread and butter. After this nourishing repast we would sit down to my Russian lesson.

One January morning, when Leningrad was buried under a soft, snowy blanket, after a difficult session on the Russian verbs of motion, Slava said he had a present for me—

something to get us outdoors for some exercise. From out of the closet he pulled a slim yellow pair of cross-country skis. They were marked with the designation "highest quality." He had a paper bag with the bindings, the old-fashioned sort that can grip on any winter shoe, and together we found the balance and attached them to the skis. I was so excited about trying them that we went right away to the only large wooded area on the island—the Smolensk cemetery.

Smolensk cemetery is huge, spanning acres from Vasilevsky's Malyi (Small) Prospect to the Smolensk River and stretching across to the Decembrists' Island on the far side. Many of my neighbors had ancestors buried there. But Smolensk was more than a graveyard. It was a tranquil place for walking among the birch trees and perhaps lighting a candle in the small church. In a more organic way than Americans think of a cemetery, it served as a park and a place for young people to be alone. The people in the neighborhood loved it. There had been talk of leveling it. But even though it was near the city center, where housing was needed, the locals knew their cemetery was safe. What protected it from destruction was not any religious sentimentality on the part of the Leningrad City Council, but the fact that every so often one black Zil limousine surrounded by a fleet of black Chaikas, would pull up to a small side entrance, and while security troops fanned out across the grounds, one man placed flowers on a nondescript grave. Smolensk cemetery was the burial place of the parents of Alexei Kosygin, then premier of the Soviet Union.

For about five minutes Slava and I glided through the snowy quiet until, as I was skiing over a small bump, one of my "highest quality" skis snapped in two. When Slava and I examined it closely we saw that under the thick yellow paint the ski was not made from one piece of wood. Incredibly, the front and the back half of the ski were two separate slats joined together with glue at a dovetail joint just two inches in front of the binding. Given this construction it was amazing that the ski lasted as long as it did. Slava was furious. That very day we went back to the small sporting-goods store where Slava had bought them. We were going to demand a refund; the whole incident turned into a lesson on Soviet product liability and quality control.

When we arrived the store was closed, but we could see employees milling about inside. We pounded and pounded and at last someone came. Cracking the door he yelled, "We're closed for inventory," and slammed it behind him. Pounding again, we finally got a brief audience with the manager.

"Look, we're closed for inventory, and anyway I don't have any more skis like the ones you bought, so I can't replace them. Maybe if you come back when inventory taking is over I can refund your money."

"When will you be done taking inventory?" Slava asked.

"Oh," said the manager, "try back in two weeks."

"Two weeks," yelled Slava, "what are we supposed to do for two weeks?"

"Look, I told you, inventory, *inventory!*" With this the manager slammed the door, breaking off further discussion. I tried to laugh it off but I could not stop Slava from feeling glum. He said he couldn't believe it. It was ridiculous. The snow was on the ground now. Leningrad could have a mid-winter thaw, as it frequently did; meanwhile we couldn't ski and we couldn't get the money back to buy another pair. How could they spend weeks taking inventory in a small shop? To console him I proposed that I would simply buy another pair that day. If he wanted it to be a present he could wait to get the refund from the broken pair and pay me back.

We caught the bus to another store that sometimes had skis, and to our good fortune found exactly twelve skis there. These were light blue and marked "second-highest quality." After our experience with "highest quality" we counted this a good sign. Slava and I made a joke out of the designation "highest quality." Whenever something fell apart right away, we would solemnly assure each other that this was proof it had been "highest quality." The "second-highest quality" skis were much fatter. They were crudely made, but this was a good sign. It would be too much trouble to put a glued joint right at their stress point. This time Slava wasn't taking chances. Despite the salesgirl's protestations, he insisted on examining each ski individually. Of the twelve skis, eleven were visibly splintered. We could not find an undamaged pair. Slava did not know any other store on the island where we could get skis. By now it was dark and despondently we trudged home, beaten by the system.

About a week later I was downtown on Nevsky Prospect and dropped into Gostiny Dvor to look for a pair of skis. Gostiny Dvor, which, freely translated, means Merchants' Arcade, is Leningrad's equivalent of the monstrous GUM (State Universal Store) across from the Kremlin on Moscow's Red Square. Gostiny Dvor takes up all four sides of a huge block on Nevsky Prospect—almost a mile of two-story continuous arcade. It was built between 1761 and 1785 by the French architect Vallin de la Mothe and at one time held hundreds of little independent shops. Now it holds hundreds of little departments, but the customer soon realizes that the departments just repeat themselves every twelve or so and have basically identical merchandise. Still, Gostiny Dvor had the largest selection in town, and sure enough I found a lovely pair of cross-country skis. They cost about eleven rubles, almost three times as much as the "highest quality" skis that had lasted five minutes. They were of varnished natural wood and, what was really lovely, had the word "NOVGOROD" written on them in old Russian letters. That night I took them over to Slava's, and we made plans to put their bindings on and go skiing that weekend.

Alas, as if some great heavenly council had decreed it, I was not to go cross-country skiing in Leningrad. That very night, just as Slava had feared, a cold rain blew in from the Baltic, and a February thaw began which reduced the parks and Smolensk cemetery to mud. Before the snow returned, my permission to leave for two months of study in Moscow finally came through. I considered hauling my skis with me; I understood that the skiing around Moscow State on Lenin Hills was quite good. But I had too much to carry on the train and reluctantly left them behind. I did not return to Leningrad until late April, when skiing was over. After an almost endless "inventory" at the sporting-goods store, when the snow was gone, Slava did manage to get his money back for the "highest quality" skis.

One day when I was playing chess with Maxim, he showed me a copy of his first-grade reader. The name of the book was *Rodnaya Rech:* in English, *Mother Tongue.* Education in the Soviet Union is standardized; every Russian first grader uses the same textbooks. In fact, probably every first grader across the entire eleven time zones of the country reads the same assignment at the same local time. As in any book printed in the Soviet Union, a number in the back shows the total number of copies printed. As the required reader for every Soviet first grader, this book had been printed in an edition of 2,750,000 copies. It sold for thirty-three kopecks (forty-five cents)—not exactly a limited edition.

Max showed me some of the stories in the reader. There were stories about animals and nature, but there were also a lot of political stories about the life of Lenin and the glories of the Red Army. Max told me he had a test the next day on a story about life in America, on page 158 of the reader. It was written by one N. Kol'ma and called "The Red Shoes." It was the only story in the reader about America, and I was interested to learn what impression the hundreds of thousands of little first graders would be given. To help Max prepare for his test we read the story together.

THE RED SHOES

The dark-skinned little girl Nancy lived with her mother in an American city.

Nancy's mother worked as a dishwasher in a restaurant and got home after midnight. But no matter how late her mother got home, Nancy always waited and did not go to bed without her.

Nancy's shoes had worn out. They were so worn out that even their neighbor, the shoemaker Bill, couldn't do anything to fix them. The sole of the left shoe was entirely torn off, and the right one had such a gaping hole that one could see the toes of Nancy's foot.

In the morning, looking over what remained of her shoes, Nancy started to cry. "How am I going to go walking without shoes?" Her mother sighed heavily, "I will stay at work until morning . . . Then, perhaps, I can manage to save enough money to buy you a new pair of shoes."

Until morning? Did that mean Nancy would be alone all night? But the desire to have new shoes was so strong that Nancy didn't pay any attention.

"Mama, buy me red shoes, you know, like the ones the little girl had that we saw in the park," she begged her mother. Her mother sighed once again, "I don't know, my little girl, if I'll be able to earn enough." However, Nancy so plaintively begged her mother to buy her the red shoes, without fail, that her mother at last promised.

On Nancy's mother's day off, they set out together for the shoestore. In the shining plate-glass show window of the store stood boots and shoes of all colors. Nancy was dazzled: she had never seen such elegant shoes. Suddenly she cried out, "Mama, Mama, look: there they are—the red shoes! Let's go quickly, Mama, and buy them!"

They went into the store. One salesman was trying a pair of yellow shoes on a fair-haired, snub-nosed little boy; the other salesman nonchalantly chattered away. The tall proprietor by the desk didn't even look over at the Negress with the little girl.

Nancy and her mother stood a long time by the counter. At

last Nancy's mother timidly requested, "Forgive me, please, wouldn't you be so kind as to show us a pair of red shoes for my little girl?"

One of the salesmen reluctantly came over to them.

"These are expensive goods," he said. "Do you have enough money for such shoes?"

The mother showed her purse. "There, sir, all last week I worked nights." Only then the salesman laid out on the counter a pair of red shoes. They were so soft, shone so nicely, and smelled so of new leather that Nancy started clapping her hands.

The salesman growled, "You can try them on if you want."

He himself was supposed to try shoes on the customers, but he wouldn't dream of stooping for these black customers. The mother herself knelt down in front of Nancy and began to pull the shoes on her. But what a pity, they were too small.

"I wonder if you might, sir, have a little bigger pair?" requested Nancy's mother.

The salesman sullenly looked over at her, "A little larger? I have them. Only you have to take the pair you tried on."

Nancy's mother rose from her knees.

"Take this pair?" she asked again. "But really, these shoes are too tight for the little girl."

The salesman quietly wrapped up the shoes in paper. "And who would want to take these shoes, which were put on your black feet? You have to take these shoes from us."

Nancy's mother clasped her hands. "My God, really all I have is enough for one pair. Does this mean my little girl must remain without shoes?"

Hearing this, Nancy loudly started to cry. Her mother approached the proprietor of the store.

"Sir," she appealed to him. "I implore you, sir, don't make me buy these shoes . . . I don't have a spare cent, sir . . ."

"I don't want to incur a loss because of you," muttered the proprietor. "You should have known that after your little girl tried them on, not one American would buy these shoes for his children."

"You're wrong about that, proprietor," a loud, friendly voice suddenly resounded.

A customer in blue work coveralls walked up to the counter and patted Nancy on the back.

"You don't have to cry, little girl," he said. "Although the shoes you tried on were expensive, I'll take them anyway; they are perfectly suitable for my little girl. And you yourself purchase other ones. I know well the meaning of hard-earned money."

He pulled out of his pocket enough money, paid the salesman, and took up the package with the shoes. Then he bowed to Nancy's mother and walked out of the store.

Successfully and happily, Nancy and her mother returned home that day. The dark-skinned little girl rejoiced at her new red shoes, which squeaked quietly with each of her steps . . .

QUESTIONS TO THE TEXT:

1. What country does Nancy live in?
2. Why was it difficult for Nancy's mother to buy shoes for her daughter?
3. How did Nancy and her mother buy the shoes? Tell the story.
4. Who helped the dark-skinned customers? Read the story.
5. Explain the expression "hard-earned money."

I could only marvel at the insincerity of the Soviet government, which while actively pursuing the policy of "détente" internationally was so unabashedly attempting to instill anti-American sentiment internally. Not that I was concerned about Max; he had met dozens of Americans and was a pretty sophisticated little boy. But the average Russian goes through life without ever meeting a Westerner. They do not believe all the propaganda, but considering that this is all they are permitted to hear, they just don't know what to believe. I remember one very sincere young man who, upon learning I was from America, asked me if it was true that Americans all had armor plate on their front doors to prevent gangsters from shooting into their homes.

He was no fool and couldn't believe this was true, but he had heard it so many times that he was beginning to wonder whether there might not be something to it. Nor could one say that an incident like that described in "The Red Shoes" did not or could not take place. It could. But to present this to impressionable seven- and eight-year-olds, as their only glimpse of American life, was outrageous.

Sensing my discomfort, Max assured me that all the little kids in Leningrad listened to the Voice of America Russian-language broadcast and weren't about to believe this kind of foolishness. Everybody knew life was better in America, Max said, because even though Americans were allowed to travel, no one he knew had ever met an American who had immigrated to the Soviet Union. Reassured, I thanked him and wished him well on his test, and we went back to our chess game.

Five /

Socialist

Socializing

Having discussed some of the difficulties of being a foreign student in the Soviet Union, I hasten to add that there are also tremendous advantages. I had also been a foreign student in Germany. I had enjoyed it; there was always plenty of *Bier, Wurst,* and *Gemütlichkeit.* But the West German people, already inundated by the waves of college-age tourists in those heady predevaluation early seventies, did not see me as particularly interesting just because I was an American. Leningrad was different. Although it had always been the home of Russian cosmopolitanism—Peter's "window on the West"—during the Soviet period contact with foreigners had been so limited that today almost the entire complement of Western young people residing in this city of four million was contained in two small dormitories. Scarce resources are much in demand. Important Leningrad writers, painters, and art collectors sought my company and invited me to their homes. In Paris or London people of their stature would not have given me the time of day. But in Leningrad these people would actually compete for my friendship. "How could you accept an invitation for dinner at Vanya's; you know I was planning to invite you." Russians can in fact smother you with their friendship and will feel really hurt if a week goes by and they have not seen you. The foreigner in Russia is a kind of reluctant aristocrat. When I told people I was from America, they would stare at me as if I were half from Mars and half from the Garden of Eden. There are other countries where travel and entry are restricted and foreigners are few, but I don't think it would be the same for a Caucasian American in places like the People's Republic of China. In Russia the people look pretty much like you and dress pretty much like you, but when they find out you are an American, they make you into a demigod. This feeling of being "special" is so pronounced that after living in the U.S.S.R. some Westerners feel a psychological letdown upon returning home. No one wants to buy their clothes anymore; no one asks in a whisper, "What's it really like in the West?"

Socializing follows a decidedly non-Western pattern. Almost all entertainment focuses on the spoken word, frequently lubricated by generous tumblers of vodka. There is little else to do. Leningrad television had two regular channels and one educational one; it was black and white and went off the air early, and with the exception of old war movies and soccer it featured little besides political lectures. There are cultural activities, concerts, and ballets, but tickets are hard to come by and, though inexpensive by Western standards, are beyond the budget of most Soviets. Most of a family's income goes for food. Little money is available for anything else. A typical Soviet family never goes to a restaurant except perhaps to give away their daughter in marriage. Entertaining is done at home around a table laden with whatever the collective efforts of the participants have been able to produce, but never without the two essentials: mountains of black bread and oceans of vodka. If a host can provide a Russian favorite in short supply, such as pickles or marinated mushrooms, he becomes an instant hero. Mustard, for example, had been absent from the stores for years. It is a real Leningrad favorite, as popular as it is in Dijon or Düsseldorf, yet not once did I see it in the shops. In the certificate-ruble stores (to which I had access, as an American exchange student) it was in abundance at a cost of only twenty U.S. cents. I would contribute a jar to every social gathering, thereby insuring my undying popularity. People would almost cry when they saw it. One woman told me that a single taste made her feel as if the czar were still in the Winter Palace.

Most of my visits to Leningrad restaurants were with Western friends, who like me had more than enough rubles and not very much to spend them on. These dinners at the Baku Caucasian restaurant or the Astoria hotel were welcome respites from the daily struggle of keeping body and soul together through the long Russian winter. We would commiserate over the latest outrage foisted upon us by Inotdel and exchange the current political jokes. A Russian restaurant dinner serves a different social function from its equivalent in the West. It is designed as an entire evening's entertainment, with music and dancing. Great importance is given to the order in which the courses are presented. In fact, it is said that the Russians, who borrowed much gastronomically from the French, in turn taught them the practice of serving a meal in courses rather than all at once. The most important element in the Russian meal is the *zakuski* (hors d'oeuvres). The elegance of the repast is determined by the variety and quality of these *zakuski*. Typical *zakuski* are sliced sturgeon, marinated mushrooms, and meat salads consisting of small pieces of vegetables, pickles, meat, and mayonnaise. The most famous *zakuski* is the very pinnacle of Russian cuisine—Beluga caviar from the Caspian Sea. *Zakuski* are frequently ordered ahead and consumed over a long period replete with toasts punctuated by jiggers of vodka drunk bottoms up. An inexperienced foreign guest is frequently sated from this course alone and shocked to hear he has only begun.

After *zakuski* comes the so-called "first one," obligatorily, soup. At dinner this may be just a bouillon with meat-filled pastries called *pirozhki*. At lunch it might be a huge bowl of beet-based *borshch*, or cabbage-based *shchi*. After soup comes "the second one," the hot plate. A smaller portion than is customary in the West, it could be beef Stroganov, chicken Kiev, or a less exotic meat and potatoes. Wine is served: if one is lucky, a dry white Tsinandali from the Georgian Republic or a Hungarian "Bull's Blood." At last comes "the sweet one," dessert. Russian ice cream is consistently good and is properly served with "cognac," actually brandy from one of the Soviet Caucasian republics, Georgia, Armenia, or occasionally Azerbaijan.

Many of my Russian friends, notably Slava, would never go to restaurants, even at my invitation. Slava considered them a waste of money for mediocre food and indifferent service, regardless of who was paying. And, Slava pointed out, you couldn't really relax in a restaurant. Slava's idea of relaxing was to sit in his kitchen with close friends and talk for hours. I had to admit that in Slava's little "salon" this could be richer than caviar. The oral tradition is strong in Russia. Almost everyone has something he can do to entertain. One may know card tricks, another can sing and play the guitar, a third can do impersonations of Soviet personalities. I remember how at Slava's parties, Tolya Putilin, a noted Leningrad abstract painter, and I would pull out guitars and try to harmonize on "Stenka Razin," "Ochi Chernye" or some other Russian folk ballad. Although our little group shouted encouragement, I'm afraid that, plied with frequent rounds of cognac, Tolya and I may have more closely approximated two wolves in Siberia than the gypsy balladeers we fancied ourselves.

Putilin was an interesting character. He and his beautiful wife, Liuda, seemed to live on nothing. They were as thin as Tolya's paintbrushes. Occasionally Tolya would sell a painting on the underground market for a substantial sum and, in typical Russian artistic fashion, fly away with Liuda to the Black Sea to squander the money in a week. They lived on the outskirts of Leningrad in a Soviet housing development. Their building was at the crossroads of Enlightenment Street and Culture Street. Notwithstanding its pretentious name, the whole area was a barren mud sea of countless dilapidated high-rise buildings studding a treeless wasteland. Inside Tolya's apartment things were different. He and Liuda had only one room, but in order to use that as Tolya's studio, they slept in the kitchen. Tolya had painted one whole wall as an impressionistic outer space, with floating pale blue orbs. Hanging everywhere were Tolya's canvases, bright avant-garde works with spheres, abstract princesses, and religious symbolism. Mimicking the United States fad of a decade earlier, we would have "happenings" and take pictures of our group in comic poses holding bright color boards and found objects.

Another artist who sometimes visited Slava was Igor Tulipanov. Tulipanov could not sell his work through official channels, but there were private collectors and foreign diplomats who were prepared to pay and pay well. He was reputed to be a rich man because sales of his finer works could bring thousands of rubles on the underground market. However, as the state plays the principal role in housing assignments, these thousands of rubles could not buy Tulipanov a private flat, and as he did not paint "socialist realism" he was not entitled to an extra room for use as a studio. So Tulipanov, despite his supposed wealth, lived in a small room in a communal apartment crowded with artwork and art supplies. He was a good chess player and we played together. At the time he was working on a series called "The Enchanted Rascals," colorful comic pornographic works about a group of cartoon hooligans. Slava was helping him with translations into English of the accompanying text, as Tulipanov hoped to eventually smuggle his works out of the country and sell them in the West. He was very skillful, combining an eclectic imagination with precision of execution.

One of the pastimes at these Leningrad social gatherings

An assortment of Russian vodkas in the hard-currency store. Russians do not have the variety of whiskies such as Scotch, bourbon, and rye that exist in the English-speaking world, but they make up for it with an array of flavored vodkas. They have lemon vodka, pepper vodka, hunter's vodka, old vodka, and my favorite, zubrowka, or bison-grass vodka, flavored with a special grass common on the Polish-Soviet border.

(*top*) Frederique Longuet-Marx, great-granddaughter of Karl Marx. Frederique was an exchange student from France.
(*bottom*) Tolya Putilin entertains David Dar, the writer, and Dar's daughter, Laura, Slava's wife, at the Dar-Paperno apartment on Vasilevsky's Island.

(*top*) A "happening" at the Putilin apartment. Tolya's wife, Liuda, is on the left, Nancy Fehsenfeld, an American exchange student studying Pushkin, is to the rear with the author and the Paperno family. Tolya and Liuda slept in the kitchen so that they could use their one room as a studio.

(*bottom*) Tolya Putilin with his work.

Igor Tulipanov, a friend and prominent Leningrad abstract artist, preparing tea for us in his communal flat.

was joke telling, and the most popular jokes were always the political ones. Told to close friends around the dinner table, political jokes are the Soviet citizen's equivalent of our political editorials, cartoons, and stand-up comedians. Unlike the official state humor published in such magazines as *Krokodil*, which is not humor at all but simpleminded anti-Western propaganda in cartoon form, these underground political jokes are not only hilarious but also reveal the people's perception of their government and its policies. Typical of Russian jokes was the "troika" format, where three individuals would express their views on a given subject. Sometimes the three individuals would be of different nationalities; sometimes they would be three leaders from different periods in Soviet history.

One such joke has Stalin, Khrushchev, and Brezhnev sitting together in a train compartment, crossing Siberia bound for communism. For no apparent reason the train slowly grinds to a halt and simply sits out in the middle of the endless *taiga*. The three leaders stare out the window and silently wonder what to do to get the train moving again. Stalin, growing madder and madder, finally jumps up and shouts, "I'll show you how to solve this problem! We'll just get every engineer, fireman, and conductor off this train and shoot them. That'll fix the wreckers and saboteurs. We'll just shoot them all." Khrushchev turns to Stalin and says, "Iosif Vissarionovich, I'm surprised at you, really surprised. If we shoot them all we'll have no one left to drive the train. What we should do is shoot one or two and kindly agree to rehabilitate the rest." Finally Brezhnev speaks, "Comrades, comrades, please, those methods may have worked in the past, but that is not the modern Soviet way. There is a much more effective way of dealing with this problem. We'll just pull down the window shade and pretend we're moving."

This reflects the average citizen's view that while mass imprisonment may have passed, so-called Soviet progress exists in government reports, speeches, and publications—but not in reality. That view notwithstanding, Brezhnev is not seen as a bad leader. He is considered a moderate. Most people worry about who will come after Brezhnev, expecting repression and a return to a neo-Stalinism. Brezhnev is seen as holding the bad guys—Andropov and his KGB—in line. He is not considered a shrewd man, but rather slow and thoughtful, like the Russian bear.

There was another joke based on the way Brezhnev begins his speeches, invariably with the formula "Respected comrades. . . ." The Russians develop a machine which, when fastened to a man's head, drains all of the intelligence from him. The "brain drain" time for a man of average intelligence is one hour. One day the Soviet embassy in Washington manages to kidnap Henry Kissinger and sneak him out of the country in a diplomatic pouch. Kissinger is brought to Moscow and strapped into the machine. An hour passes, but the machine still churns away. Night comes. Finally, the next morning, the machine slowly stops. The scientists unstrap Kissinger and listen for the first sound from a man completely drained of human intelligence. Kissinger slowly begins, "Respected comrades. . . ."

This joke demonstrates a phenomenon I found consistently in Soviet humor—self-deprecation. While the Dutch tell jokes about the Belgians, and the Swedes about the Norwegians, the Russians invariably make themselves, their living conditions, and their cultural institutions the butt of every joke. One of my favorites had three very old men, one American, one French, and one Russian, reminiscing about the best day of their lives. The American, in lengthy detail, describes a sophisticated stock-market manipulation which made him a small fortune in a single day. The Frenchman, thinking the American somewhat the philistine, describes in even greater detail the moonlight seduction of a beautiful woman he had pursued for months. The Russian listens politely and then explains that these stories are nothing compared to the best day of his life. Shivering in his six-story walk-up, one-room cold-water flat on a winter night in 1937, he heard a Black Maria prison van screech to a halt outside his building. As he lay trembling, the sound of jackboots rose floor after floor. The dreaded knock came, the door was kicked open, and the secret-police officer barked at him, "Ivan Alexandrovich, come with us to the gulag." Whereupon the Russian squealed with glee, "I'm not Ivan Alexandrovich but Alexander Ivanovich. Ivan Alexandrovich lives up one more flight!"

This self-deprecation extends even to a normally revered Soviet institution—the Red Army. There is a joke, again in the "troika" format, about three generals, one British, one German, and one Russian, who get into a dispute about which of their aides is the most efficient. The British general proposes that they conduct a little test. They should each send their aide to the liquor store to purchase a bottle of the general's favorite beverage and see how each aide performs. The others agree, and the British general sends Chauncey over to the store for a bottle of dry gin. Without any problem Chauncey expeditiously fulfills the task and courteously serves the three generals a perfect martini. Impressed, the German general decides he must demonstrate how disciplined is his aide, Fritz. He gives Fritz instructions to buy a bottle of schnapps and sends him on his way. As soon as Fritz leaves, the German general looks at his watch and begins to describe exactly what Fritz is doing. "Now Fritz is going down the stairs, now Fritz is in the street, now Fritz is in the store, now Fritz is returning, now Fritz is at the door. Are you there, Fritz?" "Jawohl, Herr General," barks Fritz and walks in with the bottle of schnapps under his arm. The Russian general is so taken with this display that he decides he must imitate the German general. He summons Ivan and instructs him to go to the liquor store for a bottle of vodka. As soon as Ivan closes the door behind him, the Russian general begins to look at his watch. "Now Ivan is going down the stairs, now Ivan is in the street, now Ivan is in the store, now Ivan is returning, now Ivan is at the door. Are you there, Ivan?" "Yeh, I'm here," comes the plaintive cry, "I can't find my cap."

As would be true anywhere, a frequent topic in evening get-togethers with Russian friends was current events. Often Russians would compare the Soviet account of a given news item with what they had heard over Voice of America or Radio Free Europe. Many Russians listen regularly to Western broadcasts, a fact well-known to Soviet authorities. The usual pattern was that if an event was embarrassing to the Soviet government, it would not be mentioned in the press at all unless the Western radio networks were giving it such play that the authorities felt they somehow had to respond. One such embarrassing item in Pravda typified for me Soviet journalistic logic. It was the official version of an interview in Japan between Soviet embassy personnel and a young Soviet fighter pilot named Belenko. Belenko was big news that fall. On duty in the Soviet Far East, he had dramatically defected by flying his supersonic Foxbat fighter to the Japanese island of Hokkaido and requesting political asylum. The Soviets insisted on speaking to him; a request the Japanese eventually granted, but only under their close observation.

The account in Pravda reminded me of what they had taught us at Harvard as "kettle pleading." In the answer to a complaint, defendant's counsel is permitted to argue a variety of defenses, even if, taken together, they would be logically inconsistent. The term supposedly arose from a legendary English case in which a man was accused of borrowing his neighbor's kettle and returning it cracked. In answering the complaint the man argued that, first, he had not borrowed the kettle, second, it was already cracked when he borrowed it, and third, when he returned it it was not cracked. The account in Pravda ran something like this: the meeting as arranged by the Japanese was a total farce because, first, at the interview attempts were made by the Japanese to prevent Belenko from speaking, but despite these efforts Belenko clearly stated that he had only landed in Japan because he was lost and out of fuel; second, poor Lieutenant Belenko was brought to the meeting so obviously drugged that he could scarcely move his lips, much less say anything comprehensible; and third, the man that the Japanese paraded at the interview was not Belenko at all.

Often my attempts to have a quiet restaurant dinner with a fellow Westerner led instead to entertaining social encounters with the local residents. This was especially true because of the manner in which seats are arranged in a Russian restaurant. In the West the typical number in a dinner party is two; a man and a woman, perhaps, or two associates discussing business. Soviet restaurants are geared much more to special celebrations with friends, and therefore the normal table size is four or six. Russian restaurants are always crowded, not because the average Russian frequently goes out to eat, but because there are so few restaurants. If you come as a couple you will almost always be seated with another couple. One night this led to a revealing conversation about Russian views on their giant southern neighbor the People's Republic of China. It was not unusual that we would be talking about China. That day everyone was talking about China, practically everyone in the world—because that day Mao Zedong had died.

That morning of September 9, 1976, I came upon the old woman who cleaned the dormitory halls doing a jig with her mop for a partner. When I inquired why she was so excited, she said, "Haven't you heard? The old Chinaman is dead. Mao Zedong is dead. There'll be a party tonight for sure." An American woman and I decided to have dinner that night at the U Prichala (At the Dock) restaurant on Vasilevsky's Island, not far from the dorm. As was usual, we were seated at a table for four with a Soviet couple. The male half of this couple was an officer in the Red Army. This was also a common occurrence. Military officers are, together with Georgian fruit salesmen and blue-jeans black marketeers, among the few individuals who have enough disposable income to go to restaurants more than once or twice a year.

We did not try to hide the fact that we were Americans, and he at first regarded us with suspicion. As always, we explained that we were on an official exchange sponsored on the Soviet side by the Ministry of Higher Education. This did little to relieve him. He was suspicious because we spoke Russian; my friend's Russian was particularly good, and in the mixture of accents that make up the Russian language she could easily be taken for a native speaker. The officer's lady friend was from Poland and did not share his sense of alarm. She found us exciting. She explained to her dull-witted companion that it was only natural that we could speak Russian; otherwise how could we go to school in the Soviet Union? At about this time the vodka arrived. One orders vodka in the Soviet Union by the hundred grams. A large flagon of about five hundred arrived, and within two minutes, before eating a bite of food, our Red Army tablemate had downed a half pint. His previous anxiety about dining with foreigners simply floated away, and suddenly we were old comrades. The conversation drifted over many topics, but owing to Mao's death that morning we inevitably turned to Sino-Soviet relations.

He did not bore us with a complex analysis of the military and diplomatic situation, but went straight to the point. He was totally convinced that war would come with China. Too drunk to make any sense verbally, he graphically showed us his view of the proper course of international relations. Extending both hands, he called one hand Russia, the other he called America. He shook hands with himself to show that these two should be friends. Then he acted out his two hands strangling someone. This unseen victim, he said, was China. His view was that the USSR and the U.S.A. should ally to destroy China.

While more dramatically presented than is usual, his feelings were representative of those of much of the Russian people. Some of this sentiment is a primordial fear of invaders from the East that stems from the more than two centuries of Mongol domination of Russia, the "Tatar Yoke" of the thirteenth and fourteenth centuries. But today much of this popular Sinophobia is government sponsored. The Soviet military and the Soviet citizenry are kept in a continual state of agitation about the "fanatics" on their heavily defended border. I recall how surprised I was when I saw, gratuitously tucked into a Soviet impressionistic movie by Andrei Tarkovski called *Zercalo (The Mirror)*, a picture of Mao—first one Mao, then the screen divided into two Maos, then four Maos, then sixteen Maos, and so on. This scene was followed by one of a long line of big Russian soldiers on a barren steppe. The soldiers' arms were linked and their eyes stared impassively ahead. Behind them was a throng of screaming Chinese shaking what appeared to be little red books of Mao's quotations. The message was clear. But for the stalwart Red Army guarding the long, lonely frontier, Russia would be deluged with screaming Chinese madmen.

The Russian populace is conditioned by this propaganda to accept war with China. The best illustration of this appeared during the border fighting between China and Vietnam in the early months of 1979. It was after my year in Leningrad, but during my return in 1980 I heard about the political climate in the city. It was as if the war had already begun. Reserves were mobilized along the Russian-Chinese border, and student meetings were called to discuss how the war effort could be supported. Grade-school children were told that they must be very good and learn to accept responsibility because soon their fathers and older brothers would have to leave home to go fight the Chinese. But with all of the talk of imminent hostilities the Russian populace greeted the news without emotion of any kind. They were not surprised or disappointed. It was what they had expected all along.

Of my many friends in the Leningrad intellectual community, a good number were Jewish—not in the sense that they practiced the religion; they were Jewish by heritage. In their internal passports, under the box marked "nationality," appeared not "Russian" or "Ukrainian" or any of the other regional designations, but instead (and through no election on their part) simply "Jewish." The position of Jews in the Soviet Union probably receives more attention in the Western press than does any other Soviet domestic issue. It is a seemingly intractable problem. The tension between the Jews and the Great Russians goes back well beyond the communist period, of course. A century ago, the reactionary penultimate czar, Alexander III, the man whom Lenin's brother tried to assassinate, was on the throne of the Russian empire. His principal advisor was Konstantin Pobedonostev, who made a frightening prediction for the future of the Russian Jews. One-third, he said would be killed, one-third would be assimilated, and one-third would emigrate. To Pobedonostev there was no possibility that the Russians and the Jews could coexist. The frightening truth is that in the last hundred years, much of Pobedonostev's prediction has come true. Perhaps a third of the Russian Jews were killed during the Second World War, either by the fighting or by the Nazis. The generally decreased role of religion in the twentieth century, coupled with increased urbanization and all the other elements of modern mass culture, have led to intermarriage and assimilation for a major portion of the Russian Jews. Finally, in the last century and continuing to the present day, there has been a constant flow, sometimes a trickle and sometimes a torrent, of Jewish emigration to the West.

I asked a Jewish scientist why the old antagonism toward

the Jews continued to exist in the Soviet Union. His answer surprised me. I thought, understandably enough, that he would just dismiss Soviet anti-Semitism as Russian barbarism and racism and nothing more. Instead he described the situation as if it were unavoidable and entirely comprehensible.

"Logan," he said, "no single group more supported or more gained from the Russian Revolution than the Russian Jews. Under czarism there were the pogroms, there was the Pale, there were the Cossacks. It was not an altogether attractive situation. The Revolution, at least until Stalin gained full control, was a tremendous event for the Jews. With most of the property-owning classes fleeing the country, Jews poured into positions of importance in the government and in the universities, from which they had previously been excluded. Because the Jews were educated, organized, and most important, urban, they were in a good position to gain from the social upheaval. Trotsky, leader of the Red Army, was Jewish; how many Jewish generals were there under the czar? Kamenev, the original Party leader of Moscow, was born Leo Rosenfeld. All of this pent-up talent at last found an outlet. In the generation after the Revolution the number of Jews in positions of importance was totally out of proportion to their numbers in the population. As the revolutionary fervor died down and the old traditions began to reassert themselves, this tremendous imbalance became untenable. The old Russian envy and chauvinistic pride came back to the fore. I have always sensed that the archetypal Russian village schoolteacher was somehow behind all this. He is the master of resentment. Often frustrated and convinced that he was destined to be a great writer or statesman, he pontificates all day to little children who are not permitted to contradict him. He is not happy with his own fate nor is he willing to accept responsibility for it—we Russians have never been much for accepting responsibility. When the Russians look around for someone else to blame, there is usually a convenient Jew to be found. If it were just him it would not be a big problem, but there are all those impressionable youngsters, and thus he passes down his own benighted resentment to the children he is supposed to be enlightening."

My friend continued, "All of these conditions existed before the Revolution, but frankly, communist ideology did nothing to improve the situation. Despite the big wall posters about workers of the world uniting and brotherhood among races, the fundamental tenet of Marxism is the class struggle. It is strictly workers against owners, proletarians against capitalists, communists against liberals, their group against our group. It takes only a slight nudge from the suspicious Russian character to have this quickly deteriorate into the Soviet Union against the West, the Russians against the Jews, 'if you are not for us you are against us.' As a consequence of this whole 'class antagonism' concept, there are quotas for jobs and educational opportunities: was your father a worker, was your father an intellectual, was your father born in Moscow, was your father a Jew? And, like so many other things in life, the prophecies become self-fulfilling. As opportunities are denied to Jews, they apply to leave, and as they apply to leave the Russians say, 'See, we were right all along, you're not really one of us, you're not really on our side, your loyalties lie elsewhere.' Soon all Jews are suspected of wanting to leave, and things are made so tough on them that most of them in fact do. Things just snowball."

While the situation for Soviet Jews is difficult, the ironies of Soviet life have paid them a small dividend. If one is Jewish and so designated in one's passport, one's chances of being permitted to emigrate are greatly enhanced. Just as Russians of indeterminate ancestry used to try to prove they were not Jewish, now many try to prove that they are. The discovery of a Jewish relative can be viewed as a tremendous windfall. As with every social phenomenon in the

Soviet Union, there are the appropriate jokes. Moshe appears uninvited at KGB headquarters and insists on a *beseda* (conversation). The KGB are flabbergasted. Nobody ever requests a *beseda*. It is something to be feared. But Moshe insists and at last his request is granted.

"Comrade colonel," says Moshe, "let me make one thing clear. I'm a happy man. I don't want to leave the Soviet Union."

"But I don't understand," says the surprised colonel, "nobody is asking you to leave the Soviet Union. It is only those who do apply to leave that get into trouble with us."

"Yes," says Moshe, "I know. But you see, it's not that simple. My children want to leave. My wife wants to leave. Even my wife's parents want to leave. And almost every day I get a call from some distant relative or another who tells me that he wants to leave. They all hate this place. I feel I'm letting everybody down. I just don't know what to do."

"But Moshe," interjects the colonel, "why is that your problem? If they want to leave let them apply and take their chances."

"Oy, colonel," Moshe sighs, "if only it could be. But you see, I'm the only Jew in the family."

The Soviet Union's lackluster record with regard to the Helsinki accords and other international agreements on human rights spawned many variations on this theme. A commissar visits a large industrial combine on the outskirts of Moscow and sits down for a chat with the director.

"Comrade director," begins the commissar, "of the thousands of workers you have employed at this factory complex, how many are Jewish?"

"Why, commissar," responds the shocked director, "none, of course. I know the Party's views on such things."

"Well, good, good," says the commissar, "that is how it should be, of course, but what with all these agreements on human rights, and considering that we sometimes bring foreign dignitaries out to see your factory, maybe it would be good if you had a Jew. Just one, we wouldn't want to overdo it, and he doesn't have to be a real Jew, just sort of a temporary Jew, until all this fuss dies down."

The director immediately picks up the phone and calls the foreman of one of the outlying shops.

"Boris," says the director, "I need a Jew. . . . Now don't give me any arguments, just pick one of your men, explain that it's for the good of the country, and appoint him the Jew. That new man, Ivan Ivanovich, will be fine."

A few months later the commissar returns to the director's office with some important foreigners he is determined to impress.

"We here in the Soviet Union just cannot understand all this vicious propaganda from the West that Soviet Jews are not given equal chances for employment in our country. Here, I'll show you. Comrade director, call in that Jewish employee of yours."

"Right away, commissar," barks the director, "comrade secretary, get me Boris . . . Boris, is that you? . . . Boris, tell that Jewish employee of yours to come up here. We want to see him. . . . What do you mean you can't? . . . . He did *what?* . . . He emigrated to Israel?"

Six /

The Soviet Lawyer

It might be said that the first Soviet lawyer was Vladimir Ilich Lenin. Lenin, born Vladimir Ilich Ulyanov, was the son of Ilya Nikolayevich Ulyanov, an actual state councillor in the czarist administration. This was a position of considerable importance. In the table of ranks originated by Peter the Great it was the civil equivalent of a major general in the Russian army. Ilya Nikolayevich was a hereditary nobleman who founded nearly five hundred provincial schools and received the order of St. Vladimir for his service to the Russian state. When he died in January 1886 in the rural town of Simbirsk, announcements mourning his passing appeared in the newspapers in faraway St. Petersburg and Moscow. At the time of his death, Ilya Nikolayevich's eldest son, Alexander, was away studying chemistry at the University of St. Petersburg, leaving his second-eldest son, fifteen-year-old Vladimir, who would later be known as Lenin, as the male head of the household.

The Ulyanovs were a family of mixed heritage, and many have sought an explanation for Lenin's character in his racial background. His father was a descendant of the Chuvash, Finno-Ugric tribes. Speaking a Turkish language, these nomads roamed the Russian steppe, the continent-wide plain that stretches from the Volga to the Pacific. In sharp contrast, his mother, born Maria Blank, was from a strict German Lutheran background. Daughter of a propertied doctor, she was educated and strong-willed. Her children were raised to be disciplined and intellectual. Vladimir grew up in a serious home, studying foreign languages and playing chess with his brother Alexander. He was always an excellent student.

Prior to his father's death in 1886, Alexander, the eldest of the Ulyanov children, is not known to have had contact with terrorist groups. How he would come in little more than a year to lead an assassination attempt on Czar Alexander III is a mystery. There was much radical ferment in St. Petersburg, where Alexander studied. Five years earlier a terrorist group known as the "People's Will" had assassinated Alexander II. Under his son, Alexander III, Russia was in a period of intense reaction. In the poorly organized conspiracy the eldest Ulyanov played a key role. Selling the gold medal he had won at the University of St. Petersburg for a paper in chemistry, he bought chemicals to make bombs. Alexander was totally committed to his purpose: to increase the bombs' effectiveness, he mixed strychnine among the shrapnel the bombs were to discharge.

The plot was a total failure. One of Alexander's young co-conspirators had mailed a letter, professing his love for the "Red Terror," to a friend in Kharkov. This letter was intercepted and the identity of the author discovered two days before the assassination attempt was to take place. On March 1, 1887, the sixth anniversary of the assassination of Czar Alexander II, the three students who were to throw the bombs were arrested on Nevsky Prospect, while waiting for the czar's carriage to go by. One of the terrorists tried to fire at the police, only to discover that his pistol would not work. Seeing that their plan was foiled, a bomb thrower decided to take all of their lives and threw one of Alexander Ulyanov's bombs to the ground. It was a dud. Alexander was arrested a few hours later in a fellow student's room.

Back in Simbirsk, the young Lenin was the first to be informed of his elder brother's arrest and broke the news to his mother. She went immediately to St. Petersburg to try and save her son. But Alexander had no desire to be saved. He felt no remorse and instead wanted to take all the blame for the group's action. At his trial he lectured his judges on socialism and the theory of revolutionary terror. After sentencing, he refused his final opportunity for a pardon, saying he wanted to die for his country. On May 8, 1887, Alexander was hanged in the courtyard of the Schlüsselburg fortress with four other ringleaders of the conspiracy. He had just turned twenty-one. It is said that when sixteen-year-old Vladimir received the telegram announcing his brother's death, he told his sister, "We must find another way."

For some time it seemed as if that other way was to be through law. While his brother awaited execution, Vladimir sat for his high-school examinations. He received the highest mark possible in all his subjects except one—logic. He applied and was accepted to the law school of the University of Kazan. At that time it seemed Vladimir wanted only to become a lawyer and had no revolutionary thoughts. He had read no revolutionary books and remarked on occasion that his brother had followed the wrong path. Ironically, despite Vladimir's strong desire to be a lawyer and his devotion to his studies, he was expelled from the law school at the University of Kazan after only ten weeks. Concerned over changes in the university and forced disbanding of fraternities, the students at Kazan held a mass meeting. Vladimir took no part but, like all the other students, was present. That night he was arrested. Police spies in the audience had taken down his name, not for what he had done—he had done nothing—but for who he was: brother of Alexander Ulyanov, the assassin. Vladimir was permanently expelled from the university and ordered by the police to leave Kazan. If the authorities had left him alone, he might well have gone on to become a provincial barrister in Kazan, and the whole course of Russian history would have changed.

Vladimir was put under police surveillance on his family's estate at Kokushkino. With any normal opportunity for a career pulled out from under him, he read and thought along increasingly radical lines. The next May his application to re-enter the University at Kazan was denied. His request to the minister of the interior to study abroad was also denied, but he was permitted to live once again in Kazan. With little else to occupy him, Vladimir continued his voracious reading. It was that autumn that he discovered Marx's *Das Kapital*. In the young Lenin's head, the ominous marriage of Russian radicalism and Marxism took place.

With determination and persistence, Vladimir's mother continued her appeals to the authorities to let her son continue his formal education. She wrote to the minister of public instruction asking whether, in view of the many services her husband had provided to the state, her son, who must now support the family, might be allowed to take the examinations in law, not as a student attending classes—this she knew would never be permitted—but as an external student. The minister at last relented and granted permission for Vladimir to sit for the examination at the university of his choice. Lenin's choice was the law faculty of St. Petersburg. He signed his letter thanking the minister as the "Nobleman Vladimir Ulyanov." Although not in its highest ranks, Lenin was born a full-fledged member of the Russian hereditary nobility.

True to his nature, Vladimir studied with great intensity, mostly at home in the town of Samara, where his family then lived, and, when in St. Petersburg, in the library of the Academy of Sciences. He took his studies so seriously that, despite not being permitted to attend classes, when he took his final exams in November 1891, he graduated first of 124. It took five more months of his mother's appeals to the authorities to obtain for Vladimir the necessary "Certificate of Loyalty and Good Character." At last he was a full-fledged member of the bar. He returned to the town of Samara and joined the law firm of A. N. Khardin. In September 1893, he moved back to St. Petersburg and joined the firm of M. F. Volkenstein. Of the eight or nine cases Lenin was to try, he is said to have lost them all.

One of my friends in the neighborhood was Irina, a recent graduate of the law faculty. She was working in a legal-consultation office on Nevsky Prospect. She was very honored by this assignment. Only about 5 percent of law-school graduates actually become "advocates." Ten times that number go to work for the police department as investigators and inspectors. At the consultation office, Irina would give advice on the aspects of Soviet law that affected the common citizen. The charge for a walk-in consultation was one ruble. I often sat with Irina when she counseled her clients. Some days she would be at the front desk, receiving incoming inquiries. She would sort them out, sending some applicants off to other agencies, telling others that their problems were not of a legal nature, and referring still others to the advocates in the back offices. Most of the time she would herself sit in a back office and advise people on their rights and duties under Soviet law.

In its theoretical aspects Soviet law is little different from the European civil-law tradition that underlies it. At the personal level, law is simplified by an elementary income tax, free medical care, and the absence of complicated property rights. In other areas, the Soviet Union has opened whole areas of legal complexity unknown to the West. The largest of these is living-space law. "Citizens of the Russian Republic have the right to housing,"proclaims Article 42 of the Constitution of the Russian Soviet Federated Socialist Republic. A stirring phrase to the rent-weary masses, but

the astute observer might wish to ask, "What type of housing, how much space, and how does one get it?" In Irina's
consultation office, over 50 percent of the questions she was
asked concerned "living space." This is not the same as
Lebensraum but rather refers to how many square meters a
Soviet citizen may have in his home.

The average Soviet citizen is permitted 9 square meters
of living space (9 square meters = 10.76 square yards or
96.84 square feet). However, in Leningrad, the city execu-
tive committee will help a citizen acquire a place in a communal apartment with more living space only if he has less
than 4.5 square meters. This is no larger than a walk-in
closet. A family unit is entitled to 9 square meters per person plus an extra family bonus of 4.5 meters. The bathroom, toilet, kitchen, and hall space are not part of the
allotment. Normally these spaces are communal—shared by
total strangers.

There is the contentious problem of "overage." What if,
in an older building, a family has a few square meters over
its allotment, but not enough (9 meters) to warrant the addition of a new person to the living unit? This space may be
retained by the family group but at a rent much higher than
for the space that falls within the allotment. Rent itself is
very low. Most families pay less than fifteen rubles a month
(10 to 15 percent of an average adult salary). Whether the
city has the right to put someone else in a family's apartment also depends on the arrangement of the rooms, the
position of the doors, the sexes of family members, and other
criteria. Through intricate questions of living-space assignments Soviet lawyers have found a replacement for Western squabbles over real estate and property law.

Soviet housing law provides that certain privileged individuals are allowed, over and above their 9 square meters,
an additional room of up to 20 square meters. This can make
an enormous difference in a cramped apartment. Above this
larger statutory allowance come the really high officials, who

have no limit whatsoever. There is nothing in the law codes about this situation, but it certainly exists. By chance I learned the situation of the vice-admiral of the Soviet Baltic Fleet. He has, for himself, his wife, and two children, and not counting halls, kitchen, or bathroom, exactly 123 square meters. For a city apartment this is quite large. I knew the exact dimensions of his apartment because he lived in a building that is designated primarily for foreigners. Each of the nine floors had identical floor plans. Emil Sveilis and his family lived in one of them, and the SAS airlines representative, Lars Lindgren, lived in another.

Of equal importance to the amount of space in an apartment is the quality of the building and its fixtures. Here, social position counted for a great deal. Unlike the "instant slums" which typify Soviet new construction, the admiral's apartment building, for example, was very modern: things worked, the ceilings didn't sag, the plaster didn't fall in. The higher one's position in the hierarchy, the more space one gets. Under Stalin, the Crimean Tatars were as a nation banished from their beautiful homeland of Crimea on the Black Sea to Siberia, ostensibly for collaborating with the Nazis. Solzhenitsyn contends that the reason they are still not permitted, almost forty years later, to return to their sunny homeland is that Brezhnev is using the whole region as a private hunting preserve.

I personally do not object to a Soviet admiral's having a little extra space. In fact, by worldwide admiralty standards, he is probably living modestly. What is offensive is the consuming Soviet hypocrisy of "equality"—the myth that no man exploits another. There is even a joke which reflects this: "In the capitalist countries, man exploits man, but here in the Soviet Union it is just the other way around." I had a long talk with my advisor about the "living space" issue. As a professor in the university, she was entitled to the increased allotment of an additional room up to 20 square meters. Combined with the 20-meter room to which her

spouse, owing to his position, was entitled, this was a substantial 40-meter increased allotment. I mentioned the
admiral's apartment and asked how she could justify his 123
square meters, a space that would accommodate thirty people in the lowest category. She glowered and said, "The
important thing is to sit quietly and work hard." She did
not deny that the situation existed, nor did she call party
headquarters and denounce the admiral for his obvious
breach of "socialist legality." She, after all, realized that the
same system which allowed her and her husband over eight
times the minimum allowed the admiral over twenty-five
times the minimum.

These allotments depend, at base, on one factor: political
reliability. For example, an artist is eligible for the twenty-
meter allotment only if he is a member of the Artists' Union.
To become a member of the Artists' Union he must paint
certain types of pictures, that is, socialist realism. His pictures are considered good or bad on a political basis. Favorite themes include Red Army soldiers killing Germans,
pictures of Lenin, and the building of BAM, the new northern railway to Siberia north of Lake Baikal (and safely away
from the Chinese border). Originality plays no role; Kan-
dinsky and Chagall would not have qualified for the larger
apartments. With professors it is no different. Although
membership in the Communist Party is not a prerequisite
for a professorship, it more than helps. If one is not in
the party he still must adhere to the general party line. Professors on the law faculty are politically reliable. Professors
on the law faculty are entitled to an extra twenty-meter room.

Although questions concerning living-space allotments
constituted about half of Irina's practice, she dealt with other
problems as well. Some of these, even though clearly of a
legal nature were, I was surprised to learn, outside the scope
of what a consultation office was permitted to handle. I
remember one Russian man of about thirty-five who presented Irina with a typically Soviet dilemma. He and his

family were in the process of attempting to emigrate. Just as I had to run around gathering signatures on petitions when I wanted to accomplish some simple task, this poor fellow had to assemble certain *zayavleniya*, or declarations, before his permission to leave could be granted. Some *zayavleniya* were prepared for the whole family and some were prepared for each individual. Basically, the *zayavleniye* is a signed statement, from someone connected with the individual or family applying to emigrate, that the signator has no outstanding claims against him and that the signator knows of no reason to object to the emigration.

This man was making the normal fitful progress with his relatives and former employers, but his wife's situation presented a particularly difficult obstacle. She was slightly older than he was and had been married before. This first marriage had been a short-lived youthful mistake; she had not even seen her former husband for fifteen years. But now the former marriage returned to haunt her. The authorities at the passport office demanded a *zayavleniye* signed by her former husband, to the effect that he had no outstanding claims against her, that he had no objection to her emigration, and that he was not himself planning to emigrate. She did not even know where the man was but fortunately found his name in the phone book. He had not left Leningrad. Feeling that he might refuse to see them, the man and his wife did not call but merely showed up at his apartment.

The former husband was totally uncooperative. He verbally acknowledged to them that he didn't care whether they emigrated or not, he didn't really care what they did, but he certainly wasn't going to help them in any way. He above all was not going to sign anything, and he never wanted to hear from them again. The family did not know what to do. They needed the *zayavleniye* to emigrate, they knew that the former husband had no legal claim, but he simply refused to sign the declaration. It occurred to them that this was a problem with which a lawyer could surely help. Perhaps there were alternative ways to demonstrate that the husband could have no claims. Perhaps the mere passage of fifteen years meant that owing to some kind of statute of limitations, he was no longer permitted to interpose any objections. They were reasonably sure that this problem had come up before; after all, it was not entirely surprising that a former husband might not be exactly gracious in rendering assistance to his estranged wife.

Although Irina was sympathetic to their situation, she reluctantly explained to the man that all matters connected with emigration were outside the scope of the consultation offices and, therefore, in a sense outside the scope of the law. Only the visa office itself could be questioned about such problems. Despondently, he left, knowing full well that the visa office, which had insisted that they get the *zayavleniye* in the first place, was not about to leap to their assistance. I wondered what would become of them.

Situations such as this one highlighted for me the limited nature of what a Soviet lawyer could do for his client. The advocate in the consultation office could clarify rules in certain areas and represent the client in court in certain disputes and criminal matters. But many areas were beyond the lawyer's authority. In the double role that a lawyer plays in any society, as an advocate of his client's interest but also as an officer of the court, the Soviet lawyer behaves almost entirely as the latter. Despite Irina's desire to help her clients as much as possible, given the Soviet system it was rare that anything much was possible. Her function was not that of the facilitator, confidential advisor, negotiator, and all-purpose advocate that is associated with practicing law in the United States. As a Soviet lawyer in a consultation office, she was more like a court-appointed information bureau—concerned, but with limited authority and limited capability.

In addition to those lawyers who work in the consultation offices, many Soviet attorneys work for industrial organizations. They are the rough equivalent of the "in-house" counsel of a Western corporation. One time I visited a factory that made little cardboard boxes and filled them with tea. The factory employed about six hundred people. I asked how they handled their legal problems and was told, to my amazement, that they had three full-time lawyers on their staff. I had no idea how a little tea-filling operation could require so much attorney time. This was especially shocking in that most of the things attorneys might do for a private Western firm were already done for them by the state planning commission, Gosplan. For example, fundamental terms and prices of contracts were already established. The factory had only to submit simplified requirements contracts to designated Georgian plantations which supplied them with tea.

I was told that the three attorneys spent a great deal of their time in state arbitration. If, for example, the tea was dropped in the Caspian or a carload got sent to Irkutsk instead of to Leningrad, all of the parties involved had to send their attorneys to state arbitration to determine which of them was at fault. If a factory were to lose such an arbitration, the effect could be quite damaging to its directors in terms of bonuses and advancement. Conveniently, however, it is not always true that someone must bear the responsibility. If the loss was "unavoidable," then it is borne by the true owner, the Soviet state. Attorneys from conflicting industrial units are always ready to agree that no one is to blame and that the loss must be borne by the entire socialist people. Given the possibility of reaching such a "no fault" result, it is not surprising that industrial and commercial losses in the Soviet Union are staggering.

I raised this problem once in a consultation with Valentina Fedorovna. In a capitalist economy, I said, if a shipment isn't delivered or if goods are damaged, one party or another must bear the loss. Normally it is the one who had title to the goods when they were lost or damaged, unless he can prove the negligence of another solvent party or unless someone else has agreed to indemnify him through, for example, a contract of insurance. It is key to any contract to specify when the risk of loss passes. Not every loss is the result of ascertainable negligence, but why should the state or the general population be responsible for losses resulting from arrangements and agreements they did not make and cannot control?

My advisor argued that it was wrong that someone should suffer when they had not been at fault. She gave a simple example. An important shipment from the manufacturer does not get to the dock before the ship must sail. The missed delivery causes great loss and inconvenience to the factory that ordered the shipment. The goods were to be delivered by truck, but it turns out that the truck driver is ill. It is not the fault of the driver that he is sick, nor is it the fault of the manufacturer. Why should they be responsible for the losses occasioned by the missed delivery? I responded that Western commercial law does not look for guilt in any moral sense; it was just that a loss had occurred and someone must bear it. That party should be the one with control over the situation, regardless of excuses. She said no, to be held accountable for a loss an individual must be shown to be blameworthy and negligent in his duties. I told her that it seemed to me that by adopting this policy the state would end up sustaining enormous commercial losses it could otherwise avoid. Rather than looking for ways to safeguard against loss, individuals and factories would spend their time dreaming up excuses as to why they personally were not to blame. Regarding the problem of "guilt," I told her that in my opinion questions of morality were better left to the criminal law rather than the commercial law. She disagreed.

Soviet officials do not maintain, as they once did, that crime is an outgrowth of the inherent inequality of capitalism and will wither away under socialist conditions. Few people alive in the Soviet Union today had much opportunity to be influenced by czarism. It is true that there is no pervasive "fear" of crime such as exists in New York City, but this may be because the press never reports criminal incidents. Even in specialized Soviet legal publications almost nothing is ever said about the crime rate. One can speculate that the reason no statistics are released on Soviet crime is that the problem is embarrassingly severe. In the absence of collected data one is forced to generalize from word-of-mouth and one's own experience. If my experience was typical, the incidence in the Soviet Union of homicide, the gravest crime, is staggering. On my small fourth-floor dormitory hall, containing perhaps forty residents, two incidents involving death under mysterious circumstances occurred during the school year.

At the end of my hall lived a crippled Bulgarian woman and her twelve-year-old son. What they were doing in our dormitory no one knew. They had been there for years and it was assumed that she had been a graduate student at Leningrad State at one time. Perhaps technically she was still registered and took a course or two. It may have been that when the time came for her to move out she had no place to go. Being crippled, she probably had trouble finding work, and as she was a foreigner, the authorities were not inclined simply to throw her out of the dormitory with no alternative accommodations. So she stayed on with her son, and they made quite a pair. Everyone thought she was slightly deranged, limping about the halls dragging her bad leg and reciting incantations. Her son was the dormitory brat. A real juvenile delinquent, he was constantly playing pranks and setting things on fire. An American woman in the room next to them reported that during the night she could hear lashing noises and cries, but she was never sure who was beating whom.

That fall, sewer-repair work was in progress around the

dormitory. Our hot water was turned off for six weeks during the long *remont* (repairs). Approaching the dormitory was like entering the first circle of Dante's Inferno. Steam clouds and geysers of hot water rose from the open mains and billowed across the dormitory grounds. Around the mains were open craters of boiling water condensing from the superheated steam. As is characteristic in the Soviet Union, no guard fences were put up, no barricades, not even a little sign. At the end of the working day the steam crew made no attempt to seal off the site or to shut off the leaking steam. They simply downed tools and headed for the beer stall. The mothers in the neighborhood tried to stop their children from playing in the area, but this was difficult. To the children it was like their own Yellowstone National Park.

One day the first-aid van came to the front of the dormitory and Zhenya carried out the Bulgarian child. He had been severely scalded. Zhenya was reluctant to talk about it but eventually told me that another child had also been involved in the accident, a five-year-old. The Bulgarian claimed that he was playing with the five-year-old when the younger child fell in. The Bulgarian jumped in himself to try to save him, but it had been too late. The five-year-old had scalded to death. However, no one else had witnessed the incident: by the people in the neighborhood, the Bulgarian's self-reported heroism was never accepted. They had seen too often how he had bullied and tormented the smaller children. The version to which they subscribed was that, hidden by the thick clouds of steam, the Bulgarian had thrown the child into the boiling water. When he realized the gravity of his prank, he had jumped in himself in a desperate attempt to save the child or at least build an alibi for himself. A few weeks in the hospital were better than a charge of homicide, and far better than facing the "peasants' justice" of the dead child's family.

While the case of the Bulgarian may have been accidental, the case of Tanya was more difficult to dismiss. Tanya was a student of languages and lived catty-cornered to Zhenya and me, across the hall and down one. Tanya was in her late twenties, blond, and an industrious student. She had literally drawers full of index cards for her thesis. Tanya spoke English passably well. I remember how she began almost all her English sentences with the phrase "to my mind," a too direct translation of a popular Russian idiom. Somehow she managed to avoid the poundage of most Russian young women, and was among the most attractive in the dormitory.

One day in spring, Tanya did not return to the dorm. Her roommate, a Norwegian exchange student, notified the dorm commandant, who alerted the authorities. Some days later, Tanya's body was found floating in the Neva. An investigation was made, and many of the Russian students in the dormitory were questioned by the police. Even while the examination was in progress the Russian students were told it was suicide. She had been "depressed," the authorities asserted, even if no one had been aware of it. The Russian students were gravely warned not to discuss the matter with the foreigners.

My recollection of Tanya's good disposition, her drawers of file cards, and her industriousness right up until the end left me entirely unconvinced that she had taken her own life. I knew that many of her Russian friends shared my feelings. The newspapers carried no word of the incident, as such matters are never reported. Tanya simply became a nonperson. It was as if she had never been there at all and we had just imagined her.

Seven /

The Other Side of

Soviet Law

Being a photographer in the Soviet Union is a trying experience: you try and try and although you get few results, you always have an experience. As if the frozen fingers, the continual darkness, and the difficulty in getting supplies were not enough, all of my film had to be sent abroad to be developed, and I was therefore unable to see any of my photographs until I left the Soviet Union. I was fortunate to be able to use the consulate diplomatic pouch for my film, as the KGB has been known to X-ray all a visitor's film as he boards an airplane to leave the country. But the photographer's worst handicap is not the cold or the KGB but the psychology of the average Russian.

One day in Gostiny Dvor, Leningrad's giant department store, I saw a lovely pile of *ushanki*, the traditional Russian fur hats, and tried to take a picture. Immediately an enormous Russian woman put her hand in front of my camera: "Nyet, Nyet!" "Why nyet, nyet," I said, "why can't I take a picture of these hats?" "Why don't you photograph the monuments in the streets?" she said. "Photographs are forbidden." "Why are they forbidden?" I said. "Show me where it says they are forbidden." "Forbidden, forbidden," said she. Experiences like this are typical. As soon as you photograph anything other than the Winter Palace some casual bystander will run up and scream, "It's forbidden, it's forbidden!"

The Soviet government does have an official list of objects that are not to be photographed. Pictures of men in uniform are forbidden. Although one rarely sees men in uniform in Moscow, Leningrad is virtually an armed camp. Probably one-third of the men on my residential island were in uniform. It is not surprising that the authorities do not want this fact well documented. Other restrictions seem to be without rational basis. One is not to take pictures from an airplane over Soviet territory. Considering the accuracy of satellite photography this is scarely a military threat. One is not to take pictures from a train window. This would rarely be possible anyway, as tourists are normally made to travel at night. Pictures of bridges are forbidden, which, in a city like Leningrad, laced with canals and hundreds of bridges, is a rule impossible for any photographer to obey. There are certainly no regulations, however, forbidding the taking of pictures in a common store.

One day I was arrested. As Solzhenitsyn said of his arrest, mine was, probably, the easiest imaginable kind of arrest. It occurred to me that as I had already documented every palace, monument, and point of historical interest, people back home might like to see something of my daily life. Across Shevchenko Street from our dormitory was a grocery store. It was typical of Soviet neighborhood grocery stores, perhaps a little better than average in the variety of products available. For instance, one day they had bananas. It did not instantly occur to me that I had never seen bananas in Leningrad before, but nevertheless I joined the queue and bought a couple of kilos. I strolled over to see Slava, who took one look, grabbed his coat, and ran out the door. He was too late; the bananas had sold out in twenty minutes. Slava admonished me for not buying far more than I needed—the traditional Soviet practice. I never saw bananas in Leningrad again.

The day of my arrest, I went to this store, did my shopping, and took a few pictures: one of the dairy section, one of the cabbages. I took only five or six pictures, neither secretively nor attracting undue attention to myself. I then put my camera away in a deep coat pocket and joined one of the queues. I had plenty of time to stroll casually out of the store, but as I didn't have a "criminal mentality" about what I was doing, I had no thought of getting away. But one of the salesgirls apparently informed the manager and pointed me out. I found myself confronted by a stout blond Russian woman of about forty screaming at me, "Who are you? What are you doing? Where is your camera?" Soviet organizational science seems to require twenty people to do the work of two; this rather small store was staffed to bursting. I was quickly surrounded by an army of Russian butchers and vegetable men. I told her I did not have the camera any longer. In fact it was in my pocket, but I did not want to have it smashed in the initial excitement. I told her I had the right to take pictures but that if she did not believe me she should call the police. I was not afraid of the police, but I did not want to have myself, any more than my camera, smashed in the initial excitement. What did frighten me was the possibility of a whole crowd of confused and agitated Russian grocery men deciding they had captured a Nazi spy. When I suggested that the manager call the police, the grocery men were visibly mollified. After all, what criminal suggests that his captor call the police? She said "Okay" and told me to accompany her to her office in the back. When in such circumstances a Russian asks you to "just step in the back for a moment," you really have to watch your step. I said I would go but I wanted the door left open.

This whole scene took place in front of fifty or sixty people in the store. We adjourned to the office. It was simply furnished, with two desks, one for the manager and one for her accountant, a young man with an abacus. We sat down, she called the local police, and they said they would send someone over. We started to wait, and she again asked me why I was taking pictures in her store. I explained that I

The grocery store, across from our dormitory, where I was arrested for taking
pictures of the baloney.

(*above*) Babushki. Owing to the phenomenal losses of Russian young men during the Second World War, there are an enormous number of widowed older women. The word babushka (plural, babushki) means "grandmother" but is applied to all women of grandmotherly age. In English it has taken on the primary meaning of the large head scarves that many of these babushki are wearing.

(*opposite, top*) A young Leningrader waits patiently for her mother.

(*opposite, bottom*) A typical winter street scene on Leningrad's Liteiny Prospect.

lived across the street and shopped in this very store several
times a week. I merely wanted to have some pictures of my
everyday life. She asked me whether I planned to publish
my pictures in order to embarrass her and the Soviet Union.
This question was the essence of the whole altercation. It
originates in what can only be explained as a massive national
inferiority complex.

The reason the Soviets have show hospitals and show
factories for foreign visitors is that they are greatly embarrassed about the true state of the country's development.
Once one leaves the large Soviet cities one is in a nation of
poverty, mud, and dilapidated wooden huts. An American
woman on our program amazed her Russian roommate when
she said she was going to call her parents in America. "How
can you call them?" asked the Russian. "You told me they
lived on a farm." She could not believe that in America
farmers have telephones. Although the Soviet Union with
all of its land and mineral resources can successfully focus
on a few high-priority projects—a space shot or a metro
system—it seems incapable of widespread economic development. It is one big banana republic without any bananas.

There are, however, many countries much poorer than
the Soviet Union which do not fear and hide from economic
reality. Fueling the inferiority complex is the Soviet ideology that "our system is better than your system," an ideology that forces comparisons. Every day the Russians hear
their media tell them that their lives are wonderful and
things are getting better and better. Yet when the citizen
looks around, he sees that everything is dirty and falling
down and stinks of cabbage. The official press tells him life
is horrible in the West, but unofficial reports indicate
otherwise. In his heart he knows that if things were so
bad in the West, Soviet citizens would be permitted to travel
there. Knowing how their own government operates, they
suspect that other governments behave the same way: any
picture a foreigner takes must be for official propaganda;

therefore anything the foreign photographer is interested in must be bad. If it's bad, it will make the individuals involved look bad, so the only rational response is to forbid it.

I repeated that I had no intention of embarrassing anyone, that I had hundreds of pictures of the museums and monuments, that this was my neighborhood and I wanted some pictures of it. By this time we had all calmed down and a new factor entered her thinking. Here was a real, live Russian-speaking American. Her store was on Shevchenko Street, right across from the dormitory for exchangees from NATO countries. Not far down the street was the dormitory for Black students from Africa. By accident of proximity, her store was the principal grocery store for all these people. Every day they came by the droves, looking very non-Russian, to buy food. She, however, had never heard them say more than "200 grams of cheese, three kilos of potatoes, and a tin of sardines." At last she had a chance to talk to a foreigner. This was a rare opportunity not to be missed.

As suited her profession, the first thing she wanted to know was how American food stores compared with hers. This was a tricky one, because after all the police were on the way, and here I was with the hot film in my pocket. I certainly did not want to antagonize her further. Unfortunately, the truth itself was antagonistic. There was simply no way in which her little store compared favorably with a typical American supermarket. This was not her fault. Prices, product availability, location, and size of the staff were all determined by the state. Her function was to use all the givens as best she could. She was helpless to improve things very much. I could see, however, that she was in no mood for a lecture on comparative economics.

So, I talked about cheese. Cheese in the Soviet Union comes in three or four varieties. There is "Russian" style, which is a kind of Mozzarella, and "Holland" style, which approximates a Gouda; then there is "Rokfort," which is like an inferior Danish bleu or a very inferior French Roquefort. Rokfort is the cheapest, at 2.30 rubles a kilo, but is usually not available. Russian and Holland were 3 rubles a kilo and usually were available. About halfway through my year a "Swiss" brand appeared, patterned on an Emmenthaler. It was more expensive, at 3.90 rubles for a kilo. By the end of the year it was frequently the only cheese available, replacing Holland and Russian. This is the pattern of Soviet inflation. First, more expensive products will be introduced, slightly different but no better. Then the cheaper product slowly disappears from the market. Technically, prices have not changed, and Rokfort still costs 2.30 rubles a kilo, but if you want to actually eat some cheese it will be Swiss at 3.90. In truth none of these cheeses was up to its namesake. The worst problem was in the distribution system; by the time the cheeses got to the store they were a little like the Politburo—old, tired, and dried out. The same cheeses, fresh from the certificate-ruble stores, were quite good. Sitting in the back of the Soviet grocery store I decided my situation called for a little "socialist realism" (which, as Solzhenitsyn has said, means a solemn pledge to abstain from the truth). I said that since we had many competing firms in the West we had more variety, but as for quality, well, cheese was cheese.

The manager's accountant asked me several questions about wages and prices in America. I reached back into my memory to recall the price of a pound of hamburger or an apartment in Ithaca, New York; how much I would make as a lawyer; how much my brother was making as a welder for the railroads. As I talked he worked away rapidly on his abacus, converting pounds into kilos and hourly wages into monthly salaries. He was actually rather well informed about Western prices, asking, for example, if a one-bedroom apartment in Manhattan might cost $500 a month. I assured him he would be lucky to find one at that price.

By this time we had become friends, and the manager

was reassured that I was not a master Western spy stealing baloney secrets. Half an hour had passed since she had first called the police. She called up again and said it was not necessary for them to come. The dispatcher said they were already "on the way," though, and would be arriving any minute. We continued our conversation.

While talking about managing a Soviet grocery store, I reflected on a joke I had heard in the neighborhood. A naive young Russian passes by a store whose sign says, "Vegetables, Fruit." As it is winter and he has not had fruit for some time, the young man joins the queue. But when he asks the clerk for fruit she tells him they never have any. Feeling foolish, the young man asks the store manager why it is that a fruit store sells no fruit. The manager tells him to wait and watch the queue a few minutes and he will understand. After observing numerous customers asking for potatoes or cabbage, the young man says to the store manager that he still doesn't understand why the fruit store carries no fruit. "Have you heard anyone ask for fruit?" the store manager asks. "Obviously, there's no demand."

At last the police came: two big men with black fur caps and dark blue jackets. The manager explained that I was an American and was taking pictures in the store. She got up, allowing one of the policemen to sit at her desk. He took out his note pad and asked if I had my passport with me. Usually I did carry my passport, but this day I did not have it, as I was only across the street from the dormitory. He didn't mind and asked me for basic information, such as my name and address. He then asked if I still had my camera. This time I admitted that I had it; I did not want to lie to the police. The officer asked for it, and I asked what he intended to do with it. He said that he would not hurt it; he wanted only to look at it and would then return it. I gave it to him. What he really wanted to do was open the camera up and expose the film. He was embarrassed to discover, however, that he had no idea how to open a Japanese camera.

The officer politely handed it back to me and told me to open it. I patiently wound the film back into its canister, opened the camera, and put the film in my pocket. This action was noted by all present; "Look, he's putting it in his pocket." "Yes, look at that, he put it right in his pocket." The officer then informed me that he wanted the canister in order to open it and expose the film. Although I was somewhat apprehensive about all this, sitting as I was in a back room with the Russian police, it occurred to me that my disadvantage was principally psychological. It was necessary somehow to ignore my feeling of weakness, and realize he too might be insecure. I had lived in the Soviet Union a half year at this point and felt I had learned some things. I refused to give him the film.

The officer was not accustomed to being refused. In the USSR there is nothing similar to the citizen's protection against the police that exists in the West. Nor do the citizens have any illusions about whom the police are protecting. Relations between the community and the police are based on fear. I explained that if he could cite any regulation stating that it was illegal to take pictures in a grocery store I would gladly give him the film. I also let drop that I was an exchange student on the law faculty at Leningrad State University. This placed him in a delicate position. He was not a top KGB officer, but merely a local policeman called to investigate a complaint at the grocery store. He could certainly have grabbed me and rifled my pockets for the film. If I had been a Soviet citizen this is exactly what he would have done. But here I was, an American, of all things. He had the good sense to know that a few pictures of cabbage did not justify risking an international incident; he had not caught me down at the missile base. What was worse, he did not want to be at the focal point of any such controversy. A minute went by while he grimaced at me; then he got up and bid me good day.

That left me still sitting with my two new acquaintances. The manager asked me where one could take pictures in America, and I told her that one could do it anywhere where the public was permitted generally. I said many military bases were fenced in and one could not go on them without permission. This permission might well forbid taking pictures. Also, some museums forbade picture taking, probably in order to boost their own postcard sales.

Before I left she wanted to discuss one other issue, the Black problem in America. It is an issue that Soviets hear a lot about in their news media. Every Soviet first grader must read the story "Nancy and the Red Shoes," which I have already narrated. Despite official statements on racial brotherhood under communism, the attitude of the average Russian is quite different. Scratch a Russian and you will find an unrepentant racist. Russians who have never seen a Black person despise Blacks anyway. The situation is complicated by the fact that the Soviet Union has chosen Africa as its number-one diplomatic target. Africans studying in the Soviet Union get privileged treatment. Whether they get an education is another question. In Moscow, Patrice Lumumba University, where many Africans study, is for ideological, not technological, development. In any altercation between Africans and Russians, the officials always take the side of the Africans. According to Russians, the Africans know they enjoy an unofficial diplomatic immunity and they exploit it. A Black American friend of mine with much experience in the Soviet Union says that at Soviet customs he gets quick, courteous service with no search until he pulls out his passport. As soon as they realize he is an American and not an African, everything changes, his suitcases are ripped open, and he gets the full treatment. I began to describe some aspects of race relations in America when she interjected, "Well, personally I can't stand the way their skin smells. And they're always in here, what with that monkey house right across the street." At this the accountant laughed at her, and said, "Listen to that, a typical Russian view."

We must have talked for another hour. As I was leaving she told me, "Listen, you're my friend now and there's no need for you to spend all your time standing in these long lines just to get the worst meat and vegetables. We never put the best produce out anyway. From now on just let me know what you need and I'll have one of the men package it up for you." This was a generous offer and I thanked her. I did not take advantage of it, because in Russia as elsewhere there is a *quo* for every *quid*. I did not want another shopping list for Western products. Also, my request to spend two months in Moscow had finally come through, and I would soon have the opportunity to go stand in line somewhere else.

With great difficulty I was able to leave the Soviet Union at Christmastime. My principal reason was vacation. But I also needed to buy books—books that were printed in the Soviet Union but only available in the West for hard currency. Like the émigrés, I had to say that I was leaving to join family (manufacturing some relatives in Western Europe). Unlike the émigrés, I was able to get an "ordinary" exit visa in about six weeks—not two years. One of the few times the exchange students were permitted to travel and see the smaller cities of the Soviet Union was when we were leaving the country. Both during the Christmas trip and at my final departure, through the Ukraine, I was able at least to spend a day, sandwiched between two night trains, seeing regional capitals.

I was traveling with a fellow American exchange student. We caught the train from Leningrad's Baltic Station. We were planning to spend two days in Riga, the capital of Latvia, before intercepting the international train which ran from Leningrad to Warsaw. In Riga we discovered that the train did not transit Riga as we had been told. It did, however, pass through Vilnius, the capital of Lithuania.

This presented a real problem. We were only 170 air miles northwest of Vilnius, but a foreigner in the Soviet Union does not simply jump on a bus. For each city one is permitted to be in, one receives a little slip of paper with the city's name and permissible dates for being there. We had Riga visas. Additionally, we had exit visas specifying exactly where we were permitted to exit the USSR, and entry visas for Poland. We were missing one link. Because we had thought we could intercept the train in Riga, we had no visas for Vilnius. As insane as it may sound, what we were expected to do in such a situation was to go all the way back to Leningrad and begin again, a retracing that would have cost us two days and many rubles. If, on the other hand, we could somehow get on an airplane for the thirty-minute flight to Vilnius, we could meet the Leningrad–Warsaw train and be across the Polish frontier by morning. We went to the Intourist office in the Hotel Riga. It was quite small, as Riga is a city not frequently visited by foreign tourists. There was only one attendant, a young Latvian. I presented her with my visa for Riga, my Soviet exit visa, and my Polish entry visa. I told her we needed to buy plane tickets for Vilnius. She looked over the documents and as I expected told me she could not sell me a ticket because I had no visa for Vilnius. I told her that visas were not required in cases where foreign guests were going to a city for the purpose of catching an international train. I was of course making up this rule out of whole cloth, but there are so many rules and procedures in the Soviet Union, most of them unpublished, that no one can keep track of them. I thought I had as much right as anyone else to promulgate a few. Apparently she agreed, because after some hesitation she said, "Well, I suppose if you're a foreign guest going to meet an international train you don't need a visa." She wrote out the tickets. I could not possibly have gotten away with this charade in Leningrad, but she probably sold so few tickets that she didn't know what the rules were. Also, the Latvians do not seem to have the same chronic desire to say "nyet" that is evident among so many Russians.

When we got to the airport the flight-security personnel were shocked to see our American passports. Foreigners had never been on that flight before. In fact, foreigners didn't even use that airport. They asked to see our visas for Vilnius. I told them we did not need visas because we were going to catch a train; if we had needed visas, Intourist would not have sold us the tickets. The officials were confused. They said they didn't think it made any difference why we were going to Vilnius, we were still required to have a visa. But they agreed that Intourist had sold us the tickets and foreigners were their responsibility. Moments later we were skidding down a snowy runway in the back of a converted cargo plane. We still did not know whether they would ask for the visa at the airport in Vilnius, but when we landed, we found that the gate to the street had been left open and we walked out and hailed a cab.

Vilnius is a beautiful city. We were fortunate enough to see the old section and have dinner before catching the train to Warsaw. We were put in a four-bed sleeping compartment. With us were two women, one about our age and one in her sixties. It never ceased to amaze me that the Soviet Union, so officially prudish about everything else, invariably threw strangers of opposite sexes together in small train sleeping compartments. Our compartment mates were unrelated and had themselves just met, but they did have one thing in common: families that were split by the many border changes that have taken place in Eastern Europe since the start of the First World War. In the region we were traveling through, many people who were born in Poland, Lithuania, or East Prussia found themselves suddenly residing on Soviet territory without ever having moved.

These women had relatives in Poland and were going there to visit. They were among a fortunate minority who were permitted to travel across the Soviet border, if only to a "fraternal socialist state." A woman conductor entered our compartment and gave us declaration forms to show what things of value we were taking out of the country. As we approached the Polish border, a green-capped soldier of the Soviet frontier guard came into our cabin and asked us to exit and wait in the hall. We stood in the narrow corridor, and, being closest, I watched him from the doorway. After examining our luggage he made a thorough search of the train compartment. There were certain places that he went to immediately: obviously, time had shown these to be favored by smugglers.

Behind one of the head rests he found a gold ring. Only I had seen where he found it. We were told to come back into the compartment and sit down. The frontier guard told the four of us he had found a ring and asked which one of us was the owner. There was a frightened silence. He waited and asked the question again. He had found a gold ring in the compartment. It was not on the declaration forms. One of us was the owner—which one? Again there was silence, but then the old woman broke down. It was her ring. She was sorry. It was a family ring. She was taking it to Poland. She hadn't meant any harm. The guard was a young man and stared at her coldly, his face devoid of emotion. The old woman was deeply afraid. We all sat frozen as seconds passed. The guard then took the ring from his pocket, handed it to her, and abruptly walked out of the compartment. The conductor, who had observed the whole incident, came in and yelled at the old woman. "Do you realize how lucky you are? Most of these guards would have just confiscated your ring and later given it to their girl friend. You were just fortunate enough to get a kind one. There aren't many." The conductor turned and stalked out, slamming the door of our compartment. The old woman stared down at the ring in her outstretched palm. Quietly she said, "It's not my ring." The young woman was also looking at it and said, "I know, it's mine. I was afraid to admit it; I thought they would arrest me." The old woman quickly looked under her seat. Wedged into a fold on the underside of the upholstery was another gold ring. They had both been smuggling. The older woman gave the first ring back to the young one and we all had a good laugh.

The reason they were smuggling the rings was that gold was one of the very few commodities that were cheaper and more readily available in the USSR than in Poland. Sold on the lucrative Polish black market, the ring would pay for the whole trip, with money left for quality Polish goods to bring home. If they had merely put the rings on their fingers, they would have had to declare them and been asked to produce them upon their return to the USSR. The border between the USSR and its Eastern European "allies" is more heavily guarded than that between Eastern and Western Europe. We were stopped for three hours on the border between the USSR and Poland while the Soviet frontier guard practically disassembled the train—so much for "fraternal socialist ties."

Poland is a world apart from Russia. While communist in name, it is composed of many different and competing economies. In Russia, black marketeering in Western currencies is a capital crime; in Poland it seems to be the national entertainment. There are special stores for Polish citizens with hard currency, and citizens may even have special hard-currency bank accounts. As a result, Poles disdain their own currency, the zloty, and seek dollars and marks. At the time one could obtain 135 zlotys for a U.S. dollar from any cabdriver. The official rate was about thirty-five zlotys to a dollar. Many shops in Poland are privately owned, as is the majority of agricultural land. The Slavic souvenirs for which I had searched in vain in Russia, such as hand-painted icons and embroidered linen, were in abundance in Poland.

I was able to communicate with Poles I met through the Russian language, but this presented a delicate diplomatic problem. Russian and Polish are similar languages, and Poles are required to study Russian in the schools. However, they resent the Russians and view the Soviet divisions in Poland as an army of occupation. They were quite pleased that we had a common language in which to talk, but Polish friends warned me not to speak Russian in crowded places or I might be in for a beating. The Poles are fanatically pro-American, and many have relatives in the States. They love to point out that after Warsaw the largest Polish-speaking city is Chicago, Illinois.

Much has changed in Warsaw since my visit. The country enters 1982 under martial law, and the fates of Lech Walesa and Solidarity are unclear. The Polish economy is in shambles and the government is in imminent peril of default on its loans from Western banks. Even then the Poles were furious about their economy, the long lines, the chronic meat shortages. The people complained about the inability of their government to raise the standard of living, feeling like poor cousins of the Western Europeans. In December 1976, I had a different vantage point. After five months in Russia I thought I was in paradise.

On January 13, 1977, I returned to Leningrad. I returned via Scandinavia and, arriving in Helsinki, Finland, I bought a ticket on the train to Leningrad. It was less than 250 miles, but as usual the train would take all night and arrive in Leningrad only the next day. I was alone in my sleeping compartment. There was only one other passenger in the whole car, a seventy-year-old Finnish woman with two gold teeth. She spoke Russian; in fact, when she was born all of Finland was part of the Russian empire.

The relationship between the Soviet Union, particularly Leningrad, and Finland is a curious one. I found it comical that the Soviet Union excuses its poor agriculture on the basis of its northerly geography, yet most of the eggs and dairy products Leningraders eat are purchased from frozen little Finland. During the Bolshevik Revolution and ensuing civil war, Lenin was having a terrible time holding the Russian empire together. Finland succeeded in seceding. The border was, for twenty years, only twenty miles north of Leningrad. The proximity to foreign soil was one consideration in Lenin's "temporarily" moving the Soviet capital to Moscow. By 1939 the Soviets had grown tired of Finnish independence and attempted to annex the country, as they were to do with Lithuania, Latvia, and Estonia. The capital of this new Soviet Republic was to be at Vyborg, in what was then Finnish Karelia. Having just divided up Poland with the Nazis, the Soviets attacked Finland on November 30, 1939. The Finns fought with a ferocity that is still legendary in Leningrad. The so-called Winter War of 1939–40 had all of Soviet Russia pitted against a nation of four million determined wild men on skis. The Russian Seventh Army could not break the Mannerheim line, while farther north the Soviet Ninth Army, supposed to slice across Finland to the Baltic, was itself torn to pieces. Bewildered Russians staggered through the snow-covered forests not knowing where they were or why they were there. The Russians finally gained some ground and pushed the border back, but dared not, in those dangerous times, obliterate their entire army just to conquer Finland.

Ironically, nowadays official Soviets like to stress what a peace-loving nation they are and have had to invent a story for why they attacked Finland. It is a prime example of how far the Soviets will go in rewriting history and pushing the truth down an Orwellian memory hole. It was Finland, they maintain, that savagely attacked the Soviet Union. The fact that the Soviet Union has more than fifty times the population and land area of Finland does not seem to dispel this fancy. The Soviet version is that so-called "White Finns" led the Finnish army against Russia even while the "people" of Finland wanted to accept all the Russian territorial demands. The term "White Finns" was developed by the Soviets to correspond in the popular mind with the term "Whites" or "White Guards" used to describe those Russians who supported the czar and the old regime during the Russian Revolution. Perhaps soon Soviet children will read stories about the "White Afghans." (In this context the term "White Russian," as opposed to simply "Whites," causes much confusion. When an English speaker uses it he generally means a czarist supporter or aristocrat, but in Russian the term has always referred to the inhabitants of a specific region, Byelorussia, a republic of the USSR bordering on Poland with its capital at Minsk. The two have no connection.)

At 11:00 P.M. we chugged out of the Helsinki main station. With the Gulf of Finland to our right and the moon overhead, I said good-bye to the West and prepared myself for another six months in the cooler. My reception was memorable. My Soviet hosts greeted me at the border with a search and interrogation lasting from 3:00 A.M. to 6:00 A.M. I don't think this was done out of meanness, but since there were so few passengers, the border police were bored and probably wanted to see the latest Western products. I'll admit I had as much as I could carry. Everything was pulled out and examined. I was given a pat-down and my shoes were carefully searched. They could have been much rougher. If I had been insolent, I would have been stripped for an anus examination. Every customs officer looks for that which his government fears the most. In the United States this is surely drugs. In the Soviet Union the greatest fear is of literature. Every art book is examined, every book title checked against a list. At the top of that list is the Bible.

My cushioned Jiffy mailing bags really intrigued them. They would pinch and poke them, stick pins in them, and peer inside. All during the search the team leader asked me questions. After I told him I was on the law faculty he asked me about my professors and what department I was in. After a half hour he would ask me the same questions again. I'm sure this was his clever way of trying to trip me up. At times like this, one can think of a million witty comebacks like "Comrade, have you already forgotten?" But such remarks would not have improved my situation. As the search continued, various attendants and conductors peered through the doorway. For our one train car the Soviets had two women attendants, two cleaners, and a conductor. When we got to the border, we were joined by three border police and four customs inspectors. We were a full car bound for Leningrad, but only the Finn and I had paid the fare.

Arrival in Leningrad yielded an unwanted lesson in Russian grammar. Russian uses the passive voice to a much greater extent than does English. In the Russian language, instead of acting, things are acted upon. Thus, "I want to see the Olympics" becomes "The Olympics must be seen," or "I drank the vodka" becomes "The vodka was drunk." In the same way, verbs in Russian are frequently put in the third person plural. "(They) say there's going to be less meat this winter." "(It) is required to serve in the army." Who says? Who requires? This construction has the characteristic of not focusing on the subject and thus seems to absolve the subject from responsibility. "Afghanistan was invaded." Similarly, transitive verbs that seem to demand or imply a human subject are replaced by intransitive verbs that do not. There is even a special particle that goes on the end of a Russian verb to make it reflexive, to show that the action reflects back on itself. This can be used stylistically to intimate that an inanimate subject somehow performed the action itself, without human interference. On that early morning in January, I arrived at the Finland Station, heavily laden with presents and things I would need for the next six months. I was still tired from my early-morning search and slowly began to move my bags to the platform. I did not wish any assistance, but one of the officious women

Statue of Lenin at the Finland Station. The present station building was completed in 1960 and is typical of Soviet functional architecture. It was to the Finland Station that Lenin triumphantly returned from Helsinki in 1917 to lead the Bolshevik Revolution. In exile in Switzerland, Lenin and his party were given special permission to transit imperial Germany, which was fighting the First World War against imperial Russia. There is some evidence that Lenin, whose mother was German, was financed by the German government to destabilize the Czarist government. After the victory of the Bolsheviks in the October Revolution, Lenin signed the treaty of Brest-Litovsk with Germany (March 3, 1918), surrendering enormous areas of Russian territory and over a quarter of the country's population. Only the victory of the Western allies over Germany changed this result.

(*above*) St. Isaac's Cathedral on an October evening. Of all Christian churches only St. Peter's in Rome and St. Paul's in London are more massive. Inside, whole pillars are faced with malachite and lapis lazuli.

(*opposite, top*) The residence of Emperor Paul I, now called the Engineer's Castle. Paul, fearing assassination, built this heavily fortified structure to protect himself. In March of 1801, forty days after moving in, he was assassinated in a corner room on the first floor. His son and heir, Alexander, is thought to have been in complicity. In the 1820s it became a school of military engineering; hence the present name. Dostoevsky was one of its graduates.

(*opposite, bottom*) Leningrad in winter. The frozen Neva with the Palace Bridge and Winter Palace in the distance. To the right is the east wing of the Admiralty. The Palace Bridge, the principal bridge to Vasilevsky's Island, was closed all winter for repairs, practically immobilizing our part of the city.

Leningrad's St. Nicholas Cathedral, one of the very few Russian Orthodox churches permitted to continue religious services. It is always jammed.

attendants insisted on grabbing one of my heavy leather bags. I turned around just in time to see her drop it off the platform and under the train. She looked up and innocently said, "Your bag fell." As I clamored around under the train after my luggage I knew I was home again in Leningrad.

One night I had been out drinking with a Norwegian friend who worked for a foreign air carrier. We had gotten quite tipsy at a foreign-currency bar. As we climbed out of the cab in front of his residence, I had to assist him in walking. It was a cold night in December, and as we passed the all-weather KGB command post, the sergeant of the guard asked if we needed assistance. Normally the guards were not so friendly; I could not help noticing that they too were sipping a little something to cut the chilly gusts from the Gulf of Finland. In what was a highly uncharacteristic gesture of goodwill, the sergeant invited us into the guardhouse for a tumbler of vodka. While we sat inside I could hear the incoming reports over the radio. "What about the German, has he arrived yet? He left the consulate a half hour ago. If he doesn't get there in five minutes, we'll have to have somebody go look for him. He might be with that new Uke [Ukrainian] girl friend of his, but she's supposed to call us before he comes over." There was a constant discussion: who was in, how long ago someone had left, who was in the car with so and so, and similar questions.

We finished our tumbler of vodka, exactly what my friend did not need. It became obvious that he would require assistance in getting up the stairs. Leaving the other soldier in the guarded post, the sergeant helped me carry him. When we got upstairs to the apartment, I asked the sergeant if I might return his hospitality and invite him in for a drink. He told me that he would love to but dared not. The apartments were bugged, he said, and if his voice were picked up by a monitor, he'd be in big trouble. I told him my friend's stereo had a quadraphonic speaker system and asked whether that would sufficiently disguise his voice. He assured me that it would. He told me that the quads posed a real problem for their electronic eavesdropping equipment, and in he went. He had, after many years of guarding these flats, never really been inside one. He was amazed at the spaciousness and fine appointments. The Norwegian thanked us for our assistance, told us to help ourselves to his flat, and promptly passed out on the couch. I asked the sergeant what he might have and showed him the liquor cabinet. Like any good Scandinavian my friend had his bar stocked with every liquor and liqueur known to man, all of which had been flown in from the West by his airline. The sergeant had never seen such things. In Russia there are vodka, flavored vodka, and brandy, and nothing further. Of all things he finally settled on a glass of blue Curaçao.

We sat down and began an inebriated discussion. He told me he had been in the army and decided when he got out to join the KGB. Benefits were a lot better than those for any other job he could have gotten. I asked him if he wasn't afraid that one of the other soldiers in the guard post might be a *stukach* and inform on him. He said no, that was not the way it worked. He said he had trained the other men on his shift and helped them out from time to time. Their first allegiance was to him, and until the guard changed at four o'clock, he was king. He no doubt wanted to impress me with his importance, and how much of this was just brave talk I don't know. He even told me that now that we were friends, if I wanted to get the lowdown on anybody, I could just contact him and he would pull their file. He told me never to trust my roommate or other Russians in the dorm. If they were living in there they had to be playing ball with the KGB. This was comical: a KGB guard solemnly warning me not to trust the people in the dormitory because they must be involved with the security services.

He told me about his training and assured me he could

take on ten men. He was very proud of the new pistol that all of the KGB guards had been issued. He took it out, removed the clip, and gave it to me. It was very light and easy to handle. I asked him if it had been fabricated in East Germany, which offended him a little, and he assured me that it had been made in the USSR and that nowadays they had first-rate technology in such things. He was very difficult to understand. We were both drunk and slurring. Moreover, he talked in a police slang I had not previously encountered. He kept referring to people who gave information to the KGB as *mokry*, soggy. I may well have been the first foreigner with whom he had ever had an extended conversation. We talked and laughed until just before four o'clock. Then, like Cinderella, he suddenly jumped up, pulled on his boots, and ran out the door and down the stairs. I still picture in my mind the ludicrous scene of my friend snoring face down on the couch with the stereo blaring, while I, with the KGB sergeant drunk as two Cossacks, was waving a pistol in one hand and clutching a glass of blue Curaçao in the other.

Eight /

The KGB

The attitude of the Russians in the dorm toward the Soviet apparatus of internal political control, in particular the KGB, exhibited a distinctly non-Western pattern of thought. The Russians, long accustomed to brutal secret-police networks (Ivan the Terrible had his dread *oprichniki* as early as 1565), have become emotionally narcotized to their effects. They do not like the KGB, nor do they praise it as a noble, patriotic organization. They do not even view it as a "necessary evil" for ostensibly protecting what is good in the state. In a way that is almost haunting, they consider it not at all a "human" but a "natural" phenomenon, and therefore no more a subject for moral comment than would be a hurricane or an earthquake. The KGB and the policies it enforces are, in the popular mind, like a swollen river or a deep ravine: one would not cross them just for the fun of it. There are dangers, of course, but if there was something worthwhile on the other side, one took the available precautions and crossed. One was not immoral or "wrong" for doing so, and the KGB was not immoral or "wrong" for punishing those whom it caught.

People would talk about a relative who ran afoul of the security police as if he had been hit by a falling tree: it was an accident, no one was really to blame, these things just happen. Even a relative who disappeared during the Great

Purges was referred to as if he had perished in a storm at sea. There is little conception of the political police as a created, human phenomenon that should be opposed, or even that could be "opposed" and not simply avoided (Westerners would not speak of "opposing" an earthquake). Indeed, if there are any "rites of passage" in becoming a Soviet dissident, they are in realizing that such things are not a natural part of the human condition, but can in fact be remedied.

A Leningrader pointed out to me that despite all the Soviet hoopla about his countrymen rising and striking against oppression, the Russian *narod*, the *Volk*, are a very docile people. Occasionally, they could get really incensed about something, as happened during the so-called Time of Troubles succession crisis (1598–1613), the great peasant revolts of Stenka Razin (1670–71) and Emelian Pugachev (1773–74), and the Bolshevik Revolution. But over the long flow of the centuries the Russians could bear any pain, any suffering, any hardship—and end by loving the tyrant who treated them so brutally. "Beat a Russian, and he'll make you a watch," goes the old Russian folk saying. The czars that the Russian people remember and love best were inhumanly vicious in their personal relations. Ivan the Terrible murdered his own son; Peter the Great lured his son back to Russia on an imperial pardon and then had him tortured to death; and Catherine the Great (a minor German princess by birth) married the Romanov Paul III, had her lover's family shoot him, and then placed herself on the imperial throne.

The Soviet period is no different. Although Joseph Stalin (another foreign ruler—a Georgian) is officially in disgrace, the common people have great respect for him. He is certain to be rehabilitated when those directly connected with him have died. My friend concluded by saying, "It's true that about once every century we get excited about something and all hell breaks loose. But in its soul Russia is not a nation of revolutionaries and individualists—Russia is a nation of sheep."

If, however, the Russians were not temperamentally inclined to oppose the KGB, they were certainly very clever about avoiding it. I have already mentioned the trick of turning up the radio when someone wanted to have a political conversation. Another way to elude the curious ears of a bugging device, or an informer with his ear to the door, was through a rudimentary political sign language. Russians are no longer hustled off in the "Black Maria" police vans of Stalin's day for having kitchen-table conversations among their family and close friends; but certain topics, including any political discussion with a foreigner, call for additional precautions. The interspersing of hand signals to define key individuals and social phenomena easily renders an overheard conversation incomprehensible. Such a conversation heard by an eavesdropping *stukach* (political informer) would sound something like this:

"Yea, old _____ has certainly had his troubles with the _____. It's not like the old days with _____ and the big _____. They were the best of friends. Understood each other, I suppose. Even used to throw the occasional _____. Of course, in those days you never knew who was a _____. They were dangerous times, that's for sure."

This conversation would, with hand signals, be translated:

"Yea, old *Brezhnev* [both hands placed on the forehead with the palms forward and open like two giant eyebrows] has certainly had his troubles with the *Chinese* [one finger pulling back the skin at the corner of the right eye]. It's not like the old days with *Stalin* [a military posture and a stern, scowling demeanor] and the big *Mao* [again the slanted eye]. They were the best of friends. Understood each other, I suppose. Even used to throw the occasional *drinking bout* [finger against the thumb of the right hand as if to snick at something, then, with the head tilted to the left, snapped against the back of the right jaw. This also signified one who was drunk, or almost anything to do with vodka]. Of course, in those days you never knew who was a *stukach* (*political informer*) [two quick sharp raps on the table]. They were dangerous times, that's for sure."

One day, after several months of waiting, Slava and his family were brought a telephone. Not every household in Leningrad had a telephone, so they were very proud, especially as it was very modern, the kind that could be unplugged and moved around the house. When the telephone man brought the new phone, he had several black ones and one shiny red one. Slava was home at the time and answered the door. The telephone man handed him the red phone. "Why do I get a red phone?" asked Slava. "I would just as soon have a simple black one." "Oh no," said the phone man, "they told me you were to have this exact phone. It is the only red one they gave me, so I would be sure not to make a mistake." It did not take a particularly suspicious mind to guess the special characteristics of the new red phone. Slava told me he believed that the bugging device was in the phone itself, not in the line. Just as long as the phone was plugged in, it would pick up the conversation in the room whether or not someone was actually using the phone. The new phone was treated with great respect. When guests would drop by it was given a special place of honor—unplugged and in the closet.

Under Soviet law a citizen has the right to apply for a declaration by the Presidium of the Supreme Soviet that he is no longer a Soviet citizen. In addition, the freedom to leave one's country is mentioned in some international agreements to which the USSR is a party, but if the Soviet Union actually facilitated citizens' petitions to emigrate, people might leave by the hundreds of thousands. Some who left would be disappointed or unable to cope in the West and would long to return to their socialist homeland. If they thought the border would not slam shut again, many of them might return. But the dislocations and loss of manpower resulting from such large-scale population movement would make Soviet-style economic planning impossible. The USSR would not be suddenly emptied of people, but it would, as did East Germany before the Berlin Wall, lose the most in the groups it can least afford to lose—skilled workers, scientists, and professionals. More important, the system could not retain its harsh, monolithic character if a real choice were continuously available to the citizens. Thus the necessity for the less obvious but equally forbidding Soviet equivalent of the Berlin Wall. A barrier must be placed in front of those who wish to emigrate. This barrier may be surmounted, but the cost is high, and certainly higher than the unsure are prepared to pay. One must be prepared to be slung into prison, confined in a mental institution with drugs and shock therapy, physically assaulted, even (though rarely) mutilated or killed. But if the dissident toughs it out, eventually he will be allowed to go—maybe.

Frequently the most brutal tactics are reserved for the unknown and inconspicuous small fry. If the prospective émigré has well-connected friends abroad, the authorities may in fact facilitate his departure. Many with international reputations are persuaded to leave in return for keeping their big mouths shut.

Such was the case of Slava's father-in-law, David Dar. Dar was well known in literary circles on both sides of the Soviet border. He had written many works published in the Soviet Union, including a popular spoof called *Mr. Gorillus*, ridiculing Hitler's rise to power, and a biography of Tsiolkovsky, the Russian Leonardo da Vinci. For himself, or "for the desk drawer," as the Russians say, he was writing a collection of philosophical essays called *Confessions of an Irresponsible Reader*.

Dar had fought and suffered for his country. In the Second World War, during the 900-day siege, he served on the Leningrad front. The troops at the front were permitted 1,200 calories a day. They had to be strong enough to fire back, but the city itself was starving. One horrible day he received a letter from a neighbor in Leningrad. Dar's wife had starved to death, and his children, Laura and her older brother, had been taken away by soldiers. The neighbor did not know where. Not only had Dar lost his wife, but he knew that in the chaos of death and war which the center of Leningrad had become, he might never find his children again either. Laura was only three and, given the trauma of death and separation, might even forget her name. Even if all three survived the siege, they might never be reunited. But for the tenacity of Laura's older brother, this might well have occurred. When the soldiers took the children away from their dead mother, they tried to place Laura in a separate nursery for infants. But Laura's brother, though only twelve himself, raised such a howl that the soldiers relented and let Laura stay with him. Dar and his children found each other and all three survived. For twenty-five years after the war, Dar remembered how hard things had been and did not openly question his government's policy. But he observed that while other nations had rebuilt and put the tragedy of the Second World War behind them, the Soviet people were held by their leaders in a continual state of siege and sacrifice. His success as a writer exposed him to creative people, many of whom became increasingly dissatisfied with the rigidity and senselessness of the state's control over the arts. Literary friends of his began to emigrate; others, to be arrested. Dar felt compelled to raise his voice. He started writing for *samizdat* (self-published), underground journals by which dissident works are circulated. When in the spring of 1977 his involvement became known to the authorities, he was called to KGB headquarters for a *beseda* (conversation). He protested that he was sick and it was a long way to go all the way to Bolshoi Dom, the "Big House" on Liteiny Prospect which houses KGB headquarters.

Very obligingly the KGB said he could come to the local office; there were several in his area and they would be happy to send over a car. He really couldn't refuse. At his "conversation" he was told frankly that the KGB was going to shut down the journal and there was nothing he could do about it. Many of the minor figures connected with it were to be arrested, and there was nothing he could do about that either. But if he kept his mouth shut and did not raise a scandal with his friends in the West, then he would be left in peace. Moreover, if he wanted to emigrate he could do so immediately. If he was good there would be no repercussions against his family. Six weeks later he was in the West. For him to stay and fight would have helped no one.

Not everyone who leaves Russia is a well-known figure like Solzhenitsyn or Rostropovich. While an appeal from an international group, such as a professional organization, can work wonders for someone desiring to leave, the vast majority of potential émigrés do not have international contacts or credentials. As soon as the average Russian applies to emigrate, his career is ruined; his family is severely criticized and demoted from any responsible positions they may have. As his situation in the Soviet Union collapses, his desire to leave increases. Years may go by. If the aspiring émigré doesn't make himself something of a problem, the authorities will sit forever on his application. The people who have gotten out usually do so because they make themselves such thorns in the side that the Soviets don't want to put up with them any longer. But most émigrés are not the type to throw bricks through windows. Nor do they wish to do anything that would risk a sentence for "hooliganism" (this term, borrowed from English, is the legal designation for all rowdy behavior, brawling, and disturbing the peace in the USSR). One of the few things they can do to accelerate the process is to openly solicit foreign contacts.

Such was the case with a Latvian cousin of Emil Sveilis's. Emil's cousin had founded the Soviet Olympic luge (one-man bobsled) team. He and the team even built the run in Latvia. When the Soviets wanted to send the team to the Olympics in Austria, he was not permitted to go, for political reasons. After all, he had relatives abroad, such as Emil, whom he might try to contact. This was the last straw; he applied to emigrate. He immediately lost his job. His wife, a doctor, lost hers as well. She knew that she was well liked at the hospital, but her superiors had no alternative. They entertained Westerners as often as possible in their one room in a communal apartment. A man from the KGB moved in to the next room. They share the same toilet and kitchen.

In the course of a year I got to know all sorts of people like this. I did not seek out dissidents, but it seemed that as soon as I'd talk to anyone for fifteen minutes, the stories would start to come out. I think we in the West feel that a Soviet dissident is either a determined revolutionary or a deep political thinker like Sakharov. This is seldom the case. The Communist Party of the Soviet Union draws a narrow line between orthodoxy and heresy. It is all conditioned by an "if you're not with us, you're against us" psychology. Most dissidents I met were not political, in a Western sense, at all. For the most part they were professional people—writers, translators, architects, lawyers—who simply had their field of inquiry or endeavor severely limited for arbitrary and artificial reasons. Imagine telling the American artistic community that the purpose of their art must be the glorification of manual labor, and its expression simplistic enough for everyone to understand. Follow this up by branding the rest of the artistic community "dissidents," and slinging prominent ones among them into the insane asylum. Although absurd, this is exactly what happens to Soviet artists. Such was the situation for Mikhail Chemiakin and the Petersburg group (now mostly in Paris). Chemiakin was subjected to six months of shock therapy before the KGB threw in the towel and permitted him to emigrate. The vast number of Soviet dissidents are pro-West: it is not capitalism they seek but some type of freedom, perhaps artistic, perhaps religious, perhaps intellectual. The Soviet authorities agree with conservative writers, however, that the concepts are somehow entwined—free enterprise and intellectual freedom. At least they strongly support its converse, that under socialism there can be no nonconformity.

In February 1977 I attended an underground art exhibit on Dresden Street in Leningrad. The term "underground" as applied to art or literature has come to mean, in the West, "not reflecting official mores." These official mores are first explained by the underground artist and then ridiculed by his art. In Eastern Europe "underground art" means what it has always meant—illegal and subjecting the artist to arrest. I had heard about this exhibit from a Canadian who was planning to go with the American teacher who ran the school for consulate children. They said I could come, and the three of us drove over through the snow. We knew when we were close because of the police cars lining the street. We turned into the approach drive of a large communal apartment building. As soon as we stopped, two policemen came out and started to question the teacher who was driving. While they wrote out a traffic ticket for some imaginary offense, the Canadian and I went upstairs. On the fifth floor we entered a typical Soviet flat. The woman who was giving the exhibit took our coats. There were about twenty people, mostly artists who had something on exhibit.

Although some say the Russian avant-garde is merely what was done in the West fifty years ago, I feel that it has great vitality. The art represented there was impressive. The canvases were neither political nor pornographic, but socialist realism they were not. I noticed one pen-on-paper sketch and asked about it. I was told that the artist who drew it had had all his work taken away by the police as he was on his way up the stairs. He had come up anyway, sat down, and started anew. His one sketch signified that the police had not prevented him from exhibiting. He was lucky; other artists had been taken away along with their canvases.

Two days later I returned with Slava and David Dar. We separated so as not to establish any personal links dangerous for them. There were again many police around the apartment building, but they had not shut down the exhibit. As I reached the fourth-floor landing I passed two uniformed policemen and one man in nicely cut civilian clothes. When I was already past, the civilian asked me for some identification and an explanation as to why I was there. I said that as he was not in uniform he would first have to show me some identification. He scowled but pulled out a green Committee for State Security card (KGB). I showed him my passport. He said, "You were here before, weren't you?" I agreed that I had been. "Listen," he told me, "if you want to see an art exhibit, go to the Hermitage." I said I had been to the Hermitage and wanted to see this one too. I then asked him why the KGB was so afraid of such a harmless exhibit.

Needling him with such a question was not as foolhardy as it may seem. The KGB had made the decision not to shut down the exhibit but instead to harass and intimidate the participants. This officer was there to make trouble but probably not to arrest—not, in any case, to arrest me. I was perfectly within my rights to go to that family's apartment. I was in the Leningrad visa boundary and the area was not restricted. The question of rights in the USSR reminds me of the famous driving poster that reads, "You may be right—dead right! Drive defensively." For a Soviet citizen, being right is not always sufficient. But I was not a Soviet citizen and could crouch behind my blue bicentennial American passport. My passport and my friendly local consulate were my assurance that for me, right would make might and not the other way around. I wouldn't have talked back to the KGB my first month in the Soviet Union, but after a half year I felt that I had a sense for what I could get away with. I found it worked well to say the most outrageous things in the most courteous possible manner.

We did not get to finish our repartee, as at that moment David Dar came up the stairs and tried to pass through the police on the landing. The KGB officer said, "Where are you going, old man? Let's see some identification." The old fellow pulled out a membership card in the Soviet Writers' Union. The officer responded, "I guess anybody can get into the Writers' Union these days." Hearing this altercation on the landing below, the woman who was giving the exhibit came down from her fifth-floor flat and, seeing that we were having trouble, did something that took great personal courage. She yelled at the police, "These are my friends, my guests; you have no right to prevent them from visiting." She then came downstairs and led us up to her apartment. Meanwhile the KGB official on the landing below screamed up at her, "You have too many guests, you have too many friends!"

Once inside she took my coat and said, "You see how we live; it's like this all the time, continual harassment." I took pictures of the exhibit and visited with the artists. I showed the hostess a picture that the artist Michael Chemiakin had given me in Paris of him with Rostropovich, the great Soviet-émigré cellist. When I left, the police detachment was standing under the stairs on the ground floor. They had not prevented me from seeing the exhibit, but they certainly discouraged all except the most brazen Russians from doing the same. Later I was to find out that the husband of the woman who organized the exhibition was ordered to

(*top*) The House of Political Enlightenment in Leningrad.
(*bottom*) The Big House, central KGB headquarters in Leningrad. "KGB" are
the Russian initials for Committee for State Security.

The Dresden Street art exhibit. This exhibit was organized in a private apartment in Leningrad on Dresden Street to exhibit the work of Leningrad avantgarde painters who were not permitted to show their work. The Soviet Union approves only the artistic style known as socialist realism, meaning the unabashed glorification of manual labor, the life of Lenin, the victories of the Red Army, or similar themes. Other artists are considered "nonconformists" and live in a twilight zone ranging from just being ignored to being committed to insane asylums. Mysterious "suicides" are not unknown. This exhibit was organized by the woman in the center of the picture. David Dar, the writer and Leningrad intellectual, is on the left. The KGB did not stop the showing but kept a close watch on those who attended and arrested several artists. Afterwards the organizer's husband, a scientist, was ordered to divorce her. When he refused he was fired from his research post and given a menial job.

Some representative canvases from the Dresden Street exhibit. The small pen-and-ink drawing on the right is particularly interesting. The artist was grabbed by the KGB on his way to the exhibit, and all his work was confiscated. He came to the showing anyway, sat down, and penned this sketch. They had not stopped him from exhibiting. The woman is Nancy Fehsenfeld, an American. It was sometimes useful for Americans, particularly diplomats and press correspondents, to be seen at underground art exhibits or the apartments of known dissidents. Not only did it bolster the spirits of the "unofficial" artists and writers to receive international attention, but in addition the Soviet authorities were sometimes reluctant simply to go in and bust the place up if they knew this would be reported in the Western press.

divorce her. When he refused, he was deprived of his position as a scientist and given a job sorting paper clips.

It should be mentioned that the handling of the Dresden Street art exhibit follows the pattern of modern internal-security measures in the Soviet Union. It is not, at present, the cattle car to Siberia for a minor infraction. It is harassment, intimidation, and social pressure against the dissident, his co-workers, and his family. Like Ionesco's Rhinoceros, one sees those around him slowly turning into something else. As vicious as the treatment can be, the observer must admit that it is not Stalinism. The KGB has, however, retained its more brutal tactics for some individuals. Such a case was that of Ilya Levin, the former Leningrad representative of Amnesty International. I met him at a small dinner party and saw him frequently during my stay in Leningrad. In the summer of 1977 he was allowed to emigrate. As he is now safely in the West, his story can be told without disguising his identity.

Ilya often remarked to me that Russia was a country in which one could die of many things, but not of boredom. Ilya had managed to graduate from the Herzen Institute of Education in spite of being expelled from the Komsomol for "keeping and disseminating anti-Soviet propaganda." Given such a charge one would imagine Ilya had been running a printing press in his basement and distributing anti-Soviet broadsides on the street corner. In fact, this virulent propaganda turned out to be a couple of old copies of *Newsweek*. Serious trouble began for him in the summer of 1975, when he applied to emigrate from the Soviet Union. With that act began a macabre two-year adventure that lasted until his emigration. There followed every month one incident or another: sometimes a search, sometimes an interrogation, sometimes a detention. There was never more than one incident per month. It was as if the KGB had some giant chart. Once they could check off Ilya's box for that month they would leave him alone. In the beginning of January 1976 he was detained for resisting the police. In the beginning of January 1977 he was arrested again, and charged with the same crime. Both times he was confined in the same cell. Interestingly, it was on the same row of cells where Lenin himself had been confined.

Lenin's actual cell was no longer used. In one important way it differed from Ilya's. On the outside window Lenin's cell still had the old czarist bars. As can be seen from any painting of the socialist-realism school, these czarist bars permitted a bony hand to reach out and wave a red flag. To prevent any such untoward display among present-day prisoners, Ilya's and the other cells now have jalousies, a type of blind that prevents people inside the cell from reaching out and people outside the cell from seeing who is inside. The jalousie also greatly reduces the prisoner's light and air. Ilya argued that conditions in the prison had deteriorated greatly in the sixty years since czarist rule. Lenin had been permitted to borrow books from the St. Petersburg public library. With milk from his pitcher he had written between the lines in these books. Later his relatives would take the books home. Holding the pages near the flame of a candle would cause the milk to scald, revealing the latest proclamation. This advantageous arrangement would not be feasible for latter-day Lenins. The cells now have no books and no pitchers of milk. Lenin, moreover, had been alone. Today the same cells hold six.

After Januaries in jail, Ilya's "box" was checked off and he was allowed to rest a little before February's confrontation. During these resting periods Ilya would get his chance to match wits with his persecutors in little chats, or *besedas*. During his periodic *besedas* with the KGB, Ilya would often assert that his interrogator was violating one paragraph or another of the criminal-procedure code. The interrogator would explain that decent people did not need to know the criminal-procedure code. Ilya wrote letters protesting violations of Soviet law to the district and city procurators and finally to Roman Rudenko, then procurator general of the USSR. He wrote not because he felt that these appeals would do him any good; in fact, he realized that these people were probably directing the campaign against him. He wrote because he wanted to feel in his own mind that he had done everything a good citizen could do. If they took no action the onus was on them. This is an example of the so-called legalist approach to Soviet law. This school argues that the Soviet Union has sufficiently humane laws on the books, if the Soviets could only be made to enforce them.

On the very day Ilya received his reply from the deputy procurator of Leningrad he was, for the first time in his life, severely beaten. The beating occurred under particularly sinister circumstances. Ilya was working as an elevator watchman on the night shift in a freight yard, the only job available to him after he applied to emigrate. That night someone tripped the emergency signal, signifying that something was wrong with the elevator. When Ilya went to investigate he was beaten and kicked by three total strangers. As required, he recorded the entire event in the watchmen's log book on a numbered and sealed page. The next night he found that this page had been ripped from the book. He left and did not return to work. After the incident he said he understood why citizens were not permitted to have guns in the Soviet Union. Without a gun a citizen is defenseless against a gang of police provocateurs.

By not returning to work Ilya ran the risk of becoming ensnared in a peculiarly Soviet dilemma. Everyone in the Soviet Union is required to work. If one doesn't get the job he wants that is too bad, he still must work even if he could support himself otherwise. Article 38 of the Russian Republican Constitution of 1978 (earlier Soviet constitutions contain the same principle) states that citizens have the right to work, including the right to choose a profession, in accordance with their ability, taking into account the needs of society. Article 58 works in tandem with Article 38, making clear that "avoiding socially useful work is incompatible with the principles of a socialist society." Article 209 of the Russian Criminal Code enforces the constitutional principle: if one does not work one may be charged with "leading a parasitic way of life" and sent to work camp. This is in keeping with a fundamental principle of Marxism. The state provides all, but the citizen also has a duty to the state. That duty is to work according to one's abilities. This sounds reasonable, but one must remember that the state determines what "abilities" one has. The privileged bureaucratic elite will perform the "taking into account the needs of society" mandated by the constitution. As the state controls all jobs, a falling out with one's employer has permanent consequences. The implications of such a system are particularly eerie in situations like Ilya's. If he went to work, he was beaten up; if he didn't, he could be sent to prison.

Ilya never faced charges of parasitism, as one must be without a job for six months before one can be prosecuted. Ilya was slated for more bizarre encounters before this time could elapse. In February 1977, Ilya became the head of Amnesty International in Leningrad. His was not a large chapter: in fact it had only one other member. A few days after he heard from the headquarters of Amnesty in London, an article appeared on page 3 of the February 24, 1977, edition of the newspaper *Evening Leningrad*, entitled "The Strange Hobby of Mister Boden." Boden was the cultural attaché of the West German consulate in Leningrad. The article concerned three friends of Mister Boden, one of whom was Ilya. The article is typical of Soviet accusatory journalism, in which the author of the charges, usually writing under a pseudonym, has no fear of being prosecuted for libel or even of rebuttal by the individual denounced. The portion of the lengthy article concerning Ilya read as follows:

I. D. Levin in his time evaded criminal responsibility for black marketeering only because he connived to occupy himself with his trafficking prior to reaching his legal majority. He was kindly and humanely dealt with then and even later when he was caught distributing anti-Soviet slander. [*Note:* two copies of *Newsweek*]

Notwithstanding this [the authorities] did not try to place obstacles in his path. He graduated from the Herzen school of education, served in the army, and returned to his old haunts, but with a different manifestation: a sycophant and toad to those gentry from across the ocean who need exactly such bums in our country. It is not difficult to guess what kind of information they await from their "buddy" Ilya.

[Two other dissidents, A. D. Aref'ev and V. I. Filimonov are denounced.]

These are just a few brush strokes in the portrait of the three "Leningrad friends" of Mister Boden, whom the refined diplomat did not shun from meeting and even invited as guests to his apartment. It was not so much the intoxicating liquor poured out by the generous hand of the hospitable diplomat, but other absolutely nonalcoholic interests and schemes which heated up the friendship. Being accustomed to a parasitic and do-nothing existence, the personal friends of Mr. Boden stood ready to provide him with information he most valued; most of all this "brooding among the creative intelligentsia"—any dissatisfaction expressed by anybody with our way of life, and our obligations as members of society to obey the laws.

The ones principally dissatisfied were Levin, Filimonov, Aref'ev, and their cohorts. Not living in harmony with Soviet law and order, consciously breaking it, there was no shortage of facts from their own biographies which, if turned on their heads, could be presented as persecution for their beliefs and reprisals for free thinking.

At the end of December of last year Levin was sentenced to fifteen days for minor hooliganism. This fact was made to appear to his "friends from the West" as the persecution of a freedom fighter.

His "friends from the West" of course used these fantasies in a broadcast on Voice of America in which, in a tearful voice, condolences were given to the hooligan.

The article continues including attacks on Levin for attending sessions of the People's Court in Leningrad and reporting to Boden on what he saw there. Although Soviet law does permit suits for libel, the state controls the press as well as the court, and there is no realistic possibility for a dissident or refusenik to bring a successful legal action.

On March 1, 1977, Ilya made one of his frequent visits to the Leningrad Writers' Union. He perused some of the books on the stand, looked at the exhibits, and went to the snack bar for coffee. As he took a chair he was startled by a sharp burning sensation below his right knee. He was sure he had sat on a cigarette, but when he looked he saw nothing. He wanted to find out how badly he was burnt, but he could not simply drop his trousers in public. The burning sensation was not incapacitating at that time. Upon returning home, he discovered a bright red patch of skin not unlike a severe sunburn. By the next morning an ominous ring of blisters had developed around the red area. His leg had contracted during the night from the now severe pain. He could not rise. For two weeks he stayed at home, hoping the burn would show some signs of healing. Ilya was afraid of going to the hospital, but finally he had no alternative.

After being examined he was immediately admitted to the Leningrad Military Academy Hospital, the leading Soviet institution for the treatment of severe burns and injuries caused by military irritants. Ilya's injury was diagnosed as a third-degree chemical burn. The fourth degree is charcoal. The probable chemical agent was a form of enhanced liquefied mustard gas, a substance unknown out-side of modern warfare. Ilya conjectured that his trousers must have been sprayed from behind while he was at the Writers' Union. When he sat down the liquid contacted his skin. The trousers themselves were undamaged. The doctors in the Military Academy were mystified as to how Ilya had contracted such a burn. When he told them the story about the Writers' Union they sent for the psychiatrist. While the doctors never completely accepted Ilya's account and kept urging him to tell the "complete truth," they were unable to offer an alternative explanation. Ilya received excellent care. Had his leg remained contracted any longer he would never have walked again. The doctors straightened the leg under general anesthesia and kept it in a plastic cast until the skin could regenerate. After two months he was permitted to leave the hospital.

Ilya was aware of two other cases of the use of military irritants against Leningrad dissidents. The first occurred in December 1973 under circumstances so perverse that Gogol himself might have been shocked. There had been talk of a peaceful demonstration in St. Isaac's Square. Among those involved was one Rubinstein, a refusenik. He was summoned to the office of the director of the division that gives out emigration visas. Naturally he lost no time in going. The director, one Bokov, ushered him in and asked if he would just take a seat for a minute while he attended to a small interruption. There was only one seat to be taken. Rubinstein sat down and waited. Bokov never returned. After twenty minutes Rubinstein went to the outside office and asked the receptionist what had become of the director. He was told the director had gone home for the day. Confused, Rubinstein got his coat and left. That evening his friends carried him unconscious to the hospital. Every area of his body that had come into contact with the chair had third-degree chemical burns of the same nature as Ilya's.

The second case had involved the nonconformist artist

Yuri Kharkev. On May 23, 1975, there was a meeting in Leningrad of unofficial artists. Plans were made to have an open-air art exhibit that summer. That very night Kharkev returned to Moscow on the night train to spread the word about the exhibit. Having left his shoes and socks at the foot of his bunk he enjoyed a good night's sleep. The next day his feet, up to stocking height, developed the mysterious burns. Interestingly, Kharkev also ended up in the burn clinic of the Leningrad Military Academy Hospital. One arm of the Soviet state caused the injuries; the other spared no effort in treating them.

Ilya faced his continuing ordeal with a philosophical detachment. One time he remarked to me how ironic it was that the Soviet Union, having signed international agreements limiting chemical warfare, now elected to employ them on the domestic front. He also wondered whether Mikhail Bulgakov, the author of *The Master and Margarita*, a book still suppressed in the Soviet Union for its parody of the Writers' Union in the earliest days of Soviet rule, could ever have imagined the Leningrad Writers' Union as being the chosen location for chemical attacks upon nonconformist authors.

While its more primitive tactics are directed against the citizens it is ostensibly protecting, the KGB is quite active against foreigners as well. Americans are particularly well attended to. My closest American friend in our little Leningrad community was Emil Sveilis, the UPI correspondent. Although there were hundreds of Western newsmen based in Moscow, Emil was the sole Western correspondent in Leningrad. Before he came, in the fall of 1976, there had been no Western coverage at all of the second-largest Soviet city. Holding such a position, Emil became something of a reluctant lightning rod for KGB dirty tricks.

Emil's Soviet experience dated from the time of his birth and had been less than cordial. A native Latvian, he was one year old when, clutched to his mother's breast, he escaped on the last boat out of Riga before the Russians captured the city. As a young child in Sweden he remembers the Soviet embassy officials coming in the afternoon to his mother's apartment and asking them to return to Riga to help build the "New Socialist Latvia." When his mother refused, they left but returned after dark. The message changed. If Mrs. Sveilis and her son did not return, all of their relatives still in Riga would be shot. At that time the Swedes were anxious about Russian intentions and did not want to be provocative. There were rumors of kidnappings from Stockholm of Eastern European refugees. Emil and his mother emigrated to America.

Emil spoke both Swedish and Latvian, and, despite the earlier Soviet threats, still had many relatives in Riga. When he went to Latvia he got very special treatment, not only from his relatives, among whom he was a celebrity, but also from the local KGB. Sometimes as many as seven people, on all modes of transportation—cars, bicycles, motorbikes, and foot—would follow him down the street. When Emil first arrived in Leningrad, he was cordially received, Soviet style. It was his first night in town, the beginning of a two-year assignment.

Arriving in a new country, a visitor is excited by every new sight and sensation. There is an overwhelming desire to "do as the Romans do." This feeling increases the more unusual the country visited. It is my experience that Americans are particularly disposed to let down their defenses, to defer cross-cultural judgments, and to identify behavior that in their own country would quickly be branded perverse as being simply "native." Emil was no exception. He had never been in Leningrad and had not been in the Soviet Union since his departure from Riga as an infant. He was willing to greet the Russians and their society with an open mind.

Emil checked in to the Astoria hotel on St. Isaac's Square.

His family was to follow in a few weeks after he arranged for an apartment. The bar at the Astoria is a foreign-currency bar, that is, rubles are not accepted. For that matter no currencies from socialist countries are accepted. Customers must pay in dollars, marks, francs, or other major capitalist currencies. For a Russian, it is illegal even to possess these currencies without official permission: if a Russian had official permission it would certainly not be to buy drinks in the tourist bar. Any Soviet citizen in such a place is immediately suspect, but one does not realize this on one's first night in town. Within thirty seconds of Emil's arrival in the bar a Russian sat down next to him and started a conversation in reasonably good English. This is also suspect. The Soviet Union is not like Western Europe. Almost no one outside the foreign-trade, tourism, or diplomatic organizations can carry on a simple English conversation. But Emil wasn't thinking about that. He was, after all, talking to his first Russian.

This first Russian asked Emil what he did and was very excited to hear that Emil was a foreign correspondent. He said that he worked "in the harbor." After a few more drinks the Russian lowered his voice and said, "Listen, I can get you some interesting information on military shipments to Cuba out there at the port." Emil immediately said that he was just a journalist and those things were not any of his business. Emil excused himself to go to the bathroom. Round two took place at the urinal. At a moment when any man is vulnerable, an enormous Armenian put his arm around Emil and in pidgin English said, "Americanski gut, gut." While trying to avoid urinating on this jovial stranger, Emil slowly extracted himself from his bear hug. It was only later that Emil realized that his wallet and address book were gone.

Returning to the bar, Emil was again approached by the fellow who ostensibly worked at the harbor. This time the man, so full of confidence before, announced that he had stayed too late and that if he left now he would surely be picked up by the KGB, who were all around the hotel. If they picked him up, he told Emil, he was a goner for sure; could he possibly spend the night in Emil's suite? His story was preposterous. Why were the KGB all around the hotel but not in the hotel? Was the Astoria some privileged sanctuary where KGB feared to tread? (Quite the contrary, there are more KGB per square meter in the Astoria than anywhere else in Leningrad save KGB headquarters.) Why was it now too late for him to leave, when earlier it would have been all right? Was there a certain time when the bell tolled and all Russians in the Astoria turned into pumpkins? However, these are exactly the informed, pragmatic reactions that do not break through that heady feeling of the first evening on a new assignment in a strange country.

This plea is one that Americans are characteristically susceptible to: "Please help me, I'm oppressed." The American heart, with its idealistic and puritanical sense of social justice, responds instinctively to the call of state repression and deprivation of human rights. I was in the Soviet Union when Carter was elected and when he initiated his human-rights campaign, which in the USSR was symbolized by his correspondence with Andrei Sakharov, the dissident Nobel laureate. Many Western Europeans criticized this policy as a counterproductive way to deal with the Soviet Union. What they found difficult to understand was that such a policy might be advanced not for any reasons of geopolitical benefit, but because President Carter and much of his domestic constituency felt such positions to be morally correct. The crusading spirit is still very much a part of the American psyche. Among exchange students this manifests itself in a terrific desire to free the Soviet people of their many burdens. It seems that every American girl who goes to Russia meets some "oppressed" poet or artist who immediately asks her to volunteer to marry him and spend the next few years helping him emigrate. Frequently they agree, not out of love, but out of this all-consuming desire to save the world.

Emil agreed to let the man stay until dawn in the ante-room of his suite. As soon as they got upstairs, however, his new acquaintance tried to seduce him. This led to some inebriated pushing and shouting (the Russian suddenly having forgotten his English) before Emil was able to evict his first Russian "experience."

Emil was to face many such incidents during his two-year tour. Once he came out of an appointment to find two men running from his car. Inspecting it carefully, he found that the wheel bolts had been loosened so that at high speeds a tire could easily break loose of its rim. His wife, Charlotte, who worked at the consulate, was picked up outside the consulate by a cabdriver who drove her all around Leningrad, would not let her out, would not talk or pay attention to her protests, picked up his equally threatening but silent friend, and after two hours, when Charlotte wondered if she would ever see her family again, spoke to her in good English and let her out. Not only was Emil followed in an obvious manner, but he also occasionally observed security police setting up parabolic "ears" to listen to his conversations on the street. Things became so intolerable that when Emil returned home, UPI decided not to send a replacement.

Ironically, Emil, like most Westerners, went to the Soviet Union with an open mind and in the spirit of objective journalism, only to be met immediately with ferocious hostility by the Soviet authorities. Frequently the only people who were even courteous to him were the dissidents. Why, when the Soviet Union goes to such trouble and expense to propagandize among tourists and visiting dignitaries, would they not strive to make a positive impression on the West's sole correspondent in Leningrad? One can only speculate, but a possible answer is that the Soviet authorities cannot believe that anyone the United States would send as a correspondent could be other than a violently anti-Soviet agitator sent to write vicious and fraudulent reports for the home press. The reason they arrive at such a conclusion is that, when given the same opportunity, that is exactly the kind of person the Soviet Union sends. One need only glance at a Soviet newspaper article about the United States to appreciate this. The concept of objective journalism being unknown in the Soviet Union, why should they suspect it in a foreigner?

Emil's confrontation with the homosexual raises another interesting issue. Article 121 of the Russian Criminal Code makes sexual relations between consenting adult males punishable by up to five years in prison. The official Party line is that homosexuality has been all but eliminated, yet many foreigners in diplomatic or scholarly exchanges are propositioned or molested soon after their arrival. Some of this has no ulterior motive. Soviet homosexuals are as much interested in Westerners as are Soviet heterosexuals. However, the frequency and circumstances of these incidents seem to lead to no conclusion other than espionage. One officer at the consulate seemed to be particularly knowledgeable about Soviet espionage activity. Many suspected that he was connected with the CIA. As the American community was very small, I frequently had a chance to talk with him. Tuesday was movie night at the consulate, and we would often have a beer together before the show. I asked him what the Soviets hoped to gain from attempts at homosexual entrapment.

He told me that the modern world of computerized record keeping and electronic information transfer made it almost impossible for a Russian-born Soviet spy to directly penetrate the United States military, political, or diplomatic establishment. Such a spy would have to command accent-free English and be given a phony identity that would survive periodic security checks. It would be unlikely the spy would have immediate access to anything confidential, so he would have to rise slowly on his own merit through the

defense establishment, intelligence community, or whatever hierarchy he was in. During this time he would have
to maintain his loyalty to the Soviet Union and its changing
policies while being entirely out of contact with it. For perhaps decades, he would be required to masquerade as a loyal
American, disguising his politics, *Weltanschauung*, intentions, and origins, all of this without a slip. Moreover, the
agent would have to be, even as a youth, so dedicated that
he would want to spend his life in this schizophrenic manner. Owing to these difficulties, the Soviet Union had little
hope for the success of a Russian-born spy. Therefore, the
consulate officer said, agent recruitment must be from a target country's native population.

He contended that the face of Soviet espionage had
changed. In the thirties, when the depression dragged on,
when much of Europe and Asia were drifting toward fas-
cism, and before the world became aware of the Great
Purges, the Gulag, and the grim reality of Stalinism, there
were those who spied for the Soviet Union out of ideological commitment. This was the time of the mole. In Great
Britain it was the time of the "bluebloods with red hearts,"
the Kim Philbys and Anthony Blounts. There are few today
so ignorant. Agent recruitment by the Soviets can no longer
be based on ideology but must be based on fear. This fear
is not necessarily of a physical nature; more often it is fear
for one's career or reputation. To make such a program
effective it must be done over a long term and with many
prospects. As the Russian saying goes, "Plant a thousand
potatoes; you never know which ones will come up." The
Soviets try desperately to get something on everybody. Not
on tourists, of course, unless they are important people, but
everyone in the field of Soviet studies is a possible target.
Everyone has his weakness and it is up to the KGB to find
it. But times change. Twenty years ago, pictures of a man
in bed with some Siberian beauty while his wife was home
in Cincinnati could normally be played to some advantage.
Today they might not be so damaging.

I heard a story, which, while probably apocryphal, frequently made the rounds in the Soviet Union. During
negotiations in Moscow, Sukarno, president of Indonesia
until 1967, was invited to a screening of a short film "of
mutual interest." The star of the film turned out to be
Sukarno himself cavorting about with two Ukrainian girls
in his suite at the Hotel Metropol the evening before. After
the movie, he was asked if he wasn't prepared to liberalize
the terms of the latest Soviet-Indonesian trade agreement.
He responded that the only change he'd be willing to make
was to add a purchase order for a hundred copies of that
film for immediate release in the Indonesian home market.
He informed the astounded KGB colonel that if his people
saw an old man like him carrying on like that, he would
never fall from power.

The consul argued that while the stigma against extra-
marital sex had moderated in recent years, the one against
homosexual sex had not. A homosexual liaison or even some
pictures, perhaps taken while the victim was drugged,
could be a useful tool for modifying his later behavior. This
seemed to me only a partial answer. This kind of activity
was, after all, just garden-variety blackmail. The reason the
Sukarno pictures didn't work was that Sukarno wasn't
embarrassed. Similarly, if someone was already a declared
homosexual, how could photographs have any effect on him?
The consul agreed that if the person entrapped just didn't
care, pictures were worthless. But, he continued, in the
connection between homosexuality and espionage there was
another consideration. Emotionally, he said, homosexuals
are unstable. It is a condition perhaps forced on them by
society, but the homosexual basically views himself as an
outcast. By virtue of his sexual preference, he is already cut
off from, and ridiculed by, the mainstream of his countrymen. Already disaffected and alienated, it is much easier
for him to supplant loyalty to country with loyalty to an
abstraction, such as the "progress of history," or to an
individual, such as a foreign boyfriend. This may be chang-

ing, the consul agreed, because as toleration of homosexuality increases, the alienation felt by homosexuals would be reduced. But the Soviets, always somewhat behind the times, continue to feel that foreign homosexuals offer a fertile ground for agent recruitment, and as a consequence, anyone they view as of espionage interest is likely to be tested.

During my exchange, three of my Western friends experienced this tactic. Like Emil, they would be lured into a room and, on the pretext of friendship between peoples or Slavic warm fellowship, be all but raped. Perhaps these were not KGB efforts at all: one can begin to see KGB behind every small unpleasantry in the Soviet Union. But living in a rigidly controlled society one views any aberration with suspicion. In one incident the Russian, right before making his advance, pounded three times on the wall. In Emil's case the whole three-step—espionage entrapment, pickpocketing, and homosexual attack—was surely the KGB's way of saying "Welcome to Leningrad" to the new American correspondent.

Getting something on everyone need not take such dramatic forms. For example, one of the American exchange students in our program in Moscow applied for a two-month extension to continue his research in Russian history. A Russian friend of his was approached by the KGB and told, "Tell your American friend we can arrange the extension, but we want a little favor in return." Hearing this, the American instead applied to leave immediately. The year before my exchange an American was caught out of Leningrad without a visa and brought to the KGB regional office. When they were sure he had been doing nothing of any consequence his interviewer told him, "Look, we can very easily let this incident pass and not say a word, or we can create a big scandal, accuse you of spying, and have you thrown out of the country. You'll never get a visa again, and what will that do for your work? It's hard enough in America to get a job in your field without losing all access to archival materials and Soviet research. All we want, in return for letting this drop, is a little routine information on your consulate."

This particular individual was wise enough to refuse to say anything until he had seen a United States consul. Others fall into a web of deception. No one starts by giving away vital military secrets to cover up some peccadillo, but that is not what the Soviets are after. At this point all they want is for the target to cooperate in any way at all. Some people, given the stress of a KGB interview and wondering whether a reservation is being provided on the next train to the distant north, reason that they don't know anything that the Soviets don't know already. After all, exchange students aren't allowed anywhere out of the cultural and administrative sections of the consulate, and these sections have Soviet citizens working in them as secretaries and interpreters. Why not tell the KGB some little fact that exists in a hundred files already?

If one does in fact cooperate, everything goes just as promised. Nothing is said, no one is informed, and the next time the individual tries to get a visa to the Soviet Union he has no problem, the trip goes extremely well: perhaps he is able to arrange difficult interviews or is invited to a conference. If the individual spends his life teaching at a small community college he will never hear about the incident again. But if instead, because of his expertise in Soviet affairs he begins to advise his local congressman, or perhaps goes into State Department work, then one fine day, maybe twenty years later and long after he's forgotten his little conversation, he will get the opportunity to hear it again. His unexpected visitor will point out to him how well his career is going and how something like this, a tape of his giving information to the KGB about the American diplomatic organization in Russia, just might not be understood by his new associates and the American people. Now they'd like a little more information.

Nine /

The Nitty-Gritty

Dirt Band Tour

April found me at the conclusion of a two-month stay in Moscow. I had asked to extend my time there. My advisor, a helpful young Russian who had been an exchange student in the Netherlands, finally managed to arrange for me to visit several days of Soviet international commercial arbitration. Unfortunately this arbitration, between Cuba and the Soviet Union, was scheduled for early May, and my permission to be in Moscow expired on April 21. Urgent appeals from the United States embassy for a three-week extension came to nothing. It was pointed out to the Soviet Ministry of Education that observing Soviet arbitration was a principal purpose of my exchange. They were unmoved. My final attempt to see Soviet law in action through official channels had been thwarted. On the evening of April 20 I returned to Leningrad on the Red Arrow. I was exhausted with the whole endeavor and had lost all desire even to speak Russian, determined to sit out the last forty days of my "sentence" and head for the Mediterranean. Such was not to be my fate.

I returned to a different Leningrad. Equinox was long past; each day brought several more minutes of light, fourteen-hour days, sixteen-hour days, eighteen-hour days. Leningrad, farther north than Juneau, Alaska, has the dramatic seasonal variations of the subarctic. The cataclysmic alternation of endless day for endless night cannot but affect one's disposition—even the disposition of an entire city. Things suddenly seem possible again. I walked down Nevsky to Liteiny Prospect. Color had returned to the broad avenue. Reaching Petra Lavrova Street, I decided to check in at the United States consulate.

As I was sorting through my mail, the chief of the cultural section asked me if I might do him a favor. The Nitty-Gritty Dirt Band was in Russia. It was the first time Soviet audiences were to see an American rock-and-roll band. The Leningrad consulate had responsibility for the arrangements in Riga, the capital of Latvia, and in Leningrad. Five concerts were to be given in each city. The cultural-affairs office wanted to know if I might help out as an interpreter.

The negotiations to bring an American group to Russia on the United States–Soviet cultural exchange had taken some three years. The Dirt Band had been chosen for a variety of reasons. Soviet officials, knowing the popularity of Western music in the Soviet Union—where Rolling Stones and Beatles records are second only to blue jeans as lucrative black-market commodities—refused even to mention the term "rock and roll." The Soviets could be cajoled into accepting a "folk" group, however, and the Dirt Band, despite their amplifiers, could be marketed as a folk group. In addition to electric guitars and drums, they used traditional American folk-music instruments: banjo, pedal steel guitar, violin, and mandolin. The Dirt Band's album *Will the Circle Be Unbroken,* recorded in Nashville with the Grand Ole Opry, had as its inspiration the desire to keep the "circle" of country music alive. Neither the Americans nor the Soviets even contemplated sending a hard-rock group of the Alice Cooper variety.

I enthusiastically accepted the offer but was immediately concerned about getting a visa to Riga, where I was to meet the Dirt Band. The cultural-affairs officer assured me that this would be no problem; he would use his influence with

Inotdel. Having suffered so many trials, I could not be so confident. The regular procedure for obtaining permission to buy a train ticket took four separate negotiations and a minimum of two weeks, assuming that nobody was deliberately stalling and that one was on good terms with all the right people. One spent this two-week minimum sitting in outer offices behind long lines of Russians, Mongols, Armenians, and Ukrainians who had been trying for a month to see the official in question. I recalled the well-known Soviet axiom that out of any four minor Soviet officials, one would certainly be in Moscow and another would be sick. Hence, like the German army in Russian mud, one's advance grinds to a halt. My relations with Ioffe, Sidorchenko, and Valentina Fedorovna were at that time not the best. They had never wanted me to go to Moscow in the first place, and to now request permission to leave Leningrad again in order to go on tour with a rock-and-roll band would not have inspired their enthusiasm.

Even if the political climate had been favorable, I could not possibly make all the necessary arrangements in those few days before the Dirt Band reached Riga. The only hope was the direct intercession of the consulate. The cultural-affairs officer called Dean Speshnev, head of Inotdel, and asked as a personal favor that I be given a visa for Riga. As these two frequently worked together, there was some hope for the success of personal leverage. Speshnev supposedly acceded to this request and told the consul that I should leave my passport the next morning and come back two days later to get the visa. As the visa had to be approved by the police, it could be done no faster. This delay meant I could not accompany the cultural-affairs officer. He would go by night train; the following day I was to pick up my visa and fly to Riga to join him. This was troubling.

On the fateful Thursday I went to Speshnev's loyal assistant Vadim Anatolyevich. If the visa were ready as promised I could make the evening plane. The Dirt Band

was arriving from Armenia the next day. As I entered Inotdel I caught Vadim crossing the waiting room and asked
him for my visa. He courteously asked me if I had my
request form with the signatures of my advisor, the dean of
the law school, and the dean for work with foreigners. His
own signature would be the fourth. I explained that this
was an exceptional case; the U.S. consul and Dean Speshnev had agreed to give me a visa outside the normal procedure. I said the visa was supposed to be ready now and he
was to have it. He explained in a moderate tone that this
was not the point—Dean Speshnev was not there and I
should go and bring the regular signatures. We both knew
that I could never get three signatures in one afternoon and
still catch the evening flight. I explained the arrangement
again: that there was no time to procure the signatures, and
that the visa was supposed to be ready now. He replied in
the same moderate tone that this was not the point, that I
was supposed to get all of the proper signatures, and that
Speshnev was not there and would not return. The sicken-
ing feeling of total loss began to creep over me. I saw it all
clearly. Speshnev was not there. The American cultural-
affairs officer was in Riga. Speshnev had either not informed
Vadim or had said to squash the project. When the cultural-affairs officer returned the Russians would say that it
had been a big misunderstanding, probably the fault of my
language ability, but that in any case these things happen
and "Yes, we Russians do have too much bureaucracy; it is
the fault of our czarist heritage."

Despite my earlier attempts not to let my expectations
rise, I found myself on the verge of despair. Only one small
thing, nagging at the back of my mind, kept me from slamming the door and leaving in disgust and despondency.
Vadim was behaving abnormally. He was not yelling at
me. He was not scowling. On the contrary, he was talking
in an almost courteous tone. This was most suspicious.
Why, for the first time in a year of our bureaucratic trans-

actions, was he not marching off and slamming his door? Why was he not being rude? His whole demeanor was so considerate that my curiosity was instinctively aroused. Was he hiding something? For the fourth time I repeated the arrangement to which Dean Speshnev had agreed. I reiterated that I must leave that night; did he have the visa? Again he repeated his formula, not responding directly to the question, but not raising his voice or dashing to his office and locking the door behind him.

We were in a hilarious situation. We were in the principal waiting room of Inotdel. Along all four walls were Arabs, Afghans, and Africans watching the two of us, toe to toe, stoically repeating ourselves over and over again. On the sixth or seventh round, Vadim broke. Abruptly he went into his office, pulled my passport out of his drawer, gave it to me, and stalked off in the usual manner. I thought he was washing his hands of me and simply returning my passport untouched. But when I looked inside there was a crisp little visa to Riga. I had won a great diplomatic victory and was congratulated by all present.

Lest it be thought that Vadim had some personal grudge against me, I got on with him comparatively well. It helped that I was an American; our group had by far more clout than any of the other foreign students at Inotdel. As I discovered with Sidorchenko, Russian officials seem to respect the nationals of a country in direct correspondence to the military power of their homeland. Americans at least eventually could get in to see a *chinovnik*, whereas Third Worlders seemed to spend all their time sitting in waiting rooms. Eastern Europeans from "fraternal socialist countries" got no respect whatsoever. It must be admitted, however, that as bad as things were for us, compared to native Russians, the foreign community was dealing with a responsive bureaucracy.

A few hours later I was airborne and bound for Riga. I nestled back into my seat, exhausted from the day's maneuvers. As we skirted the Baltic Sea it started to rain. I relaxed and let my mind wander. I speculated on what the members of the Dirt Band would be like. They had been a band for some ten years but had undergone several personnel changes. Although they had never been a super group, their albums had a strong market and they were well known on the college circuit. They were among the originators of the country-rock genre, but had never captured the center ring as had Linda Ronstadt or the Eagles. For me, meeting and working with the members of a nationally known group was a special thrill. One reason the State Department singled me out to help with the tour was that I was myself a musician. I frequently joined in with local Russian bands at consulate functions. Ten years earlier I had played with a high-school rock-and-roll band, the "Steps of Stone," in Fayetteville, North Carolina. I had written the lyrics for two songs we had recorded at a country and gospel music studio in Charlotte. My cousins went to school in Chapel Hill with James and Livingston Taylor. I followed the records of the big groups and wondered what such success would be like. When time came for college I left my group and went north to Cornell. As the Baltic rain beat against the plane window, I wondered about the road not taken, and about what had become of my musician friends in North Carolina.

This was not my first trip to Riga. I had passed through the city on my way out to Western Europe at Christmastime. Though it is only a few hundred miles from Leningrad, Riga is an older city with a different past. When I learned that the Leningrad consulate wanted me to serve as an unofficial tour guide for the Dirt Band, I studiously reviewed the history of the city and the Latvian people.

Riga was founded by the Teutonic Knights in 1201. Situated in a key geographical position on the Baltic Sea, Latvia, along with its neighbors, Estonia and Lithuania, had always been an attractive morsel for both the Russian bear

and the Swedish lion. The Baltic countries were first
annexed to Russia in 1721 after the defeat of Charles the
XII of Sweden by Peter the Great. Following the Bolshevik
Revolution, Latvia became, in 1919, an independent republic. Independence did not last long. Following the conclusion of the Hitler-Stalin Pact, Soviet troops occupied Latvia
on July 21, 1940. A year later this occupation was replaced
by that of the German *Wehrmacht*. Caught between Nazis
and Communists, Latvia suffered greatly during the war.
Latvians I met told me that the only difference between a
Russian officer and a German officer was that the German
would excuse himself before he shot you. In 1944 Riga was
recaptured by the Red Army, and Latvia is now one of the
fifteen Soviet republics. However, the United States does
not recognize Latvia, Estonia, or Lithuania as being part of
the Soviet Union, regarding them merely as "under occupation."

Architecturally, Riga reminds me of a medieval German
city like the old section of Nuremburg. There are winding
little streets, ramparts, and fortifications—a world apart
from the wide avenues and late-empire style of St. Petersburg. While St. Petersburg was built of malachite and gold,
Riga was built of brick and timber, never luxurious, but
industrious and enterprising.

The standard of living is considerably higher in Riga than
in Leningrad. Only here did I find things on which to spend
my accumulating stock of rubles. In the Soviet Union there
are so-called commission stores, where a citizen can take his
old things and put them up for sale to the general public;
the store retains a commission of about 7 percent. In the
Baltic provinces of the Soviet Union, there is another kind
of "commission" store especially for handicrafts. In these
stores artists receive a commission on sales of their work. In
Riga this means such treasures as beautiful amber jewelry
and handmade leather goods. As the Baltic countries were
annexed to the USSR only in the 1940s, they were not

exposed to the Great Purges of the 1930s, which destroyed much of Russian independent craftsmanship. In Riga these traditions remain. Because the system of material supply is weighted much more toward consumer goods than in Russia, one has the sense of being in East Germany or Czechoslovakia and not in the Soviet Union. There is a joke about the higher Baltic standard of living. Two Russian collective farmers from the *glush* win a trip to Riga as a reward for their hard labor in the fields. After days in a train crossing the barren Russian countryside, sipping vodka the whole way, they arrive in Riga. Through their bloodshot eyes, they see that the shops are full of products, there is food in the stores, and the people are well dressed and courteous. Awestruck, they go straight to the Riga town hall and apply for political asylum.

Riga demonstrates my pet theory of Soviet "reverse colonialism." With the exception of Moscow itself, the farther one goes from the capital, the higher the standard of living. In the heartland of the Great Russian people, the living standard is at the lowest levels in the Soviet Union. But as one continues toward the border and toward the non-Russian areas of the country, the living standard gradually rises. The results can be seen in the Soviet Union's Baltic republics and in the Caucasian republics of Georgia and Armenia. As always, there is a Soviet joke which illustrates this. One day a Georgian is driving his big Chaika limousine and, around a blind curve, comes to an enormous crevasse that has opened in the poorly constructed roadway. His limousine falls into the hole, crashes, and is destroyed. As he is helped from the wreck, the Georgian sighs and exclaims, "I worked all summer to save up for that car." While the Georgian recovers on the side of the roadway, a Zhiguli, the Russian-built Fiat, rounds the curve and meets the same awful fate. The local people pull a startled Latvian from the wreckage and sit him down next to the Georgian. "I can't believe it," says the Latvian; "I saved all year for that car."

While the two motorists commiserate with each other, a third car, a little Zaporozhets, scarcely more than a go-cart, comes around the bend and hurtles into the crevasse. When the elderly Russian driver is pulled from the ruined little auto, he can't stop sobbing. The other two try to comfort him but the Russian is inconsolable. "You don't understand," he wails, "I saved all my life for that little car." "Well, I'm sorry for your loss," says the Georgian, "but really you shouldn't have bought such an expensive automobile."

As one goes beyond the Soviet border to Soviet-controlled Eastern Europe, this trend continues; the living standard continues to rise (although this has much to do with cultural and historical distinctions). This "reverse" policy removes the element of envy from Soviet-style colonialism. A Latvian may hate the Russians but he cannot envy them; the average Russian is obviously in worse shape than he is.

From the airport, I took a cab to the Hotel Riga. The Baltic breeze was warm, electric with anticipation. The next day, Emil Sveilis from UPI, the cultural-affairs officer from the American consulate in Leningrad, and I went out to the Riga airport to meet the Dirt Band. They had already played in two cities in the USSR: Tbilisi, capital of Georgia, and Erevan, capital of Armenia. Both of these republics are in the far south on the Soviet-Turkish border. The band arrived on their Aeroflot plane and were suitably attired—John McEuen in a felt hat with a feather, Jeff Hanna in a Stetson. Accompanying the musicians was an entourage of roadies, technicians, interpreters from the Soviet sponsor, Gosconcert ("state concerts"—there is no other kind), and a representative from the U.S. Department of State.

Although I had come just to interpret, my trip to Riga immediately proved essential to the tour for a quite unexpected reason. In keeping with their country-rock style, many of the Dirt Band's best songs feature harmonica.

Hoping to learn a tune or two from the members of the group, I brought along two standard Hohner "Marine Band" harmonicas, originally purchased in America. The Dirt Band had started the tour with over forty harmonicas, but sometime after their last concert in Erevan all of them were stolen. The harmonicas had not all been packed together. Suspiciously enough, someone had methodically gone through the closely watched equipment, found, and taken all the harmonicas, and only the harmonicas. In most countries the band could have promptly replaced them in any music store, but not in the Soviet Union. The only two harmonicas available in Latvia were the ones I had casually tossed into my suitcase as I raced for the flight to Riga. Those two harmonicas saved the show.

From the airport we all climbed into the bus for the Hotel Riga. I was curious to know whether the members of the band had any interest in the country they were visiting or whether they viewed this as they would any other month-long tour: set up, play, and when does the bus go back to the hotel? The question was answered as soon as we were on the bus. Someone asked how they liked Erevan, and John Cable, one of the guitarists, complained that they weren't really getting a chance to meet anyone. They had been taken on an excursion or two but mostly just sat in their hotel room and played poker.

The language barrier was partly to blame. The Dirt Band had so far played in republics of the USSR whose population did not natively speak Russian or even a related Slavic language. As Russian is a language requirement in the schools of these republics, a native who could speak English would already be on his third language, third alphabet, and third linguistic group. Although the band traveled with three competent English-Russian translators from Gosconcert, these "translators," far from providing access to the populace, were the main reason for the band's isolation. The state-provided translators were not there to facilitate spontaneous contact between the band members and Soviet young people, but rather to keep them apart. The Soviet interpreters seemed more interested in discouraging the band members from ever leaving their hotel rooms. They always had plenty of Soviet champagne available for subdued parties in the band's hotel suite, with no Russians allowed. No Georgian or Armenian in his right mind would have said anything critical or candid about the Soviet Union through an official Soviet interpreter.

The officials from our State Department could not lend much assistance, as they were, of necessity, too involved with logistics and protocol to spend time socializing with the musicians. My unofficial function was to arrange for interested members of the band to break through their linguistic curtain and meet privately with Soviet young people. Since I was younger and a musician myself, the consulate felt I would have more rapport with the group and the young Soviets they were likely to meet. I had my own Russian and Latvian friends to introduce them to, but for the most part I would just interpret for the young people who came up to us after the concerts or on walks around the city. This pleasant task was made more exciting by a phenomenon I had not witnessed previously in the Soviet Union: the presence of continuous and somewhat comical KGB surveillance.

I had hung around enough with the Western diplomats at the consulate Marine bar to hear the many theories of KGB operation. The predominant Western conception is that the whole massive apparatus works by push button from Yuri Andropov's headquarters in Moscow: every island in the Gulag, every *agent provocateur* and *stukach* is at the beck and call of the latter-day Berias. If this were true it would be in contrast to every other so-called centralized operation in the Soviet Union, the force of which diminishes with every mile from Moscow. Another theory suggests that city KGB heads are in fact more like feudal chieftains or Ori-

ental warlords. They owe fealty to Moscow but are jealous
of their private satrapies. An order may come from Moscow, for example, that the Dirt Band should be watched,
but all decisions regarding the order's execution would be
left in the hands of the Riga boss. If this speculation is
accurate, the Riga boss certainly earned himself the Order
of Lenin. Twenty minutes after the Dirt Band had arrived
at the Hotel Riga, I was walking out the front door with
Jeff Hanna, the lead singer. Parked directly in front of the
door was a taxi cab with two attractive young women and
a driver. The dark-haired girl in the front immediately called
out to us in English (what more natural language to use in
Riga?) asking us if we knew where the Dirt Band was staying. We knew very well where the Dirt Band was staying,
as did she. "Oh, you're the Dirt Band, what a coincidence!
Well, what are you doing tonight?" I whispered to Jeff that
this was highly unusual in the Soviet Union and things were
perhaps not what they seemed. He needed no persuasion,
and with a diplomatic "Thanks, but no thanks" we continued on our way. During our six days in Riga, this raven-
haired young woman was around us constantly. Later I
learned her name was Maria and she claimed to come from
Spain; I supposed Azerbaijan to be more likely. While no
other young person seemed to be able to get near the hotel,
Maria was always there sitting with her driver in her taxi
cab inviting us to come have some fun.

Tickets to the Dirt Band's concerts sold for six rubles
apiece, about a day and a half's wage for most Russians. All
the concerts were sold out. They had never been adver-
tised, and the tickets never went on public sale. With the
exception of a handful of complimentary tickets given to the
Americans, Gosconcert was responsible for ticket distribution. The last thing Soviet officials wanted to see was a wild
rock concert with the flower of socialist youth rushing the
stage in a frenzy. Yet the leadership was painfully aware
that if they permitted the tickets to go on public sale this is

exactly what would have happened. Worse still, the Americans could then have suggested that in light of the enthusiastic reception, more such concerts by rock-and-roll groups should be arranged. In official Soviet eyes, music is a leading element in what they refer to as the "putrefying influence of the West." Its very popularity with Soviet youth demonstrates the magnitude of the danger. Owing to these fears, it had taken three years to arrange the Dirt Band tour, with the Russians procrastinating every step of the way. Simply put, Soviet policy was to keep young people out of the concerts. This was done principally by giving out tickets to aging collective farmers, city *chinovniks*, and senior military officers. These old fellows were very courteous, clapped respectfully—but didn't exactly scream for more.

Large heterogeneous societies are difficult to control. Given the proclivity for anarchy inherent in the Russian character, official policy frequently (usually?) goes astray. Many feel that it is exactly this tension between official regimentation and personal irresponsibility that makes the Soviet Union more "livable" than a place like East Germany. I imagined a scene like this. Old grandpa on his collective farm 200 kilometers from Riga gets two tickets to the Nitty-Gritty Dirt Band concert along with a form letter from the local party committee saying that in view of his years of service to the motherland he is being given this opportunity to attend a concert of American popular music. The party expects he will show solidarity by attending, together with his wife. There is a note from the collective farm treasurer that he owes the collective twelve rubles. Just about this time, seventeen-year-old Masha is having tea and *pirozhki* with babushka in the kitchen. Grandpa raises a hue and cry that he doesn't want to go to Riga, that he hasn't been to a concert since he walked back from Berlin in '45, which suits him fine, and anyway he especially doesn't want to hear any rock-and-roll in a Riga skating rink. Immediately Masha starts howling that everyone in

(*above*) The Nitty-Gritty Dirt Band with the author in the Evropeiskaya Hotel in Leningrad. The American consulate asked me to tour with the Dirt Band to interpret for them and facilitate their meeting Soviet young people. From the left, the author, John McEuen, Jimmie Fadden, and Jeff Hanna.

(*opposite, top*) Emil Sveilis, correspondent for United Press International, introducing the Dirt Band at a small club date in Riga, Latvia. Emil was born in Riga and still had relatives there. The KGB gave him very special attention when he was in town.

(*opposite, bottom*) John McEuen, leader of the Dirt Band, entertains Max Paperno at Slava's apartment. McEuen took a serious interest in what Russian life was like; while the others went on their official tour, I took him to see Slava.

technical school said an American band was coming but nobody could get tickets and could she please, please have them. Grandpa is now on the horns of a dilemma. Nothing would please him more than giving Masha the tickets, but that note from the party said he was supposed to go. Masha's pleas continue; Grandpa hesitates, equivocates, vacillates, and finally abdicates. After all, he rationalizes, they won't shoot him. Everybody would understand a grandfather's wanting to make his granddaughter happy. Owing to familial situations like this, enough young people were present, perhaps 40 percent, to make the concerts exciting. True to the most morbid fears of the Soviet leadership, they yelled, screamed, threw flowers, and rushed the stage.

After the first concert, KGB troops formed a tight shoulder-to-shoulder corridor from the backstage theater door to the bus. Ostensibly this was done to protect the band from contact with the crowds. One suspected it might be to protect the crowds from contact with the band. But there were no crowds when the band left the hall, merely thirty sparsely scattered well-wishers. Here was a choice opportunity to meet the Latvian young people, but we were locked in a salmon run between two rows of KGB. There were far more KGB on the scene than fans. John McEuen, leader of the Dirt Band, decided to break through. The troops were well prepared for the Latvians to push in, but were dumbfounded when we tried to push out. They didn't know what to do, whether to resist or let us through. Here one had a handful of scrawny musicians on one side, thirty Latvian young people on the other, and a wall of steely-eyed internal-security police in between. McEuen slithered through and the wall closed behind him. What were the police to do then, leave him on the other side? Confusion reigned. We all started pushing and the wall broke. Members of the Dirt Band were surrounded by enthusiastic small groups of Latvians. A few of the Latvians tried out their halting English, and I went from group to group interpreting through Russian. It was an altogether harmless scene, but the KGB, who had been made to look silly, were not amused. Slowly the band drifted back to the bus. On the ride back one of the Soviet interpreters began pontificating about Lenin's triumphant return by train to St. Petersburg's Finland Station. Jeff Hanna quipped, "What's this about Lenin at the filling station?"

Back at the Hotel Riga the situation was reminiscent of a grade B detective story. There were heavyweights on every landing, reading the newspaper in the dark. Volga sedans at points around the hotel sat with their motors running. At a fixed time every day one Volga would pull out and another pull in right behind. Agents paced every corner. Inside the hotel a young Russian approached us. Immediately two plainclothesmen came over and just stared at him from six inches away. Finally one said to him in Russian, "What do you think you are doing?" The Russian had the good sense to respond in broken English. The operatives were confused and backed off.

This fellow, who had come all the way from Minsk to hear the Dirt Band play, was soon joined by a Latvian couple with whom he was staying. They were taking an enormous risk, sitting with us in the Hotel Riga describing to the band the grim reality of Soviet life. They told us an interesting story. During the summer of 1976 the American embassy sponsored a bicentennial exhibit in Moscow. Thousands of Russians a day came to see it, partly because they were each given colorful plastic carry bags and pins. There was a guest book where visitors could put down their remarks. Everyone who signed the guest book, even those who just said "Thank you," were called in by the KGB for a *beseda*. Nothing very tough, just a kind of "We are watching you, be careful." Personally I felt this had to be an exaggeration, if only because of the thousands of people involved, but they averred it was true. I believed these young people made quite an impression on the band. It was clear that they were taking great personal risks and were not trouble-makers. Far from it; they were concerned citizens. Later, some of the band members visited the flat of the Latvian couple, their first opportunity to see a Soviet home.

At that time, there was no meat in Riga and there had been some minor food riots earlier that spring. By contrast our tables were well laden. The authorities did not want these musical ambassadors to take home a negative impression. At dinner that night I heard from one of the roadies that Maria, who had called to us the first day in front of the hotel, was asking for me by name. How did she know my name? Had somebody called out to me on the street, or had she read my file? Intrigued, Emil and I decided to take a walk. True to form, as soon as we were out on the street, Maria—we called her Black Maria, because of her hair and because of the association with the infamous "Black Maria" sedans that were used to haul people off during the Great Purges—pulled up with her driver.

Though usually I felt quite safe in the Soviet Union, on those nights in Riga I would not have gone out alone for anything. While I talked to Maria, Emil watched our flanks and rear. We were just off to the side of the hotel. One of the KGB stake-out men—obvious by his pink shirt, he'd been pacing the corner for three hours—was only twenty feet from us. Normally I would not be interested in stand-ing outside a big metropolitan hotel and chatting with the local prostitutes, but being in the Soviet Union immedi-ately adds that sense of intrigue, that touch of electricity in the air. How does she operate? What's her real story? Emil and I invited her to come into the hotel to have a drink with us at the foreign-currency bar. She declined, inviting us instead to go for a ride in her taxi. She assured us that important Westerners did so all the time. Attractive as she was, we had no intention of getting into that taxi. She told us she was afraid to go into the hotel because of the security police. This was really humorous. Maria had been making herself as obvious as possible since our arrival while security men hovered all about us, so close by that Emil and I were concerned lest they hit us over the head and dump us into the trunk of Maria's cab.

We had quite a lively banter going, I speaking Russian and Emil speaking Latvian, when abruptly another taxi pulled up next to Black Maria's. Two stout uniformed women jumped out, each carrying a big black-and-white nightstick. They ran around to the back of Maria's cab, opened the door, and got in. To judge from the looks on their faces it was no social call. We backed off ten feet and watched; Maria rolled up her window. It appeared at first that she and her driver were going to be arrested. There was animated talk, but we couldn't hear what was being said. Maria showed some papers; the women wrote on a clipboard, and two or three minutes went by. Abruptly the women got out of the cab, got back into their own cab, and left. Maria waited a minute, then nonchalantly rolled the window back down. We asked her what had happened. She said they were taxi police and wanted to check the registration and see whether the driver was working. It looked to me like a bit more than a registration check. It was my guess that the two women were local police who had intended to arrest her for solicitation. She had let them know that she was there on a matter of state security; they should delay in order to preserve her cover, but then clear out and stay away. Come-hither looks notwithstanding, we retired in cowardice to the hotel.

After the fifth concert we flew to Leningrad. The Dirt Band stayed at the Yevropayskaya (European) Hotel, just off Nevsky Prospect. Built in the czarist past as the Hotel de L'Europe, it was matched only by the Astoria in charm and genteel elegance. The band's three short days in Leningrad were filled with protocol. There were receptions at the consul general's residence and at Marine House, at the consulate. The members of the group had little time to see the important sights of the city. Even on that tight schedule, John McEuen insisted that he wanted to meet the Russian people, and if it meant missing Peterhof, well, people were more important than palaces. I was truly impressed and hastily made arrangements for him to meet Slava. I cannot describe how honored Slava's family felt to have McEuen entertain them with a private banjo medley. Eight-year-old Maxim was curled up at McEuen's feet in absolute rapture. After the visit, I showed John around the neighborhood, the shops for the citizens and the yellow-curtained shops for the privileged few. I remember John's sad fascination with a Russian Orthodox church on the corner of Slava's street that had been converted into a department store.

A brief incident after the last Leningrad concert dramatized for me the psychological power of a strong-willed individual unwilling to accept the behavioral norms of a regimented state. As we boarded the bus to take the band to the train station, John McEuen grabbed a handful of bright-red souvenir guitar picks with "Nitty-Gritty Dirt Band" stamped on them, opened the window of the bus, and threw them to a throng of excited fans. Before the young Russians could get to them, the police, who were surrounding the bus, waved the crowd back and began to collect the guitar picks for confiscation. McEuen was furious and, shaking his fist, yelled at the police to give the guitar picks to the crowd. Needing no prompting, I vociferously translated the command. Looking up at John's stern demeanor in the bus window, the police, who were used to obeying direct orders, made no protest and began to distribute the guitar picks. The crowd had never seen anything like this before and roared its approval.

When I described this incident to Slava, he made an interesting observation. The admirable thing about John, Slava told me, was that John had not left his American values on the doorstep before entering the Soviet Union. He brought his values with him and interpreted his Russian experiences accordingly. Most visitors to the Soviet Union, said Slava, took the position that as they were "guests" they should not question the values of their "host": when in Rome do as the Romans do. But, Slava said, this acceptance of foreign rules of behavior should not be taken to the extreme that when in an unjust situation, one should behave unjustly. In the United States, Slava asked me, wouldn't Americans be ashamed of special stores for restricted "certificate dollars"; wouldn't they refuse to tolerate bars for currencies that the common people were not permitted to own? I answered that I thought he was right.

"Yet," Slava continued, "when those same freedom-loving Americans come to Russia they adopt some meek feeling of 'judge not lest ye be judged,' and go along with the whole system. This is particularly disappointing in the case of the American exchange students, and I have met enough of them over the years to have a basis for generalizing. They aren't tourists; they are in the country for a long time. Presumably they know a few things about Soviet society, yet they never want to rock the boat or irritate the authorities in any way." Slava felt this rose to the level of a moral question.

Slava told me that I had impressed him because I would assert myself. With Inotdel, with my advisor, in my fleeting contacts with the police and the KGB, I did not simply abandon any thought of right and wrong and do exactly what I was told to do. "And," Slava said, "those American Slavicists who think that this submissive behavior will endear them to the Soviet authorities have learned very little about this country. When you are dealing with the Russians a compliant attitude accomplishes nothing. When an American from a strong and free country becomes docile and cowardly before some minor *chinovnik*, the *chinovnik* despises him for it and will usually make more outrageous demands just to see how far the silly person can be pushed." Slava had a sip of tea and continued, "You have seen many things and accomplished a great deal here, more than your fellow exchange students. Russian officials are impressed that you will stand up to them. They don't mind a little pounding on the table. That is what they expect Americans to do."

I was flattered by Slava's praise and agreed with his assessment of how to deal with Soviet officialdom, but I did feel that my relatively "confrontationist" attitude stemmed not from any great courage on my part but because in a way, I had much less to lose. I was not struck dumb by the threat of becoming *persona non grata* in the Soviet Union. In some ways I would have considered it an honor. But I, after all, had a secure position in a law firm awaiting my return. My colleagues on the exchange, planning their careers in academia, had much more to lose. In addition, my training as a lawyer made me more disposed to arm-wrestle with the bureaucrats than the other exchange students might have found appealing.

Following the incident with the guitar picks, the bus took all of us to the train station. The Dirt Band's time in Leningrad was at a close. They had a few remaining concerts in Moscow before they were to leave the Soviet Union, but I would remain in Leningrad. There were warm good-byes at the Moscow station; a great adventure was ending. It would be less than two weeks until I would myself be at the Moscow station taking the Red Arrow south and away from Leningrad.

Everything seemed anticlimactic after the Dirt Band's departure, but an important obligation remained before I could depart from Leningrad. I had to prepare and present my *otchet*, or accounting, to the Civil Law Faculty. I had some cause for apprehension about this. The *otchet* for graduate students is the year-end report describing the extent to which they have fulfilled their scientific plan. Given my situation, this could be nothing but a debacle. From the beginning there had been a direct conflict between what the law faculty wanted me to do and what I wanted to do. From my point of view, the world these scholars inhabited was a dream world of theories and norms and hypotheses that had no connection with the reality of the Russia I had seen. My every legitimate attempt to see Soviet law through the proper channels had been thwarted. The only thing to which I had been able to gain access through the good offices of the law school was the university library. I wanted to go into my *otchet* screaming, but to what purpose? The faculty had been good to me and I had not behaved in the manner they had hoped. Probably they had done as much for me as their limited powers permitted. From their point of view, they should be screaming at me. The second semester I had hardly been in attendance at all. First I was in Moscow, and then I was on tour with a rock-and-roll band. They could not help being angry and disappointed. I did not relish the impending confrontation. In such situations I have found it an advantage to be speaking in a foreign language. It is easier to remain detached when you have to say hard things or when hard things are said to you. It is as if it's not really you they're talking to, but a translator.

On the fateful day, I was the third student and the only foreigner to present my *otchet*, and I listened while the first two cataloged how many of Ioffe's texts they had read and waxed eloquent on the marvelous ways in which Soviet jurisprudence had refined the coarse concepts of bourgeois jurisprudence. When my turn came I told the faculty about my progress in Russian and my attendance at classes in the first semester. I told about my many talks with Valentina Fedorovna. But I also described my frustration in trying to see a Soviet trial or arbitration. I explained that I had spent a very large part of my year preparing petitions and requesting signatures. I told them that I was very disappointed about being denied permission to stay in Moscow long enough to see a foreign-trade arbitration, particularly as that was a primary objective of my study plan. There were no disturbances during my *otchet*.

When I finished Ioffe spoke. He said that I had not read enough books, that there had been plenty to do without my seeing arbitration, and that I should have done what was available instead of worrying about what was not available. My mind had been on other things and not on the research I was supposed to be doing at the law faculty. Of course he was right. After the meeting, Valentina Fedorovna said she was sorry she couldn't be proud of me, but she bore me no ill will. So, with a whimper ended my appointment to the Civil Law Faculty of Leningrad State University.

As luck would have it, it was that very day that the acting consul general in Leningrad, George L. Rueckert, had told me he was available to perform the ceremonies to swear me in to the Ohio Bar (My admission to the New York Bar would come after my return.) Outside the law school named for A. A. Zhdanov, I caught the trolley car to take me to the consulate. As I rattled through the rain-soaked streets I thought it ironic that I would be sworn in to the American legal fraternity within an hour of having been so ignominiously ejected from the Soviet one. Arriving at the consulate, I was flattered to learn that the entire Western press corps in Leningrad had turned out for my swearing in. In other words, Emil had shown up with his camera. That night, Emil and I and our Swedish friends Lars and Karl got drunk together, turned up the stereo, laughed, and said horrible and perfidious things about the Soviet Union.

The evening of June 1, I was standing on the platform of Leningrad's Moscow station waiting to board the Red Arrow. Although it was after eleven, it had only just gotten dark. I would spend the next three nights on the train— Leningrad to Moscow, Moscow to Kiev, Kiev to Odessa. In Odessa I would catch a Soviet cruise ship, which would take me along the Bulgarian coast, through the Bosphorus past Istanbul, and deposit me, a week's journey from Len-

My induction into the Ohio bar at the American consulate in Leningrad. George Rueckert, acting consul general, performed the ceremony.

ingrad, on the Greek island of Mykonos. Two more different places I could not imagine. To my disappointment, I
was going to miss the peak of the White Nights, the time
when you can read a book on the streets of Leningrad at
midnight.

There is a poignancy about leaving a place where you
have learned so much and laughed so much, and to which
you feel you may never return. No other city has left me
with such indelible impressions. As I stood there with
Slava, neither of us knew whether we would ever meet again.
Neither of us had any encouraging thoughts on internal
developments in the USSR or on the future of United
States–Soviet relations. We had seen too much to have any
illusions about that. It seemed inevitable that our nations
would slide down the path to increasing confrontation.
Sadly, the course of events has yet to prove us wrong.

Ten /

Return:

Chicken Kiev, Hold the Chicken

O_n *October 24, 1980,* I boarded Finnair flight AY-102 bound for Helsinki, to connect the next day with Aeroflot flight 646. I was returning to Leningrad. Three and a half years had passed since I stood with Slava on the train-station quay waiting for the Red Arrow. Much had happened in those three and a half years. I had not written to Slava or other Russians. Such letters would be read, and no matter how innocent the contents were, the mere fact of corresponding with a foreigner could endanger my friends' careers. Occasionally reports came to me when Americans I knew went through Leningrad or when someone there emigrated to the West. Through the potato vine I had heard that Slava himself had at last applied to emigrate. His request had been denied: he too was now a refusenik.

My life had also changed. No longer in academics, I was a practicing international lawyer in New York City. Books on Russian grammar had been replaced by licenses, leases, and loan agreements. Because of the declining trade between the United States and the Soviet Union, my work had been primarily with the Japanese and Western Europeans. But the most significant change in the years I had been away was the continued deterioration in political relations between the two countries. As the DC-10 winged across the black

Atlantic, I reviewed in my own mind the events that had contributed to that decline.

When I was still studying in Leningrad, Neto, then president of Angola (he would later die in a Moscow hospital), frequently appeared on Soviet television thanking the Russian people for intervening in Angola's struggle against "imperialism." The Angola situation had presaged a new pattern of Soviet international involvement. It was the first of the so-called proxy wars fought in the Third World with Soviet equipment, advisors, money, and diplomatic support, but stopping short of using Russian combat troops. Troops themselves were supplied by a dutiful Soviet ally. In the case of Angola and other African countries that ally was Cuba. Many in the United States thought this activity should not be tolerated, but the aftertaste of Vietnam had left the country as a whole unwilling to get involved. In the years since I had left Russia, proxy wars had become commonplace. Like a hotel burglar the Soviet Union went down the hall of nations trying every door. The Soviet Union intervened in, if not in fact precipitated, the war in the Horn of Africa, first supporting Somalia and then switching sides to its enemy Ethiopia. In Southeast Asia, Vietnamese troops with full Soviet patronage pacified Laos, then invaded, a slice at a time, neighboring Cambodia. Southern Yemen, a Soviet client, attacked Northern Yemen. By and large, the United States and its allies did nothing about these Third World adventures, displaying an apathy that could only entice the Soviets into more aggressive actions.

Opportunities were soon to present themselves on Russia's oil-rich southern border. In April 1978 there had been a bloody and successful coup in Afghanistan, led by the Marxists Noor Mohammed Taraki and Hafizullah Amin. By the beginning of 1979 Soviet advisors were in every important Afghan ministry and military organization. In February 1979 the American ambassador to Kabul, Eugene Debs, was killed in a gun battle between his guerrilla captors and the Afghan police, while Soviet "advisors" coolly looked on. In September, Amin purged Taraki. When on November 4 the American embassy in Tehran was seized and on November 21 a street mob burnt the American embassy in Islamabad, Pakistan, America's weakness in the region proved too tempting. During November and December 1979, over 50,000 Soviet combat troops poured over the border into Afghanistan. The Soviet army was instrumental in having the independent Amin overthrown and executed and installing their man, Babrak Karmal, fresh from exile in Czechoslovakia, as the puppet leader of the country.

The invasion of Afghanistan galvanized the Carter administration into action. On January 2, 1980, Thomas Watson, the American ambassador to Moscow, was recalled—a diplomatic protest that had not occurred during the invasion of Hungary in 1956 or of Czechoslovakia in 1968. On January 4, Carter ordered a partial embargo on grain and the sale of high-technology and strategic items. The Olympic boycott was announced. Plans for new consulates, an American one in Kiev and a Soviet counterpart in New York City, were terminated. The SALT II treaty, for which the Carter administration had fought for years, was quietly shelved. On January 21 Andrei Sakharov, winner of the Nobel Peace Prize, was denounced by the Soviet government and exiled from Moscow to Gorky. In retaliation the National Academy of Sciences of the United States canceled scientific exchanges with the USSR. On January 5, 1980, Secretary of Defense Harold Brown arrived in the People's Republic; the United States was playing the "China card." In August, hundreds of thousands of Polish workers went on strike, and the United States warned against a possible Soviet invasion. The whole matrix of Soviet-American relations was put in the deep freeze. Détente was dead.

The collapse of relations greatly reduced the possibility of anyone's repeating the experience I had had. The USA-

USSR Intergovernmental Agreement on Cultural and Educational Exchanges under which my exchange operated had expired and not been renewed. Inertia carried the program forward on a reduced level, so that some candidates continued to be exchanged for shorter periods. No American law students had been accepted by the Soviets. Restrictions on the American exchange students, severe in my time, had increased; most assumed that the whole program was in its last year.

While I was ruminating on these disconcerting themes, the Finnair stewardess offered me a complimentary copy of the day's *New York Times*. There on the front page was a story that took me back, "Ailing Kosygin Quits as Soviet Premier; Tikhonov Is Named." Kosygin was ill and stepping down (his death was announced on December 20, 1980). The new premier of the Soviet Union was to be Nikolai A. Tikhonov, whose name meant the "Quiet One." He was one of the so-called Dnepropetrovsk group, the members of which had known Brezhnev in his days in the Ukraine. Brezhnev's success had been their success, and Tikhonov was now one of the small clique that controlled the Politburo and the largest nation in the world. The article went on to say that Kosygin's resignation left Leonid Brezhnev "as the only survivor of the troika that ran the Soviet Union after Mr. Khrushchev was sent into retirement." The other member of that "troika" had been Nikolai V. Podgorny. I recalled that it was in the closing weeks of my time in Leningrad that he had been ousted as president of the Soviet Union. I remembered Sasha's fondness for Podgorny and wondered what had become of the man Sasha called the last of the "men of the people." Every account I could find used some euphemism such as "forced out" or "pushed aside." But what had really happened to Podgorny? I could not find out. No one knew. Was he living quietly in a suburb of Moscow, as most Russians assumed;

or was he holding some clerical post in Vladivostok? From the total absence of any news in the Soviet press, one could just as well conclude that the man who had served as president of the Soviet Union for two decades had been shot behind the ear in a basement cell in Lubyanka prison. The fate of the third horse was unknown.

For a long time I had thought about whether I wanted to return to Russia. There had always been an ambivalence within me; half of me saying "Never Again" and half of me longing to go. Filling out the visa application had brought back many of the police-state memories. Questions were asked, such as "What is your home address and telephone number? List dates of previous visits to the USSR. Do you have any relatives in the Soviet Union?" At last my desire to make another visit won out, not least because, given the Olympic boycott, Afghanistan invasion, and strikes in Poland, I felt that relations might get so bad that the Russians would close their border and, as happened to China specialists in the fifties, that it would be years before I could go again.

I had never been a "tourist" in the Soviet Union before. Every foreigner in the USSR must be sponsored by some Soviet organization. As a student I was there by authority of the Ministry of Higher Education. As a tourist, I would travel through Inostranny Turist literally "foreign tourist," known to all by its abbreviation, Intourist. My travel plans had to be confirmed in advance by a New York travel agent accredited by Intourist. Although almost all Westerners who travel to the Soviet Union do so in groups, it is possible to make independent arrangements. In the summer and fall of 1980, American groups to Russia were almost nonexistent; and as I already knew the country and what I wanted to see, I chose to travel independently. As required, I worked out with the accredited travel agent a detailed itinerary: each train I would be on, every hotel I would be staying in. Telexes were exchanged with Moscow; changes were made and telexed again. Each detail had to be confirmed by Intourist's central office. While not all of my proposed travel plan was permitted, one special request of mine was accepted and confirmed. I could stay in the Astoria Hotel in Leningrad.

The Astoria was built in 1912 and in its day was among the grandest hotels of Europe. It is a hotel heavy with the weight of Leningrad history, and that history was often grim. It is rumored that Hitler printed invitations for a grand ball at the Astoria to celebrate the capture of the city by the German army. Owing to the courage and tenacity of the Leningraders, the ball never took place. A revolution and two world wars after its founding, the Astoria retains a gentility unknown to modern Soviet hotels. Its location is a tremendous advantage. While most of the Intourist hotels are isolated in the suburbs, the Astoria stands right in the shadow of the massive granite and malachite St. Isaac's Cathedral—the heart of Leningrad. It is a five-minute walk to the Hermitage and the Nevsky Prospect. As a student I had frequented the restaurant off the hotel lobby and knew I wanted to stay at the Astoria if I ever returned.

After the exhausting night flight from New York, with a two-hour layover in Finland, I approached the Intourist desk at the Leningrad Airport. Thoroughly jet-lagged from the eight-hour time difference, I wanted nothing more than to be whisked to the Astoria and to climb into bed. I did not realize how soon after my return my skirmishing with Soviet officialdom would resume.

"Your hotel will be the Prebaltiskaya," said the Intourist clerk. "No," I said in English, "my hotel is the Astoria. That has been confirmed by Moscow." "I'm sorry," said the clerk, "but *we* were informed by Moscow that your hotel was the Prebaltiskaya." It seemed that while the traveler is bound by his confirmed itinerary, Intourist was not playing by the same rules. The memory of all of the frustrations of my year in Leningrad washed over me, but with the sinking sensation I also recalled some of the tactics I had learned. I insisted that I was going to stay in the Astoria and showed them my prepaid voucher, which showed my reservation there. To placate me they generously agreed to call the hotel, but as I expected the answer came back "mest net" (no places). During my student year, every request I made to get a train, restaurant, or hotel reservation had always been initially greeted with this response, "mest net." There were always places. The game was whether you were enterprising enough to get one. I told the clerk that I was sure the manager could make room, and I would just go to the Astoria and speak with him directly.

Intourist then tried to dissuade me by arguing that the Prebaltiskaya was really a better hotel; I should be pleased with the change, it had been done for my benefit. While I was a student, a Swedish construction company had been building the Prebaltiskaya (the name means "Baltic region"). After a long subway ride from the center of Leningrad, one could catch a trolley bus and, after a walk through the mud and cold, arrive at the new hotel on the Gulf of Finland. The only convenient way to get out of the place was on an Intourist excursion. This is precisely as Intourist planned it; the chance of meeting any extraneous Russian was remote. Although the Prebaltiskaya is reputed to be comfortable and modern, a new Swedish hotel could not compare with the historical ambience of the czarist Astoria. I again insisted that I had a reservation for the Astoria and that was where I was going to stay.

They called the Astoria again. This time the response was "They say there are no rooms tonight, but after tonight it will be all right." I saw in this another classic Soviet stratagem. If there is anything the Russians understand, it is the impact of territory and inertia. These are as effective in dealing with a foreign tourist as they are in international relations. As they well knew, once I was in a warm hotel room, my desire to waste time trying to move would evaporate. Having situated me and my things anywhere else, their responsibility would have been discharged. But as long as I was standing in front of them at the airport with my baggage scattered about, they had to do something with me. I had to make them believe that doing what I wanted would in the end prove less troublesome than refusing me. I again said I would simply go to the Astoria and speak to the manager. They protested that they had no authority to permit the car to go there. I said that in that case I would just take the bus. At this they shrugged and nodded to the driver to take me.

As night fell I was standing with my bags at the Astoria reception desk, a porter beside me eagerly hoping for a tip. I had told the car not to wait. I showed the receptionist my voucher. She looked through her book but could not find my name. I again showed my voucher, explained that the Intourist officials at the Leningrad Airport had sent me to the Astoria, that the car had left, it was dark, and I was exhausted from my trip. She surveyed the situation and called the hotel director on the phone. At no time did I let on that I could speak or understand Russian. It is a tremendous advantage to force Intourist personnel to speak English with you. They have some respect for you as a "foreign guest," but if you speak to them in Russian they forget who you are and begin to treat you like one of their own—none too courteously. She said to the director in Russian, "He's not down here in our books, but it is written in his voucher that he is to stay here." Pause. "What can we do, he's here and the car is gone. It's more trouble to send him somewhere else. Let's permit him to stay." Pause. "Right, okay." She turned to me and said in English, "Passport, please." My fifth-floor room was lovely, with a breathtaking view of the square and St. Isaac's Cathedral lit up in the night. Most of the other rooms on my floor were empty.

One's satisfaction is in relation to one's expectations.

Anywhere else I would not have felt the exhilaration of a diplomatic triumph from the simple matter of getting into the hotel where I had had reservations for weeks. Admittedly, the room was unheated and, considering it was snowing outside, rather cold. But it didn't matter, I had gotten in. I was thrilled to discover there was hot water. The room key was a magnificent monster, weighing perhaps two pounds. One of the originals from the hotel, it said in raised brass letters: "Astoria Hotel, Saint Petersburg."

Why, one might ask, when there are plenty of rooms available, would a hotel turn you away? The answer can be found in the fundamentally different motivation of the administrators of a hotel or any service industry in the Soviet Union. There is absolutely no profit motive in the Western sense. The Astoria management cared not at all how many rooms were full. A full house would not have meant any more money in their pockets or even any promotions or bonuses for good management. To the contrary, it is a positive disadvantage to have a full house—the more guests, the more work. More important, there is a political risk. Many Soviet officials have special priority regarding space, whether for trains, planes, hotels, or restaurants. Upon the mere flashing of certain cards, doors are expected to fly open. Woe to the hotel manager who does not have a suite ready for an unexpected guest from the Central Committee.

After washing up I made a quick tour of my floor and its sumptuous nineteenth-century furnishings. As I passed by the fire exit, I was not surprised to find it locked. The authorities did not want people going from floor to floor out of view of the severe eyes of the *dezhurnye*, the duty ladies who sit on guard at the top of the main staircase on each floor. Over to the side of the fire door was a little box, which contained a key hanging from twisted baling wire. I wondered whether in the smoke and panic of a fire anyone would be able to find the box, untie the key, and manage to unlock the door. My thoughts were motivated by more than idle paranoia. I was reminded of an incident that had occurred at the Rossiya Hotel in Moscow during my student year. The Rossiya Hotel, as Intourist guides assert, is the biggest hotel in the world. It is situated in view of St. Basil's Cathedral, just off Red Square. The hotel is symmetrical in design, a large square of 6,000 rooms enclosing a central courtyard. Guests complain of never being able to find their rooms, because every floor, corridor, and lobby is identical. You practically need a compass to find the elevator. The Rossiya has no fire escapes, which is not unusual; the entire time I was in the Soviet Union I never saw a fire escape. The Rossiya does have interior emergency fire exits, but given the symmetry of the halls and the enormous distances, these are difficult to find.

In February 1977 a major fire broke out on the upper floors of the Rossiya. As at the Astoria and any other hotel in the Soviet Union, babushka-age duty ladies were at their posts on every corridor. These old matrons, notorious for raising the alarm if a man tries to sneak a girl into his room, inexplicably vanished at the first sign of peril. The guests were left to discover the danger when their rooms began to fill with smoke.

An English acquaintance of mine was in the hotel on the evening of the fire. He had been reading in bed when he smelled smoke. He walked to the door and to his horror found it hot to his touch. Remembering his British public-school training, he got a wet towel from the bathroom to breathe through. Crouching low to the floor, where it would be coolest, he opened the door. The heat struck him as if he had stuck his face into an oven. The hall was black with smoke. Unable to see, he began to crawl along the wall feeling for the door to the stairs. He had stayed in the hotel before and had at least a vague idea where it was. Breathing through the towel, he made his way along the endless corridor. Faint from the heat, he found the stairwell door,

The Astoria Hotel. Built in 1912, its appointments reflect its prerevolutionary construction. Despite the cold at the time this picture was taken, my top-floor room was unheated.

(*top*) Palace Square in preparation for November seventh. From the Winter Palace one sees the General Staff Arch and the Alexander Column.

(*bottom*) Troops on the march across the Palace Bridge. About one-third of the men in Leningrad are in uniform, and there are constant troop movements in the city. To the rear is one of the rostral columns, adorned with *rostra*, the symbolic prows of defeated enemy ships. Hempseed oil was formerly burned in the copper bowls on top of the columns to enable merchant ships to find their moorings. Now they are lighted only on national holidays.

(*top*) Wall decoration for the November Seventh celebration of the Bolshevik Revolution.
(*bottom*) Return to Leningrad in October of 1980. Slava and Max Paperno with the author in Smolny Cemetery. The Papernos were refuseniks at that time, meaning they had applied to emigrate and been refused.

pushed himself through, fell down two flights of steps, and passed out. He was pulled to safety from the lower floor.

Interestingly, one's nationality played a key role in whether, and how, one survived. The English and Americans took to the halls at the first sign of danger. Several Japanese guests tied bed sheets together and, hanging from the burning seventh floor, were pulled to safety by people on the fifth. By acting quickly, all of the foreign guests managed to save themselves. By far the largest group in the hotel, however, was the Russians. They did not attempt to escape, but even as the fire grew worse, stayed in their rooms awaiting instructions. Instructions never came, and over a hundred and fifty died. The next morning, crews were out on scaffolding trying to paint over the blackened areas before the Western press could photograph the damage.

With these cheerful thoughts on my mind, I set out for the warmth of the hotel restaurant and my first meal back in Russia. The Astoria's grand stairway spiraled around a brocaded elevator shaft; on each floor were luxurious lobbies complete with babushki and czarist appointments. I stopped off in the Beriozka shop for a bottle of good vodka: "central heating" to ward off the cold of my unheated room. As I have described, one must pay in Western currency for Beriozka purchases. Prices are stated in terms of rubles and then converted to an equivalent amount of Western currency at the official exchange rate. Ruble prices were considerably higher than in my student year, and to make matters worse, the official exchange rate between the dollar and the ruble had deteriorated from $1.33 = 1 ruble to $1.65 = 1 ruble. (As usual, as soon as I have more money, prices have already gone up.) It looked as if the lovely hand-painted Russian souvenirs, such as the small lacquered boxes from the village of Palekh, would once again be beyond my budget. I laughed when I got change for my dollars. There was one Finnish mark, a French 50-centime piece, and a few Austrian groschen. Although I was not going to those countries and did not need their coins, I knew it would do no good to protest. Beriozkas are required to give you change in hard currency and so they do, with whatever they happen to have in the till.

I walked into the restaurant of the Astoria and was seated by the head waiter. I felt a tinge of nostalgia. During my student year this dining room had been my gastronomic refuge. Because it catered to foreign visitors, sometimes influential foreign visitors, the Astoria was always at the top of the food priority list for Leningrad. Frequently during the long winter the Astoria would have the only salad in the city. It had always been a little Western enclave. One could even buy the *International Herald Tribune* from under the counter at the newsstand, provided, of course, one asked in good English and looked sufficiently like a visiting Western businessman. If a Russian entered the hotel lobby he was rudely accosted by the battery of doormen—What do *you* want? Off the lobby was a sign at the door of the restaurant that said in Russian, "Guests only." What it meant was "foreigners only," and those Russians with money and connections.

As I leafed through the elaborate, multipage menu, I had no illusions about being able to order anything I saw there. This was never possible, many of the choices were rarely, if ever, available. Nevertheless, the Astoria had always had a good selection, so, as is customary, I asked the waiter what *was* available. Black caviar was available, red was not. To my surprise, of the many other *zakuski* (appetizers), the waiter said they had only strips of roast beef. There was no beer. My favorite salad, the "capital" salad of potatoes, turkey, and pickles, was not available. There was no bouillon. When it came to the hot course, the waiter said, "I recommend you take chopped meat with mushrooms." "What else is available?" I asked. "Well, there are other things," he said with embarrassment, "it's just that they will take a long time." "What other things?" I asked. "No, no, really," he responded, "I strongly recommend you take chopped meat with mushrooms." This was my first encounter with the serious food shortage that has developed in the Soviet Union in the last few years.

Although the food supply in Poland receives much more attention, the situation in the Soviet Union is far worse in terms of actual quantity and quality of food obtainable. Russians, however, inured to hardship and out of touch with standards in the rest of the world, do not do much beyond complaining to their friends while drinking a bit more vodka. Rumors are heard about food riots in rural villages, but the government, it is said, quickly placates isolated trouble spots with increased shipments. Lines were far longer than in my previous experience, and the variety of food was also reduced. There was little or no pork. In 1976 it had always been possible to get three or four different kinds of cheese. In 1980 only one was available—occasionally. The food shortage in Leningrad was severe, but the situation in the countryside was said to be far worse. Milk might be available once a week, and people would stand in line from four in the morning waiting to buy it. It has always been Soviet doctrine that if the government takes care of the cities the countryside will take care of itself. The leadership remembers that it was not ideology but spontaneous bread riots in St. Petersburg that brought down the czar in 1917. The Soviet government feels that the peasants, no matter how desperate, are simply too scattered and isolated to cause any political problems. As a result, food allocation was organized so that the countryside would bear the brunt of the food shortage. However, knowing the food supply was better in the cities, peasants from the collective farms would descend like locusts every Saturday and Sunday, searching for food. The situation had become so bad that the Leningrad City Council ordered that no food stores, other than those exclusively for bread, could remain open on the weekends. In typical Soviet fashion, this policy backfired completely. The peasants would instead just come during the week and not work the fields, thereby aggravating the problem.

In the restaurants there were few choices. In some towns, no matter what I ordered I would be brought the same thing, stew beef and potatoes in a crock. The chicken dishes I tried consisted of a few bits of meat on a sparrow-sized bird. The experience that best exemplified the food problem to me was ordering chicken Kiev. This Ukrainian classic consists of butter surrounded by boned chicken breasts. This oblong is then breaded and deep fried. When I received my order it was on the small side but looked fine. It was only after biting into it that I realized that it was merely deep-fried crumb batter—they had left out the chicken!

Everyone I met spoke of the food shortage. In small cafeterias signs would say, "It is the duty of every citizen to conserve bread." I do not mean to suggest that the situation bordered on famine. As long as the Russian peasant gets his bread, cabbage, and potatoes, he can persevere, provided, of course, that his expectations do not rise. It seemed to me that the United States embargo of grain shipments was causing great difficulty. However, if the intent was to starve the peasant into toppling the Soviet government, it was unlikely that any embargo could have this effect. The Russian peasant is known for his stoicism. Meanwhile, the bureaucrats in Moscow were still eating pretty well.

Later, over a scrawny shashlik at Leningrad's Baku Caucasian restaurant, I discussed this problem with my lawyer friend Irina. Her career had gone well in the three and a half years since I had last seen her. After two years of work in the store-front consultation offices, she had returned to the law faculty and finished her candidate's (master's) degree. She had been working on a book on family law which she hoped would lead to a doctorate. She told me that it was her impression that the government had aggravated the food shortage by trying to hold down prices on basic foodstuffs.

She gave me an example that seemed straight out of classical, not Marxist, economics. Peasants who worked on collective farms are legally permitted to own a cow and sell its milk. But, she told me, they were no longer interested in doing so. To maintain a cow was expensive, and milking it was troublesome. Though they were permitted to sell the milk, this meant spending another day traveling to market. It was forbidden to arrange for a neighbor to do it on commission. On the other hand, the government had a policy of subsidizing the production of essential foods, and the price of milk in the state stores was therefore low. Many young farmers thought, "Why bother to own a cow when I have enough rubles to buy milk?" The fallacy, she explained, was that as less milk was produced privately, the demand for milk in the state stores increased. There was soon not enough to go around. Eventually the government had to begin de facto rationing by delivering only small quantities to each store. In addition, people felt the government had begun to debase the quality of dairy products. It was rumored that access to butter-producing facilities had become as restricted as access to military bases. With the cuts in supply, it became necessary to wait in line for hours on the few days when dairy products might be available. Granted, the price was still low—when you could find any. Artificially depressing certain prices had caused such dislocation, Irina said, that the government was periodically chastizing the peasants for buying scarce bread from the state stores and feeding it to their hogs and chickens!

The next morning I left the Astoria in order to fulfill one of my principal purposes for returning. Visiting Slava and his family was an emotional homecoming. They had no idea they would ever see me again. Totally unannounced, I climbed the stairs and rang the bell. Laura answered and was astonished to see me. Slava was out on his bicycle gathering some groceries. Laura had lost weight from a sparse diet and from worrying about her family's possible emigration. Max came home from school; bigger now, he gave me a hug. As so often in the past, I had arrived cold and hungry. Laura quickly warmed me up with tea and kasha (buckwheat groats). The family was living mainly on bread and butter, kasha, cabbage, and, surprisingly, pumpkin. Pumpkin had come into the state stores at a low price, and Slava, aware that it would keep all winter, quickly hoarded a hundred kilos. At last, Slava himself strolled in to find me smiling in the kitchen. He said he felt twice the joy in seeing me because it was so unexpected.

Later on, Slava, Max, and I took a long stroll in Smolensk cemetery to discuss their proposed emigration. It was not the sort of talk Slava wanted to have in a possibly bugged apartment. The family's first application to emigrate had been denied that summer, and Slava was told he must wait six months before applying again. After years of seeing others go through it, Slava too had become a refusenik.

Slava's situation was different from that of most individuals in the Soviet Union. As a translator who worked on short-term contracts with several Soviet publishing houses, Slava had no "employer" in the usual sense. He was at that time working with an important Soviet publishing house called Iskusstvo. When Slava's editor at Iskusstvo learned of his intention to emigrate, he was horrified. Because Slava worked on a contract basis only, the house was not accountable for Slava's political failings. But Slava's emigration posed an even more delicate problem. Iskusstvo was about to publish the sixth volume of the complete definitive Russian translation of the plays of George Bernard Shaw. Translations for two of these plays had been put out on contract, completed, and accepted by the publisher. The translator was none other than Slava. Were this sixth volume to appear with Slava's name on it while Slava was already living in the West, it would be for the publisher what is known ominously in the Soviet Union as a "serious political mistake." What made all this especially foolish was that Slava had already translated plays in earlier volumes of the series. But the publisher wasn't concerned about that. There he had a defense in the event he was personally accused. "How did I know that Slava was planning to emigrate? The organs of state security didn't tell me about it. How was I personally to know?" But now that he did know, he was open to attack. Even though Slava's name was on the earlier volumes, from Iskusstvo's political point of view his name could not appear on a later volume that might appear after his emigration—as if anyone else would know or care that Slava had decided to emigrate after volume four had come out, but before volume six. Still, this is the phenomenon of personal political accountability in the Soviet Union, and Slava's publisher was in a pickle because of it. Iskusstvo did not have to publish Slava's translation, of course, but the other options available to the house were also unsatisfactory. They could get someone else to do the translation. However, the fraternity of competent English literary translators in Russia is small, and its members have some degree of professional pride. For one of them to do another translation of a work that had just been translated by one of their colleagues would have seemed demeaning and useless. Others might say that the second translator had merely plagiarized Slava's work. No respected translator wanted to touch it. There was another alternative: Iskusstvo, possibly the most respected literary publisher in the Soviet Union, could simply publish the complete plays of George Bernard Shaw in the definitive Russian translation without including translations of *Geneva* or *A Village Wooing*, and simply hope that no one would notice. While Iskusstvo pondered this dilemma, one thing was definitely decided: while Slava waited to emigrate he would get no new contracts from anyone.

Slava told me that since he viewed himself as an outsider anyway, the blacklisting did little to change his life. Laura, on the other hand, had always held a regular job and was upset about her discharge from the bookstore. Having been in the workaday world for so long, it took her some time to adjust to her newfound idleness. What concerned her even more than the loss of her job was that much of their personal library, which she had spent most of her life collecting, would have to be left behind. The Soviet law that forbade exporting books published before 1946 had that fall been changed to forbid exporting any book published prior to 1976. Most of their library was published prior to 1976. Laura's great passion was reading, and she had read most of her books more than once. To her it would be like saying good-bye to old friends, and all because of a senseless change in a senseless rule. It was possible to get special permission waiving the prohibition on certain books, if one was prepared to pay a staggering export duty. Slava and Laura were beginning the necessary procedures to have determinations made on which books could be exported and for what price.

Things had been hard on Max, too. He had thought he was leaving forever, until Slava told him that their application had been denied. The family would be in Leningrad for at least six more months. It is hard to get an eleven-year-old to take his studies seriously under the best of circumstances, but for him to know that any day he might be saying good-bye to his school and friends forever rendered the whole endeavor meaningless. One part of everyone's curriculum acquired new importance—foreign languages. Slava and Max studied French together every evening; Laura was learning English.

The family just tried to get by. Slava tended to his hoard of pumpkins in the apartment-building cellar; Laura had found a dozen different ways to prepare them. Slava and Laura had at last obtained a swimming pass. This had entailed a medical examination and a long wait. They had received permission to use the pool between the hours of eleven and twelve P.M. on Monday nights. It was over an hour each way to the pool, but it didn't matter. Laura was elated, and modeled her new bathing cap for me. The family lived on a barter system. Slava would help someone with his English, and that person would help Slava feed the family. Both of Slava's parents were working and helped the family as much as possible. Laura's parents were both deceased. Her mother had starved to death during the siege of Leningrad, and her father, David Dar, had recently died while living in the West. In addition to causing grief, his death posed a serious legal problem for the family.

One of the few ways an individual may receive permission to emigrate from the USSR is for the "reunification of family." This principle is contained in the famous 1975 Helsinki accords. The Soviets in theory accept it but in practice scrutinize each application on political grounds. Still, having a living relative abroad was at least a beginning. It meant that one could submit an application; whether anything would come of it, beyond the loss of one's job, was another question. Without a relative abroad one didn't even have a pretext for applying.

The family's only relative abroad had been David Dar. While I was still a student, Dar had been ordered by the KGB to emigrate. He was the relative whom Slava and his family were ostensibly seeking to join. Dar had signed the necessary documents that had begun the family's application. The summer before my return, Slava had heard from the Soviet passport office that his visa petition had been denied and wrote to Dar to inform him. Some weeks later Slava heard that Dar was dead. For many months Slava assumed that the news of the family's rejection had killed the old survivor of the Leningrad blockade. In breaking the news to Laura, Slava altered the time sequence slightly so that she would not draw the same conclusion. Later Slava learned that Dar had already been in a coma when the letter arrived; he had never known one way or the other.

Dar's death put the family in a serious predicament. In

addition to their grief for Laura's father, they had lost their jobs, their application to leave had been rejected, and now the relative abroad on whom their application depended was dead. If the authorities who monitored their correspondence were in touch with the authorities who handled their visa application, they might not be permitted to reapply. Slava obviously could not inquire about his status, because that would only focus attention on the inadequacy of their application. Unemployed, and living a pariahlike existence, they could be trapped forever in the limbo of having applied to leave but now not qualifying to go. For months Slava silently bore his anxiety. It was while I was in Leningrad that at least this part of Slava's torment was resolved. His sister who lived in Soviet Estonia received her visa to emigrate. She was free, and Slava again had the necessary relative abroad. The family's application could go forward.

Eleven /

Beyond Détente

Election Day, 1980 found me in Moscow. It was not the first time I had been in the Soviet Union at the time of the American presidential election. Exactly four years earlier, Zhenya and I had sat in the dawn light huddled around a muffled shortwave radio, listening to the results come in over the Voice of America. Leningrad is eight hours ahead of Eastern Standard Time, so the Tuesday-evening returns were coming to us early Wednesday morning. A crackling transmission announced that James Earl Carter had become the thirty-ninth president of the United States. In the weeks before I had been at the consulate to hear tapes of the debates between Ford and Carter. Ford's statement, later retracted, that Eastern Europe was not dominated by the Soviet Union hit the consulate staff like a thunderbolt. Some analysts would later say the offhand remark had cost Ford the close election.

Though the fact was not immediately apparent, by the time of Carter's election the era of détente was coming to an end. In the early seventies, books with such titles as *Détente and Dollars* and *Coexistence and Commerce* had postulated a new future in East-West trade. For the United States, at least, trade with the Soviet Union had never fulfilled those buoyant expectations. The Trade Act of 1974 had, through the Jackson-Vanik amendment, tied the issue of freedom of emigration to the granting of most-favored-nation status. Without this status, Soviet imports faced high United States tariff walls, and U.S. exports to the Soviet Union were not accompanied by the subsidized low-interest loans available from other trading partners. Any Soviet hope that Carter would improve the diplomatic climate quickly evaporated when Carter, who had proclaimed human rights to be a major principle of his administration, put the principle into practice by writing personally to Andrei Sakharov, the Nobel laureate and leading Soviet dissident. At about the same time there were reports that Soviet high-energy-wave bombardment of the United States embassy in Moscow, designed to interfere with communications, was so intense as to injure the health of the American ambassador. Things were off to a roaring start.

Now it was four years later. Policy toward the Soviet Union, highlighted by such issues as the SALT II treaty and military expenditures, had been a major issue of the Reagan-Carter campaign. Thomas J. Watson, Carter's appointed ambassador to Moscow, who earlier that year had been temporarily recalled as a protest over the Afghanistan invasion, invited the entire American community over to his official residence to hear the early-morning results. It was expected that the results would come in starting Wednesday at four in the morning, local time. When I arrived at eight I was greeted with the news that Carter had conceded two hours earlier. A new era in Soviet-American relations had begun. The career diplomats broke into small groups to discuss what it would mean, and the political appointees, like Watson himself, began, I suppose, to think about packing.

I too had to think about packing, because right after our national event of electing a new president, the Soviet Union had their national event, the November 7 anniversary of the Bolshevik Revolution. From the time of my arrival, the troops and crowds had been practicing for the "spontaneous" demonstrations. Early in those November mornings masses of troops regularly lined up in Red Square. Over the loudspeakers blared, "Now remember, soldiers, when I talk about the peace the Soviet Union is bringing to the world, you shout out spontaneously and in unison, 'Yes, and it's all true.' " The practice went on for hours. As a nonresident foreigner I was not permitted to stay in the capital during the four-day celebration. Banished to the Soviet hinterland, I had decided to visit part of the Zolotoe Koltso, the "Golden Ring" of historic cities and villages that surrounds the capital.

Before leaving Moscow, however, I had the opportunity to speak to a very unusual Soviet citizen about the meaning of the elections—Roy A. Medvedev. With Solzhenitsyn exiled externally and Sakharov exiled internally, Medvedev is the best-known dissident intellectual left in Moscow, the last clear voice left to the opposition. His books include *Let History Judge* (Knopf, 1971); with his twin brother, Zhores, *Khrushchev, The Years in Power* (Columbia University Press, 1976); *The October Revolution* (Columbia University Press, 1979); as editor, *The Samizdat Register* (Norton, 1977); and *On Socialist Democracy* (Norton, 1977). Presently he is working on a biography of Nikita Khrushchev. He is a man who has long fascinated American correspondents resident in Moscow, and their books about their experience use him as a principal source. He has been careful never to infuriate the Kremlin completely, the way Solzhenitsyn or Sakharov did, choosing rather to deliver his critique as one against neo-Stalinism but not against socialism or the Soviet system of government. This "reformist," "socialism with a human face" positioning does not endear Medvedev to the authorities, but having established an important international reputation, he is grudgingly endured by them.

This was one of the first rules that Zhenya explained to me. The Soviet system tolerates, even encourages, all sorts of criticism: "This is bad, that is bad," and so on. Brezhnev himself traditionally begins his economic speeches with a critique of Soviet shortcomings. Soviet newspapers regularly print scathing letters to the editor, complaining of some inefficiency or other. What is not tolerated is for a person to go one step further, to make the logical connection that if everything is such a mess it must be because the system itself is bad. This would never be permitted. It is Medvedev's reluctance to take this last logical step that has kept him at large through the years.

Medvedev is a man who knows something of the dark side of Soviet reality. He last saw his father in 1938, when he was dragged off by Stalin's secret police in the middle of the night. His twin brother, Zhores, who now lives in London, was thrown into one of the notorious Soviet "mental hospitals" for voicing opposition to the regime. After Roy had raised an international scandal and gotten Zhores released, they collaborated on *A Question of Madness*, one of the first exposés of the use and abuse of psychiatry in the Soviet Union. At present Medvedev lives in a comfortable apartment on the outskirts of Moscow on the way to Sheremetova Olympic airport. His flat is so crowded with books that you can't see the wallpaper. He is a charming man with a professor's white hair and spectacles, and looks every inch the old-world scholar.

That day we spoke about the impact of the elections. Medvedev pointed out that despite what was said about Reagan's being so hawkish and anti-Soviet, there were at least three good reasons why the Kremlin might prefer him to Carter. Carter, explained Medvedev, had made human rights a main tenet of his administration. He had no qualms whatsoever about involving himself in the internal affairs of other countries. Carter's correspondence with Sakharov had been a boon to the dissidents but had greatly embarrassed the Soviet leaders. It was unlikely that Reagan would make any similar public display. Second, the Republicans were more in favor of free trade, and Reagan had declared himself to be against the grain embargo. It was likely that the restrictions on exports of U.S. technology would be relaxed under a Republican, "the business of America is business" administration. (The Polish crisis changed this situation dramatically.) Finally, and what Medvedev felt to be most important from the Kremlin's point of view, were Reagan's cooler feelings toward the People's Republic of China. The Kremlin was horrified about what they saw to be the near certainty of a formal military alliance between a Carter-led United States and mainland China. By contrast, Reagan had made various pro-Taiwan, anti-Peking remarks during the campaign.

Medvedev pointed out the interesting paradox that the Soviets usually got along better with Republican presidents than with Democratic ones. Despite Republicans' being supposedly less "progressive," to a conservative Moscow regime they were in fact preferable to the volatile Democrats. Carter, whom they did not feel they knew, and who had never visited the USSR, was particularly frightening because of his powerful national-security advisor, Zbigniew Brzezinski. The Kremlin did know Brzezinski and viewed him as an emotional anti-Soviet Polish aristocrat and nationalist. From the leadership's point of view, Carter, inexperienced in foreign affairs, could be easily maneuvered by the wily Pole Brzezinski—a situation that could only lead to trouble for the Soviet Union. All in all, Medvedev opined, the Kremlin was ready for a change.

I asked him briefly about his plans and whether he felt that like his twin brother he would eventually emigrate to the West. He said that he expected not, or at least not voluntarily. His brother was a biologist and as such could work anywhere, but he was a historian of the recent Soviet past. Given the unpublished state of most of his sources, it would be impossible for him to work outside the USSR. His present work on Khrushchev, for example, was primarily based on the oral recollections of individual Soviet citizens. It was not the kind of thing one could do as an émigré. I took some pictures and we finished our chat. He bid me adieu, and I left Medvedev's small enclave of calm in the turbulent world all about him.

My visit had delayed my departure, and it was not until four in the afternoon that I pulled out of the lot at the Ukraina Hotel in my rented Zhiguli. It is now possible to rent a car in Moscow and drive on specified highways to other cities. Everything must be approved in advance, and I would not recommend it to one who cannot speak Russian. By that hour of the day in early November the sky was already darkening, and a light snow was beginning to fall. My destination was 150 miles away, not far, but the driving conditions were abysmal. The road was two-lane and icy. The falling snow, the headlights of oncoming truck convoys, and the diesel fumes blanketing the busy highway made for very bad visibility. Although this was among the most difficult driving experiences I have ever had, by Russian standards the road was a good one—the main route between Moscow and Gorky, a town of two million people, seventh-biggest in the USSR.

I was not going all the way to Gorky, however. As I have mentioned, Gorky is closed to foreigners. It is the city of internal exile for Sakharov, who, the authorities felt, had too much contact with the Western press in Moscow. At the ancient town of Vladimir I turned off the Moscow-Gorky road for Suzdal. Suzdal is first mentioned in the Russian chronicles in 1024, long before the founding of Moscow. Although of great importance in medieval Russia, it is really not more than a village now—a village of golden domes, monastery walls, wooden churches, icons, and iconostases. Because of its small size and its position well east of Moscow, Suzdal is one of the few ancient towns that escaped the wholesale destruction of the Second World War. It is a virtual museum of old Russian life.

After an almost five-hour drive, half-blinded by the driv-

ing snow, I was exhausted. I looked forward to some hot
borshch, black bread, and vodka. I hoped my room would be
heated. I arrived in Suzdal to find an enormous new tourist
complex built to accommodate the numerous visitors the
Soviet Union hopes to attract to the historic town. As I
registered in the train-station-size lobby, the administrator
told me that the restaurant was closed for "sanitary day."
At eight-thirty at night in a tourist complex with hundreds
of rooms, a pool, and a sauna, there was no place within
miles to get anything to eat. I was starving. I went to get
my bags. There was no porter; in fact, the whole staff was
crowded around the lobby TV set watching a soap opera.
The only one on duty was the doorman who had watched
me register. When I returned from the snowy street with
my bags he did not open the door but instead blocked my
way and demanded to see proof that I was registered. I
pushed past him and staggered down seemingly endless,
empty corridors of burnt-out overhead lights and grandiose
lobbies. In an empty, porterless hotel they had given me
a room as far from the lobby as possible. As I turned the
final corridor I noticed a man entering the room next door.
I thought it odd that in this monstrous complex probably
the only two guests in the whole place were housed at the
far end in adjoining rooms.

I returned to the reception desk and explained that I had
just driven from Moscow and was very hungry. I knew it
was not unusual for a restaurant to be closed. Russian service establishments, not fettered by the need for profits, are
always looking for excuses to close for the day. What was
unusual was that there was no way to get anything at all at
the dinner hour. There is usually a little "buffet" attached
to a hotel, which serves open-faced sandwiches and tea. The
"buffet" is in service precisely to make food available when
the main restaurant is closed. This is important because
there are no late-night delis or coffee shops in the Soviet
Union. In a small town there are few restaurants, and they

Roy Medvedev, the famous Soviet writer and intellectual dissident, with the author in Medvedev's apartment in Moscow. President Reagan had been elected only hours before, and Medvedev was giving his views on the impact of Reagan's election on United States–Soviet relations.

(*above*) In the country, laundry is still done by hand in the stream. If the stream happens to be frozen, what of it!

(*opposite*) Although Peter the Great insisted that St. Petersburg be built of stone and brick, the great genius of the early Russian architects was in wood. This reconstructed church is in Suzdal, 200 miles east of Moscow.

close early. If nothing is available at the hotel, you just go hungry.

The night manager was unmoved by my plight. He looked at me with wounded pride that I could even suggest that the "tourist complex" should have some dinner facility available. He kept repeating, "But I told you, it's sanitary day, *sanitary day!*" In Russian a characteristic way of arguing is simply to repeat the phrase in question with increasing vigor. How can one explain to a Russian hotel manager that in America every day is sanitary day but this doesn't mean you have to close down the restaurant? The receptionist was more sympathetic. What makes the Soviet Union's official rigidity tolerable is the contervailing basic good nature of the populace. Many times, when I was blocked by the official "nyet," some kind Russian would take me aside and say "da." The receptionist called a friend of hers who managed a small restaurant in the town. It was already closing, but they agreed to prepare something for me, and I was told to hurry into the village.

I drove about two miles to a small restaurant called "Merchants' Arcade," located in the old trading house of Suzdal. When I arrived, two young men, fighting and surrounded by their howling friends and girl friends, were being shoved by the doorman out into the street. The door was locked behind them, and a drunken donnybrook broke out right in the entranceway. It was quite a problem to get the doorman, who had not been alerted to my arrival, to open the door while the drunks around me were punching each other and demanding to be let in for more vodka. It was all I could do to avoid being dragged into the melee. At last I managed to get the doorman's attention, convince him I was an American, and squeeze inside. I was alone in a restaurant that seated perhaps fifty people. The manager came out, welcomed me, and told me that they didn't have a wide selection but would do their best. I assured her that I was too hungry to be particular; she should bring me whatever they had. To my great joy I was soon blessed with a steaming bowl of cabbage soup and pungent black bread. As I ate the screams and taunts of the local youth were faintly audible from their continuing brawl.

As the waitress brought me the main course of stew beef and potatoes, a young man in his late twenties walked into the restaurant and sat down a few tables in front of me. How had he gotten in? I wondered. I then recognized him as the person I had seen in the dimly lit hotel hallway, my next-door neighbor. There was no doubt in my mind that he was from the KGB and had been sent there to make my acquaintance. I immediately suspected that he would ask me for a ride back to the hotel. Calling for the waitress, he demanded in stentorian tones, "Can't a man get anything to eat in this place?" The manager brought him some food. I finished my main course and ice cream in leisurely fashion, paid, thanked the manager again, and prepared to leave. When I passed the man's table he leaped up with a big grin. I noticed that he had not bothered to pay. "My name's Misha," he said. "I'm in the same situation as you. I was hungry and the restaurant at the hotel was closed so I had to hitchhike into town. Can I have a ride back to the hotel?" It was interesting that he was so well aware of my situation. Though I knew exactly what he was up to, I felt it would be unwise to refuse his request. If the KGB wanted to hit me over the head or shoot me up with drugs, they could choose their time and place. I was in no position to stop them. But leaving "Misha" to freeze in the snow was not a good strategy. It would have irritated him and possibly started a personal vendetta against me, out of what was intended as mere routine surveillance. More likely this was just a little reconnaissance mission, a half-hearted attempt to find out what I was doing and, if I were foolish, to somehow lure me into a compromising situation. It was better to be civil but to keep him at a distance.

As we walked out to the car my new friend told me that

he was a chemistry student and had been at a conference in neighboring Vladimir. He had come to Suzdal for a few days to see the sights. As we drove back he was very talkative. He asked me if I was studying at Moscow State. I told him I had been there for a while in the faculty of international law but that was already four years ago. Misha said he asked because he had an American friend at Moscow State. He told me that the hotel restaurant was not really closed; rather a private reception was going on for some "big shots," as he put it. He said that the corruption in the Soviet Union was dreadful and asked if I didn't agree. I said that those things happened everywhere and there was much good in the Soviet Union also. We spoke in Russian and he told me he had always wanted to study English. Curiously, if I didn't recognize a word he used, he seemed to remember the English for just that word. When we got back to the hotel he asked to be let out so that he would not be seen with a foreigner. I knew very well that this was the old game Zhenya used to play of "Meet me by the bus stop" and would soon be followed by the "Please, you can trust me, see, I'm afraid of the authorities, too" charade. I assured him that the entire staff was parked in front of the television anyway, so he really had nothing to worry about. He thanked me for my kindness and asked if he could offer me some wine in his room. I could imagine the bag of tricks he would have for me if I accepted. I thanked him profusely but assured him I was too tired, having driven through a snowstorm from Moscow; perhaps the next night. This seemed to satisfy him and we retired to our respective rooms.

For the next few days, Misha seemed to be everywhere. If I went to the lobby he would stand next to me and buy a paper. If I tried to use the phone, so would he. He was remarkably parsimonious, however, never bothering to actually drop his two-kopeck coin into the slot. He would even knock on the door, at first not identifying himself, and then when I wouldn't open up, would pretend to be room service asking at what time I wanted to make a dinner reservation. For my part, I was just plain unsociable. Although always considerate, and always suggesting the possibility of a later meeting, I kept close to my room and did not go out after dark. Misha must have found me a very boring fellow indeed, spending my days staring at icons and the nights locked in my room. After a few days he just gave up and disappeared.

I do not know what brought on the KGB's sudden interest in me. It could well have been my meeting with Medvedev the day of my departure for Suzdal. Medvedev is watched, and anyone who goes to visit him comes to the attention of the authorities. Another explanation is that I was probably the only American in Suzdal during those few days in November. The KGB's interest was nothing personal, just that the "plan" had to be fulfilled and I was the only game in town. As beautiful as Suzdal was, I was relieved when the November 7 celebrations were over and I could return to the relative anonymity of Moscow, as just another tourist in the big city.

I left Suzdal in the morning to avoid the night drive I had experienced on the way out. In contrast to that journey, there was little traffic on the road and the drive through forests of birch trees was pleasant and relaxing. I returned to the aging Ukraina Hotel, where I had stayed prior to my departure for Suzdal. The Ukraina is one of the Stalinist baroque buildings that brood about Moscow's skyline. Moscow State University and another dozen major structures from the Stalin period are in the same drip-sandcastle style. They cause much confusion to tourists, because they all look the same but are so big, that people tend to use them for landmarks. Many an exhausted tourist has staggered up to what he thought was his hotel only to find himself at the Ministry of Foreign Affairs.

When I tried to check back in to the Ukraina the clerk

said they did not have me registered; I would have to see
Intourist. I showed the Intourist official my travel voucher,
which listed solely the Ukraina Hotel. She began to make
some phone calls. About two hours went by while Intourist
tried to determine what would be done with me. In the
meantime night fell, and I wondered what I was to do about
my rented Zhiguli. At last they decided I would be put up
in the centrally located luxury-class Hotel Intourist. I wondered what I had done to bolster my status. The only reason I could imagine was that the Ukraina, on the banks of
the Moscow River, is just across Kutuzov Prospect from the
residential compound for foreigners. I had been there on
the eve of the presidential election visiting Kevin Klose, the
correspondent for the *Washington Post*. Intourist may have
felt I should see a little more of Red Square and a little less
of the foreign correspondents.

The Intourist is a new hotel with a view of the Kremlin.
Exclusively for foreigners, it is considered one of the best
hotels in the Soviet Union. Important business delegations
and deluxe-class tour groups stay there. President Nixon
used it for various functions during his 1972 visit. Unlike
in Suzdal, porters at the Intourist fought with each other to
carry my bags. But when I tried to tip the winner, he
declined to accept the ruble I offered him and begged instead
for some small souvenir from the West—a pen, a trinket,
anything I had. The next morning I went down to the
"Swedish table," or buffet, offered by the hotel for breakfast. I couldn't believe my eyes. For a ruble and forty
kopecks (officially about $2.30) there was a buffet heaped
high with sweet rolls, fresh fruit, sausages, eggs, cold cuts,
porridge, imported jam, toast, and a variety of juices. At
the Astoria in Leningrad, breakfast consisted of a slice of
fat on white bread. Like any good Russian peasant arriving
in Moscow from the provinces, I heaped my plate high,
figuring that the Lord only knew when I would see food
like that again. As I got a second plateful I thought to myself

what a distorted view of Soviet life Western businessmen would have if the Hotel Intourist were all they saw of Russia. This buffet would give them a totally erroneous impression of the cost and availability of food. It reminded me again how Moscow was always on display, and how uncharacteristic and un-Russian life there could be.

As I was leaving the restaurant, several of the waiters followed me, asking to buy various articles I was wearing, my blue jeans, my camera bag. From the moment of my arrival in Leningrad I had noticed this changed nature of the eternal Russian black market. In my student year, transactions had been done on a clandestine basis and on a comparatively small scale. Young men would come by and ask in Russian what time it was. If you did not react they would ask again, but this time in broken English. If you responded, in hushed tones they inquired if you had anything to sell. In fact the Russian word for these entrepreneurs, *fartsovshchiki*, derives from the English phrase "for sale." This unofficial commerce in clothing, records, and currency, which the Russians refer to as "on the left," was nothing new, but never had I seen it so widespread or so seemingly tolerated by the authorities. At the Astoria, young men would jump into the elevator with me and on the way up to my floor try to strike a bargain. A little old lady who did my wash begged me for payment in my socks. Porters and coat checkers would shrug disappointedly if I tried to tip them in Soviet currency. As always, individuals who owned private cars tried to make extra money by using them illegally as taxis. Now government vehicles were pressed into service as well; socialist chauffeurs by day became private taxi men by night. I was shocked when, on my way back to the Astoria after the ballet at Leningrad's Kirov Theater, I was given a ride in a black Volga sedan with the license plate MNN—an official car of the KGB. The massive scale of black-market activity reminded me of what I had seen in Warsaw four years earlier. Upon my return I mentioned to a Polish diplomat what I had seen. He remarked that with the food shortages and the widespread black marketeering I described, it sounded to him as if the Russians were taking the "Polish road to socialism."

At my meeting in Leningrad with my lawyer friend Irina, I had mentioned what seemed to me the open toleration of the "second" economy. Thousands of Leningrad young people were now living "on the left." After the food shortage it was the most significant social change I had noticed since my student days. Irina, as a member of the law faculty, was certainly no radical, but like many educated Russians of her generation she was totally candid about the need for widespread reform. She acknowledged everything I had observed and, while not claiming to have the definitive answer, offered the following explanation.

The Soviet Union's consumer economy was in dire straits, she said, and that was plain for anyone to see. Official figures showed that economic growth had been sluggish, and no one believed that the standard of living had improved in the last ten years. The food problem had clearly gotten worse. Product quality had reached a new low. Quality is difficult to quantify, but those Western economists who accepted Soviet production statistics on anything—tractors, for example, as an indication of how many tractors were actually plowing the fields, as opposed to those broken and stripped for parts—had clearly not seen the Soviet economy in action.

Given this unhappy situation, there were only two ways for the country to go. One was toward increased repression and force in the economic area, in a word, neo-Stalinism. Under Stalin, work discipline was very strong. If someone overslept and was twenty minutes late for work, he risked Draconian punishment. This was no longer true. In fact, things had gone so far the other way that it was normal for a bad worker to make more money than a good one. After all, Irina continued, a good worker lives only on his salary.

A bad worker has time while malingering to do a little private business on his own. A joking curse that used to apply only to the crafty Georgians but was now universal is "May your life become so hard that you have to live on just your salary." Good workers were so fed up with this situation, and with the poor products available for their wages, that they now loafed around all day. Their saying was "We pretend to work and they pretend to pay us." There was another path open to the leadership, Irina argued, namely, a return to an incentive system with rewards determined by a controlled market. Such a system had been tried before. It was called the NEP, the New Economic Policy.

The NEP was a masterstroke by Lenin that was totally undone after his death. The new Soviet state had in 1920 and 1921 lost over twenty million people to civil war and famine. Another million professionals and skilled workers had fled the country. The economy was devastated. The value of the ruble had fallen from two rubles to the dollar in 1914 to 1,200 rubles to the dollar in 1920. The yield from the Russian harvest was down to about one-third of its prewar level. Faced with dissatisfaction and widespread food shortages, Lenin said that capitalism was bad only in relation to socialism and that socialism must make a temporary retreat. Under the NEP the state maintained control over the so-called commanding heights of the economy—such things as finance, foreign trade, and heavy industry. In small manufacturing and retail trade, however, private enterprise could resume. Private factories could employ up to twenty workers, and hired labor was once again permitted on farms. The policy was a tremendous economic success. By 1928 the acreage under cultivation finally exceeded that prior to World War I. However, to the consternation of the communist leadership, the power of the so-called NEP-men and the prosperous peasant farmers, labeled "kulaks" by the Bolsheviks, was increasing. The NEP came to a crashing halt when Stalin achieved control of the state and, at the

1927 Congress of the Communist Party of the Soviet Union, inaugurated the first five-year plan.

Irina continued that the open toleration of so much illegal economic activity was in reality a return to the NEP through the back door. The party recognized the economic problem but did not want to confront it. It did not want to face the issue; to do so would mean acknowledging defeat. It was better simply to look the other way and let the second economy have its day. She made an interesting point. "As you know, Logan, Marxist theory taught that socialism would come first to developed capitalist economies. Marx, writing in the mid-nineteenth century, saw Germany or England as principal candidates. But Marx was wrong. Instead, socialism came to Russia, which in 1917 was still in a state of agrarian feudalism. Because Russia went straight from feudalism to socialism and skipped capitalism, the economic lessons that we were supposed to learn under capitalism were never learned. Political lessons we have had. The Russian people have had more than their share of political lessons. But economic lessons we have not had. In this area we are only beginning to learn. Socialism," Irina continued, "is really something for intellectuals. That doesn't mean it isn't worthwhile. But it is essentially a group of hard-to-understand elitist ideas, like the labor theory of value, exploitation, and concentration of capital. The workers don't understand these theories and don't care to. What the worker cares about is where his bread is coming from and what he must do to raise his standard of living a little bit. No economic theory will change this. Rather, the system should become more flexible, and not make criminals out of people who only want a pair of blue jeans."

Irina's argument brought to mind the "convergence" theory I had studied in college: that is, objective economic factors would eventually force the large Soviet and American economies toward the same middle ground, dictated not by ideology but by empirical observation of "what worked."

Although I never particularly agreed with the theory, in at least one aspect it seemed to be coming true. In the United States our high tax rates, made even higher by "bracket creep" inflation, had created a great temptation for taxpayers to do business on an unreported "cash" basis. In Russia it was not taxes that people wished to avoid. Private economic activity is itself illegal. But taken to the extreme, a high tax rate could serve the same disincentive function that a fine would serve in the Soviet Union. In both countries the financial rewards for keeping a transaction out of the view of the government are substantial. In both countries the unreported, "unofficial" sector of the economy has become enormous.

Irina agreed that taxes could be confiscatory but felt it would take a pretty walloping tax rate to approach the disincentive effect that Soviet law had upon business enterprise. To illustrate how destructive this effect could be, she told me about a case that was going on in Leningrad at that time. There was a tremendous shortage of industrial safety goggles in the city. As a result, welders and turners who could not get goggles were constantly exposed to eye injury. Their factory directors were in serious violation of safety standards in permitting them to work without goggles, but the alternative of shutting down much of Leningrad industry while waiting for Moscow Gosplan (State Planning) to issue orders for their production was out of the question. It might be a year before any goggles were delivered, and then perhaps in insufficient numbers. While everyone pondered this dilemma, nothing was done, and the incidence of industrial eye injury reported by Leningrad hospitals continued its steep rise.

In the midst of the shortage, some enterprising workers started fashioning safety goggles themselves, first just for their own use, but when they became aware of the potential market, also to sell to other workers and factories. The little factory was an instant success; the workers' eyes were protected, the managers could once again comply with the safety rules, and Leningrad industry kept chugging along. In the meantime the men who organized the business were making a handsome profit; they had cornered the market and orders kept rolling in. The goggles factory existed for quite some time because no one wanted to blow the whistle. And in a way, no one could. So desperate was the need for goggles that everyone was implicated. Even the directors of large industrial combines were quietly giving orders to do business with the little factory. Irina speculated that the authorities had probably looked the other way for as long as possible, but eventually the enterprise grew so large and profitable that everyone was talking about it. Finally the police had to act lest everyone else decide to open his own shop.

When at last the axe fell, everybody connected with the business was hauled into People's Court on the charge of violating Article 153 of the Criminal Code of the Russian Republic. This article prohibits private entrepreneurial activity and activity as a commercial middleman for the purpose of enrichment. As there were so many people involved, the trial would take a long time. Irina was sure that the men who had started the factory would go to jail. Article 153 carried a maximum sentence of five years, and, if only as an example to others, the prosecutor would have to demand some prison term. Ironically, the state had still not been able to supply Leningrad with safety goggles, and industrial eye injuries were again on the rise.

Irina felt that this result was both unjust and a foolish waste of legal resources. "The problem," she said, "is that criminal law gets involved in all sorts of ways here that it would not get involved in if the Soviet Union were a market economy. We try to use other methods of control, like social censure and administrative sanctions, but often this is not enough. As you know, Part Six of our Russian Criminal Code is devoted exclusively to economic crimes. Some of

them, like illegal use of trademarks, would be found anywhere, but others, like Article 153 on entrepreneurial activity, or Article 154 on speculation, are uniquely socialist.
There is another aspect to this problem of overcriminaliza-
tion. Not only are special laws needed to stop people from
engaging in private commercial activity, but special laws
are also needed to protect the society against the potential
abuses of having only one producer. For example, Article
157 prohibits the repeated sale of poor-quality goods by store
managers and sorters. Given the shoddy state of Soviet
merchandise, this law is rarely enforced. If it were, the
whole consumer-product distribution network would be in
jail. But such a law need only be on the books in a state that
will not permit people to engage in a free market, but, cor-
respondingly, cannot depend on the free market to enforce
its own competitive sanctions against inferior products."
Irina concluded, "It is unfortunate, but ultimately, subor-
dination of individual economic ambition to the requirements of state planning must rest on the bedrock of the
criminal law."

Throughout my year in Soviet law school, I had thought
about the functional relationship between "crime and punishment" and the economic needs of the Soviet state. Irina's
discussion focused on Soviet economic crimes, but all of
Soviet criminal procedure raises the same concerns. Criminal trials always seemed to emphasize the character, history, and socialist consciousness of the man on trial, rather
than to investigate the crime itself. Such factors as the
accused's war record, how many children he had, and
whether his supervisor felt he was a good worker took on
great importance in a Soviet trial. Although this taking into
account the "whole man" had at first a certain attraction for
me, I came to feel that it was done not at all out of altruistic
motives, but more as a kind of massive social-engineering
project. It was as if the state were trying to rationally allo-
cate its human resources. If a man were accused of some

petty crime, a simple decision would be made—is he more valuable to the state where he is, or can we use him in eastern Siberia? Reports from his neighbors, his military service, and, most important, his work record determined the outcome of the trial. Whether he had actually committed the crime, or why, seemed to be treated as secondary.

Although the Gulag Archipelago has changed since Solzhenitsyn's day, there is still plenty of room in Soviet prison work gangs for malcontents who have committed some minor infraction. Even though the propaganda articles claim that dedicated young volunteers are building the new trans-Siberian railroad (called BAM, for Baikal-Amur Mainline), it is widely accepted in Russia that it is being constructed primarily by prison labor. Even university buildings built in Novosibirsk, the largest city in Siberia, are built by guarded prison work gangs. True, the prisons and work camps are not like those of Stalin's time. Now, prisoners generally survive. They are even paid a little and can remit the money to their families. If a prisoner works hard and causes no problems, his sentence may be reduced by half. This reflects the general softening of the system since the days of the Great Purges, but it also reflects mundane and realistic economic principles—a well-fed man who wants to go home will work harder and more effectively. The Soviet state has been unable to entice sufficient labor into the many remote but rich mineral areas of the country. Even with large pay bonuses, the so-called "northern coefficient," and increased vacations, few unskilled workers are interested. Building a railroad through Siberia is not exactly a cushy job. The Soviet prison system forms a "reserve labor army" to provide manpower for the most difficult tasks. It pulls into its ranks those who are not, in the opinion of the elite, making a "positive" contribution to the state where they are. The fact that many activities that are not considered criminal elsewhere—such as acting as a commercial middleman or not working at all—are designated "criminal" in the

Soviet Union provides a dependable flow of young recruits to swell the ranks of this army.

Many of my speculations on this "economic" function of the Soviet penal system were confirmed by a chance meeting in Moscow with Pyotr, a survivor of the Nazi concentration camp at Buchenwald, who had gone on to spend much of his adult life in Soviet prisons. I met Pyotr through Kevin Klose, the Moscow correspondent for the *Washington Post*, and David Satter, the Moscow correspondent for the *Financial Times* of London. Pyotr was on the lam, one step ahead of the KGB. Not knowing how much longer he would be at liberty, he had come to Kevin's office to tell his story.

Pyotr was a tough old bird who would not submit to authority. Having survived Buchenwald, he saw the KGB as no different from his former captors, and when pushed, shouted in their faces that they were "Red Fascists." It was a wonder he was alive at all. When he was not in prison he would live in train stations, always on the move. He had just finished a prison sentence in the Ukraine, where his work camp constructed wheat-drying units. He said he was the only prisoner in the camp who could be described as "political." The other inmates were just simple workers who would one day be caught stealing some small item from their factory and be given a three-year sentence. Pyotr felt that the arrests had nothing to do with the gravity of the crime. Everybody stole a little from his factory, but suddenly they'd lower the boom on one small guy. Most of the ones arrested were young, but once imprisoned it was almost impossible for them to return to normal society. Prison made them hard, and the Soviet system of work-books, which everyone carries to describe his work history, made concealing a criminal record impossible. Typically the man would become a recidivist, arrested again for a longer term.

Pyotr felt that the state made these arrests as a cost-cutting measure. Outside the camp, a worker earned about 160 rubles a month for constructing wheat-drying units. Inside the camp, he earned 15. When more cheap labor was needed, there would be a "campaign" in the law-enforcement agencies, more arrests, more convictions, and longer terms. Sometimes in the "cooler" punishment cell, where Pyotr would be placed after explaining to his captors the similarities between themselves and the Nazis, Pyotr would compare notes with the other prisoners about different camps. From these sessions Pyotr concluded that there were over a hundred prison work camps in the Ukraine alone. His camp at that time held 1,700 inmates, and he suspected that figure was about average.

When our session with Pyotr broke up at about two in the morning, Kevin dropped him off near the Kiev Station. As Kevin drove off, he noticed a car behind him pull in at the place he had dropped Pyotr. We all wondered how far Pyotr had gotten, and what the KGB would do to him for talking to us.

Conclusion

I remember that when I was a student in Leningrad in 1976, Leonid I. Brezhnev was due to have his seventieth birthday. Many Russian friends thought that at those celebrations he would announce a more limited role for himself and make plans for retirement. Similarly, when I returned to the Soviet Union in the closing months of 1980, many Russians believed that the seventy-four-year-old Brezhnev would announce his retirement at the upcoming Twenty-sixth Congress of the Communist Party of the Soviet Union. This congress, currently held every five years, is a time for the party to take stock of its accomplishments, discuss new policies, and announce changes in the senior party hierarchy. But my friends were wrong: when the congress took place, in February and March 1981, not only did Brezhnev not step down, but for the first time in Soviet history no changes in the top leadership were made at all. Although one would normally conclude that Brezhnev must cease to be the leader of the Soviet Union at some point, predictions as to when this will occur have all proved inaccurate. In Brezhnev's behalf it must be recognized that it is risky to step down from a top position in the Kremlin; Soviet history indicates that retirement spells at best political suicide, and, considering President Podgorny's abrupt disappearance, may be tantamount to physical suicide as well.

Brezhnev was born on December 19, 1906, when Russia was a very different country from what it is today. Almost 90 percent of the people born that year, in what is today the Soviet Union, were born in rural areas. Health care was so primitive that of the over six million babies born in 1906, one in four would die before its first birthday. Illiteracy was high. By the age of twenty, a quarter of the men and half of the women of the "Brezhnev generation" could still not read and write. Yet change was in the wind. Brezhnev was on the eve of his eleventh birthday when the Bolsheviks seized power, initiating a time of tremendous social and political turbulence. Russia was quickly racked by civil war. Even when the actual shooting died down, the ideological fighting remained at a fever pitch. The entire society was polarized into "classes" and "class enemies" based on birth and education. Many of those who fought for the Bolsheviks were peasants loyal to the cause but uneducated and unskilled. The experienced managers and bureaucrats who had not fled Russia during the civil war were essential to the economic survival of the nation. But having been educated under the old regime, they were feared by the Bolshevik leadership, who suspected them of counterrevolutionary tendencies.

As soon as Stalin attained power, he decreed that the working class must have its own technical intelligentsia, and during his first five-year plan (1928–32) established technical and engineering schools around the country. Typical of the new young "socialist" technicians was Leonid Brezhnev, who joined the Communist Party in 1931 and graduated from the Metallurgy Institute in Dneprodzerzhinsk in 1935. Those like Brezhnev who received their college education in the early days of Stalinism fully expected to spend the next forty years working their way up. Then came the

Great Purges. Stalin was able to eliminate all those he considered a threat. Experienced men educated before the Revolution were denounced as counterrevolutionaries, wreckers, and saboteurs. From industry to the Red Army, the higher up one was, the more chance one had of being liquidated. Suddenly there were vacancies at the top for people of the right "class" background. The young Communists of Brezhnev's generation, only a few years out of college themselves, rose rapidly into this vacuum. Although many of these untested young men were incompetent, to Stalin, loyalty was an infinitely more valuable trait. Some proved their worth. By 1938, Brezhnev was a regional party senior secretary. Others rose even faster. Dimitri Ustinov, the present Minister of Defense of the Soviet Union, graduated from college in 1934. Seven years later, in the year the Germans invaded Russia, he joined Stalin's cabinet as people's commissar of armaments. He has been in the top leadership for over forty years.

The generation that followed Brezhnev's had no such luck. In fact they had no luck at all. Those born from 1910 to 1918 discovered that the top jobs had already gone to people not much older than themselves, blocking their own advancement for the rest of their careers. In an even less enviable position were those born from 1919 until 1925, for this was the group that bore the worst of the fighting of World War II, in which ten million Russian soldiers died at the front. Owing to the cataclysmic events of the first thirty years of Soviet history, the Russians born from 1910 to 1925 are severely underrepresented in the country's leadership. This group, in their late fifties and sixties today, is the "missing generation" of the Soviet elite. Almost thirty years after Stalin's death, his legacy is now coming home. Tikhonov, at age seventy-five, replaces Kosygin, dead at seventy-six—but the septuagenarians cannot replace each other forever. Because of the missing generation, the instability of the eventual transition is increased. This generation-wide hole in the chain of command makes gauging the Soviet leadership after Brezhnev especially difficult.

It is not just that Brezhnev himself is so old but that the whole Politburo is old. If Brezhnev were to die tomorrow, an interim "collective leadership" of Brezhnev's long-term associates could hold things together for a while. But these men are no younger than Brezhnev. The average age of the inner circle of voting members of the Politburo in 1981 was seventy-five. It is also possible that Brezhnev could be around for a while. Josip Broz Tito of Yugoslavia held firmly to the tiller until just before his death at age eighty-seven. But whether Brezhnev or any other individual lives or dies in the next few years will not alter the actuarially inescapable conclusion that within the decade of the eighties, the entire leadership of the Communist Party and the Soviet foreign-policy establishment will change. Because of the "missing generation," the reins of power will fall abruptly to men fifteen to twenty years younger than the present leaders. These younger men, by and large, the West does not know.

When I asked Russian friends whom they expected to succeed Brezhnev, they professed ignorance, but a few interesting theories emerged. One Moscow acquaintance argued that, like any strong man, Brezhnev has surrounded himself with weak men who are dependent upon him; therefore the new leader would not come from the present Politburo. Podgorny, the last of the Khrushchev protégés, was not weak enough to survive. But the theory that Brezhnev has surrounded himself with those dependent on him is contradicted by the fact that Brezhnev, unlike both Stalin and Khrushchev, did not replace the other men of his generation in the course of consolidating his position. When Lenin died there were seven voting members on the Politburo; within seven years only Joseph Stalin remained. When Stalin died there were ten voting members on the Politburo; within seven years, only Khrushchev and the foreign-trade specialist Anastas I. Mikoyan remained. In both cases the new leader preferred younger men who were politically indebted to him. Brezhnev's pattern was different. Perhaps because of the strength of the other Politburo members, few changes were made. The experienced men stayed on, adding close personal associates they had known for many years. It is because Brezhnev did not, or could not, replace the old guard that the Soviet leadership has reached its present advanced age. As just one example of how long they have been around, Andrei A. Gromyko, minister of foreign affairs, was serving as ambassador to Washington when Franklin D. Roosevelt was president.

The other members of the elite feel safe with Brezhnev. They might not feel so safe with a youngster of fifty who might quickly seek to replace them. It may be for this reason that so few younger men have found a seat on the Politburo. The new leader, my Russian friends assure me, must be a man whom no one fears. He must appear to be a moderate who will preserve the interests of the status quo. Later he may surprise them all, as did both Stalin and Khrushchev, but none of the present elite will willingly risk a return to the assassinations and purges in the upper ranks that the Soviet Union knew for so long. But there is a paradox in all this: change having so long been resisted, when it comes it is likely to be dramatic. The leadership has not planned for continuity. Brezhnev and his septuagenarians have chosen to face the eighties with a program of intervention abroad and ossification at home. No one has been groomed for the succession.

The sensitive nature of the impending across-the-board change in the Soviet leadership becomes even more delicate when one considers the economic problems the Soviet Union will be facing as the turnover occurs. Brezhnev may have provided no cultural flowering or elegant life-style to the man in the street, but he has managed until recently to deliver modest increases in the standard of living while vastly increasing the country's military power and global prestige. The Soviet Union has evolved, in the period since Brezhnev took power in 1964, from a European state to a great-power rival of the United States, with commitments from Cuba to Angola and Afghanistan. But considering the enormous cost of its military establishment, it is unlikely that the Soviet economy, without thorough structural reform, can maintain anything like the slow but steady progress of the Brezhnev era. The Soviet economy grew rapidly at first by bringing more and more labor into industrial production. But now, declining birth rates and competing military and agricultural demands have created an acute labor shortage. Continued growth must come primarily from using the available labor more efficiently. The introduction and diffusion of labor-saving technology is essential to the continued growth of a mature industrial economy. But this has always been the Achilles heel of centrally planned economies, which, without the spur of domestic and foreign competition, resist innovation and change. So serious are the inefficiencies in the Soviet system that in 1979 and 1980 the gross domestic product crept ahead at only a 1.5 percent rate. Economists currently predict growth of no more than 2.5 percent a year in the country with the greatest petroleum production and the richest natural-resource base in the world. In 1979 and 1980, for the first time in Soviet peacetime history, steel output declined. Soviet oil and natural gas, which have been by far the biggest export commodities of the country, and upon which they rely to pay their substantial debt to Western trading partners and banks, will increasingly be required in the domestic economy, unavailable for export. Coal output declined in both 1979 and 1980. Soviet agriculture remains unreliable at best, and is frequently a disaster. In 1980, the plan for a 235 million-ton grain crop fell 54 million tons short of its goal. In the official Soviet statistics for 1981, the figure for grain production was deliberately omitted. Little wonder; unofficially the harvest is thought to be 66 million tons below the Party's target, the third disasterous harvest in a row. Without the large surpluses of the Western grain producers, Russia could again find itself experiencing near famine. Formal rationing of food, particularly of meat, has already begun. The economy is in such disarray that I have heard the cynical but revealing observation that the Western world should be glad that Russia is communist. Considering its land area, oil, mineral wealth, and educated population, if the Soviet Union had any kind of rational economic organization, the West would never be able to compete.

Without economic reform, the eighties will be a decade of increasing scarcity, but Russia has dealt with scarcity before. In fact, that is the only condition it knows. Previously, however, Soviet scarcity was accompanied by war, revolution, or mass terror. It is an open question whether the country can live with a stagnant or decreasing living standard in a terror-free environment. In Poland this combination led to the total collapse of the status quo—the birth of Solidarity and then the imposition of martial law. This was what Irina had in mind when she referred to the choice between fundamental economic reform and neo-Stalinism. "No growth" may make the Brezhnev middle road untenable. The very stability of the Brezhnev period may have undermined the state's ability to wring continued sacrifice from its population. For example, the attempt to keep the populace in a martial psychology by constant reference to the Second World War will sound hollow indeed when Brezhnev goes and the leaders of the Soviet state come from those who were too young to fight. At some point the Russians who are told, as they are now, that they are not eating meat because it has been sent to Poland may begin to wonder if the sacrifice of empire building is really worth it.

Even if the docile Russian *narod*, the people, can be made to go along with expansion abroad and stagnation at home, they may not be the ones the new leadership will have to convince. There is something of a demographic time bomb ticking away in the southern republics of the Soviet Union. The people who live in these more traditional areas, in the Caucasus and especially in Central Asia have a much higher birth rate than the ethnic Great Russians. Officially the Russian population in the Soviet Union hovers just above 50 percent, but some feel that the non-Slavic "minorities" are deliberately undercounted. With some representation from the Ukrainians, the Russians politically dominate the Soviet Union. Yet as it is recognized that the Russians are a ruling minority, the Central Asians, a people of Mongolian ancestry and Moslem heritage, may begin to inquire whether they should not play a larger role in a state of which they are such a large part. The new Moslem assertiveness south of the Soviet border, in Iran and the other oil countries of the Gulf, can only increase this sentiment. But even if the political ramifications of the Russians' becoming a minority ruling elite can be retarded for some years, there is the immediate economic problem of manpower. Owing to low birth rates, as of 1982 the working-age population of the Russian Republic will begin to decline. In the labor-starved Soviet environment, a decision must soon be made whether to move the factories, traditionally located in European Russia, to Central Asia, or to move the Central Asians to the factories. Either economic solution will compound the political dilemma of continued Russian control.

It is the prospect of untested, untried, and unknown men competing for power in a time of economic stress and social change that makes the future of the Soviet Union and our dealings with them appear so unpredictable and alarming. British diplomats used to say that czarist Russia was an "absolute monarchy tempered by assassination." This holds equally true for the Soviet Union today. Although the Brezhnev era is a time of seeming stability and strength, the Soviet Union is fundamentally a fragile society. An incident like the coup d'état against President Podgorny is more characteristic of a banana republic than a mature political system. Khrushchev as well was the victim of a coup he did not anticipate and could not resist. When the last member of the troika that replaced Khrushchev—Podgorny, Kosygin, and Brezhnev—falls, when Brezhnev and his friends from Dnepropetrovsk can no longer rule, political power will literally be up for grabs. The death in January 1982 of Mikhail Suslov, said to be the kingmaker of Soviet politics, can only increase this instability. How many other groups twenty years younger than the group around Brezhnev would like to be next in line or, of equal concern, fear the consequences of their rivals' attaining power?

When the Brezhnev generation begins to lose its grip, one should not discount the possibility of a power struggle in the grand Bolshevik tradition. I do not see the likelihood of a grass-roots revolution, starting from the bottom, in the Soviet Union today. The workers in the Gdansk shipyards of Poland are twenty years ahead of their Soviet counterparts. But with no clear successor in sight, the fifty-year-olds may not agree on who should follow the seventy-year-olds. A "colonels' revolution" of military or political officers of the second echelon is quite possible. If this occurs or if the transition is in any way stormy, the Russian people may rapidly get involved.

Time is itself legitimation; the fifty-year-olds, unknown to the people, will not have the aura of establishment that the old boys have. Nor will they be able to claim the mantle of war leadership. The new Soviet leadership will have no more claim on the right to rule than did the czar, a claim resting on power alone. As the poem goes, "The czar has ten million bayonets," and so he had, but suddenly Lenin was standing at the Finland Station and the czar's ten million bayonets were no more. Russia has never known democracy, and the people have always accepted a strong leader, no matter how ruthless. But they will not tolerate a false czar. If the leaders themselves begin to dispute who is entitled to rule, the Russian *narod* can rise like an angry sea.

Precedents can be found in Russian history. In the sixteenth century, the son of the czar became czar. If the czar had no son, then there was, as today, no proven rule of succession and nobody knew who the next leader would be. Ivan the Terrible's son, Theodore, died in 1598 without an heir. The conflicting claims to the right to rule, based on putative links with the extinct dynasty, led to a time of war, revolution, and fantastic Kremlin intrigue known as the "Time of Troubles." The Romanov dynasty rose from the ashes of this period. Today no one knows who will follow Brezhnev and his colleagues. Technically it is true that the Central Committee has the right to elect the members of the Politburo, including the general secretary (Brezhnev). In practice the tail has wagged the dog; after it is clear who the general secretary will be, the Central Committee goes through the motions of electing him.

The contenders for Brezhnev's position will have to have issues around which to collect their support. The creation of a "crisis" from which a "strong" leader can emerge is a well-known political device. The possibility cannot be discounted that one faction, perhaps the military itself, will attempt to gain an internal political advantage by throwing the nation into some foreign-policy adventure. If Brezhnev, the aging "conservative," is prepared to invade Afghanistan, how much further would some politically threatened novitiate be willing to push the awesome military might that Brezhnev has assembled? The political phenomenon of "Bonapartism," a takeover by the military in times of alleged crisis, has generally not been a factor in the communist world. However, the creation in December 1981 of polish General Jaruzelski's "Military Council for National Salvation," and the ensuing arrest of former Polish Communist Party leaders, all done with Soviet backing, raises a significant precedent. Does the Politburo now agree that when the military perceives a threat to the status quo it is justified in seizing power from the Communist Party?

But if in the coming succession Russia enters a new "Time of Troubles," there will be a terrifying difference. In a power struggle in Red Square, many political contestants may have access to the Soviet military machine and nuclear stockpile: it will not be the Russian state alone that hangs in the balance, but the entire fate of civilization. In such a flammable situation it will not be SALT treaties or détente that would force a latter-day Stalin to look elsewhere for a political rallying point, but the military deterrent of the United States and its NATO allies. It must be painfully obvious to even the most chauvinistic new Soviet leader that a strike at the vital interests of the Western democracies could only end in total disaster.

But the coming end of the Brezhnev era is fraught not just with negative implications. Each of the four major Soviet leaders—Lenin, Stalin, Khrushchev, and Brezhnev—has left his personal imprint on his period of Soviet history. For worse, but also for better, the Soviet state does not have the elaborate system of checks and balances that limit the speed at which democratic leaders can effect change. The general secretary of the Communist Party may not be able to do anything he wants, but in instituting some bold policy, he need not worry about the reaction in *Pravda* the next morning. The initiatives of Khrushchev in breaking the yoke of Stalinism show that dramatic reform is possible, even from those who have spent their lives serving their predecessors and the Communist Party.

The men who will come to power after Brezhnev and his circle depart have had a totally different life experience from a Russian born in 1906. The Revolution, the civil war, forced collectivization, the Great Purges, even the Second World War were not for them formative experiences. What they remember are Khrushchev's exposure of the crimes of Stalinism, the flight of Sputnik, the end of the cold war, and the beginning of détente. They are as a group better educated and more widely traveled than their predecessors. Just as Brezhnev began to accept Western technology, perhaps they will begin to accept other Western ideas. The economic and social reform of the Soviet state may seem for them not a burden but a challenge. It will be a time of great possibilities, a time of enormous potential—perhaps even a time when the experiences of this author, living under Brezhnev, will seem as distant and dated as the experiences of one living under the czars.

Epilogue

When I was back in Leningrad, curiosity drew me once again to the dormitory at 25 Shevchenko Street on Vasilevsky's Island where I had lived with Zhenya. The place was spruced up a bit and newly painted. Inside, the old commandant was still dozing in the little glass-enclosed office. That much, anyway, had not changed. We talked a bit; he remembered me. He mentioned how there weren't so many Americans anymore. After a few pleasantries I asked him what had become of Zhenya. "Ah, Zhenya." He thought for a minute. "Well, finally, after Lord knows how many years, he left the dorm and went back to Saransk." The commandant supposed he was teaching there. But, the commandant allowed, Zhenya had never quite gotten around to finishing his thesis, so he returned periodically to Leningrad to see his advisor. When he was in town he would usually stop by the dorm. The commandant expected him to be there for the upcoming November 7 holidays and asked if I would be staying. I explained that I would not, but asked him to remember me to Zhenya when he next saw him.

Many of the Leningrad alumni are now living in the West. After leaving the Soviet Union with David Dar in 1977, Ilya Levin went to the University of Texas at Austin. He has become one of the very few specialists on the Russian literature of the absurd. He publishes and frequently presents papers at gatherings of Slavicists.

Tolya Putilin, the Leningrad abstract artist, emigrated to Paris with his wife, Liuda. He is active in art circles and exhibits on the Continent. One fine day I was strolling down Madison Avenue in New York City, having just visited the Metropolitan Museum of Art. As I passed the Nakhamkin Gallery, my eye caught a familiar sight. It was a canvas by Igor Tulipanov. Tulipanov had emigrated from Leningrad and was living with his wife and son in New York City, where he continues to create his unique art. That exhibit was shared with Michael Chemiakin, perhaps the best-known of the younger generation of Russian abstract artists. Chemiakin had already left Leningrad and was living in Paris at the time of my exchange, but I was fortunate to get to know him there. Exceedingly generous, Chemiakin once presented me with a copy of the rare volume *Apollon 77*, a collection of the best of modern Russian poetry and painting, a vital contribution in the struggle to keep Russian art alive outside Russia.

In the spring of 1981 I was working late one Saturday night on this manuscript when the phone rang. It was Slava. On his second application, he had received permission to emigrate. He, Laura, and Maxim had quickly followed the route of many émigrés from the Soviet Union—to Vienna, Rome, and finally New York. Slava, who is the most enterprising Russian I have ever met, has had no trouble fitting in to his new life in America. He approaches everything with gusto and is fascinated by all he sees. Shortly after his arrival he gave me a long lecture on the virtues of American automatic door closers which shut the door behind you quietly and smoothly. In Russia, he reminded me, you must either pull the heavy door shut behind you or, alternatively, an attached strong spring slams it, announcing your arrival with a thundering report. Slava is presently teaching Russian at Cornell University, in Ithaca, New York, where he is working on a Ph.D. in Slavic linguistics. He continues his writing and translating.

A fascinating case was that of Ioffe, my old professor. I did not see him when I was back in Leningrad but later heard that this man, the leading civil-law specialist in the Soviet Union, had become a refusenik. I could not believe my ears. Apparently what happened was that Ioffe's daughter decided to emigrate. As I have previously discussed, one of the bureaucratic obstacles placed in the way of any prospective emigrant is that of obtaining the necessary *zayavleniya*. When Ioffe's daughter expressed her desire to emigrate, Ioffe would have known instantly the dilemma he was in. Refusing to sign his daughter's *zayavleniye* might have meant that she would not be permitted to emigrate. On the other hand, to sign the *zayavleniye* would signify to the authorities that he implicitly agreed with her desire to leave the Soviet Union. It would mean the likely collapse of Ioffe's position at the faculty, in the profession, and in the country. Although I personally liked Ioffe, I could not help sensing the sweet irony of this man, the leading proponent of Soviet civil law, being caught in such a predicament. How many times had he explained, justified, and defended regulations just such as this one? How many times had he ridiculed and silenced students who questioned such procedures?

Ioffe had too much strength of character to refuse his daughter's request. I was told by people who were in contact with him that he signed the *zayavleniye* and, as expected, his position in the Soviet Union rapidly collapsed. On the very day that Ioffe's daughter was informed that she could emigrate, he was told by the authorities that having proven himself incompetent even to train his own daughter, he could not possibly be trusted with the students in the law faculty. There was nothing else for him to do but apply to emigrate himself. His application was refused. Like the thousands of less well placed Soviet citizens before him,

Olympiad Solomonovich Ioffe became a refusenik. I wonder how this little reversal was explained to the students at the faculty. I also wonder how Ioffe felt about his forty-year career as the leading apologist for Soviet civil law, and whether the phrase I had heard him use so often, that "in bourgeois countries they do this, but here in the Soviet Union . . . ," haunted his dreams. Although a weaker man could have avoided it, Ioffe had been caught in the very web he helped to spin.

But refuseniks may reapply. Since Ioffe was already of pensionable age and because of his reputation in the West, he was not the kind of man the Soviets like to hold for long. Delegations of international lawyers were already telegramming their protests. In the late spring of 1981, Ioffe arrived in the United States. Once again a leading Soviet professional had ended up in the West. The former head of the the Civil Law Faculty of Leningrad State University named for A. A. Zhdanov now resides in Massachusetts, where he is teaching at my alma mater, Harvard Law School. Things have come full circle.

73   12/15/8